PENGUIN BOOKS

TOGETHER

ABOUT THE AUTHOR

Richard Sennett was founder director of the New York Institute for the Humanities, and is now University Professor at New York University. He has previously won the Amalfi and Ebert prizes for sociology and in 2010 was awarded the Spinoza Prize for outstanding contributions to public debate on ethics and morality. *Together* forms part of a three-book project on 'homo faber', focusing on the skills human beings possess to make a life together; the first volume of this large project, *The Craftsman*, was published in 2008. He is the author of many celebrated books including *The Fall of Public Man*, *Flesh and Stone* and *The Corrosion of Character*.

RICHARD SENNETT

Together

The Rituals, Pleasures and Politics of Cooperation

PENGUIN BOOKS

PENGUIN BOOKS

Published by the Penguin Group
Penguin Books Ltd, 80 Strand, London WC2R ORL, England
Penguin Group (USA), Inc., 375 Hudson Street, New York, New York 10014, USA
Penguin Group (Canada), 90 Eglinton Avenue East, Suite 700, Toronto, Ontario, Canada M4P 2Y3
(a division of Pearson Penguin Canada Inc.)
Penguin Ireland, 25 St Stephen's Green, Dublin 2, Ireland (a division of Penguin Books Ltd)
Penguin Group (Australia), 707 Collins Street, Melbourne, Victoria 3008, Australia
(a division of Pearson Australia Group Pty Ltd)
Penguin Books India Pvt Ltd, 11 Community Centre, Panchsheel Park,
New Delhi – 110 017, India
Penguin Group (NZ), 67 Apollo Drive, Rosedale, Auckland 0632, New Zealand
(a division of Pearson New Zealand Ltd)
Penguin Books (South Africa) (Pty) Ltd, Block D, Rosebank Office Park,
181 Jan Smuts Avenue, Parktown North, Guateng, South Africa 2193

Penguin Books Ltd, Registered Offices: 80 Strand, London WC2R ORL, England

www.penguin.com
First published by Allen Lane 2012
Published in Penguin Books 2013
002

Copyright © Richard Sennett, 2012

The moral right of the author has been asserted

Printed in Great Britain by Clays Ltd, St Ives plc

A CIP catalogue record for this book is available from the British Library

978-0-141-02210-9

www.greenpenguin.co.uk

Penguin Books is committed to a sustainable
future for our business, our readers and our planet.
This book is made from Forest Stewardship
Council™ certified paper.

ALWAYS LEARNING   **PEARSON**

for
Stuart Proffitt
and
Elisabeth Ruge

Contents

PART THREE
Cooperation Strengthened

Preface

A few years ago I decided to write a trio of books about the skills people need to sustain everyday life. I've spun out theories my own entire life, but have tired of theorizing as a self-contained pursuit. And I've the sense, as the world clogs up with physical stuff, that we don't know how to use material objects and machines well. So I wanted to think harder about ordinary things – not a new pursuit, since many philosophers have explored the skills of everyday experience, but a subject new to me in old age.

I began with a study of craftsmanship, the quest to make physical things well. *The Craftsman* tried to show how the head and hand are connected, and more, the techniques which enable people to improve, whether they are engaged in a manual or mental activity. Doing something well for its own sake, I argued, is a capacity most human beings possess, but this skill is not honoured in modern society as it should be. The craftsman in all of us needs to be freed.

While writing this study I was struck again and again by a particular social asset in doing practical work: cooperation. Cooperation oils the machinery of getting things done, and sharing with others can make up for what we may individually lack. Cooperation is embedded in our genes, but cannot remain stuck in routine behaviour; it needs to be developed and deepened. This is particularly true when we are dealing with people unlike ourselves; with them, cooperation becomes a demanding effort.

My focus in *Together* is on responsiveness to others, such as listening skills in conversation, and on the practical application of responsiveness at work or in the community. There's certainly an ethical aspect to listening well and working sympathetically with others; still, thinking about cooperation just as an ethical positive cramps our understanding. Just as the good craftsman-scientist may devote his energies to making the best atom bomb possible, so people can collaborate effectively in a robbery. Moreover, though we may cooperate because our own resources are not self-sustaining, in many social relations we do not know exactly what we need from others – or what they ought to want from us.

I've thus sought to explore cooperation as a craft. It requires of people the skill of understanding and responding to one another in order to act together, but this is a thorny process, full of difficulty and ambiguity and often leading to destructive consequences.

The last lap of my project lies before me, a book on making cities. They aren't made very well today; urban design is a craft in peril. Physically, too much urban design is homogeneous and rigid in form; socially, modern built forms frequently take only a faint imprint of personal and shared experience. These are unfortunately familiar complaints. I'll try to draw on the work in previous volumes to address them; my hope is that understanding material craftsmanship and social cooperation can generate new ideas about how cities might become better made.

I've baptized these three books the 'homo faber project', drawing on the ancient idea of Man as his or her own maker – a maker of life through concrete practices. My quest is to relate how people shape personal effort, social relations and the physical environment. I emphasize skill and competency because in my view modern society is de-skilling people in the conduct of everyday life. We have many more machines than our ancestors but less idea of how to use them well; we have greater conduits between people thanks to modern forms of communication, but less understanding of how to communicate well. Practical skill is a tool rather than a salvation, but, lacking it, issues of Meaning and Value remain abstractions.

The homo faber project does have an ethical centre, focused on just how much we can become our own masters. In social and personal life we all come up against the limits on desire and will, or the experience of other people's needs which cannot be reconciled with our own. This experience ought to teach modesty, and so promote an ethical life in which we recognize and honour what lies beyond us. Still, no one could survive as a passive creature without will; we have at least to attempt to make the way we live. As a philosopher, I'm interested throughout these studies in that fraught, ambiguous zone of experience where skill and competence encounter resistance and intractable difference.

Though my three volumes are meant to add up to a whole, each is written to stand on its own. They are written for the intelligent general reader who quite properly asks: why does it matter? Why is it interesting? I've tried to eliminate academic bickering – a blood sport which is never of much value to the general reader – from the pages of these books, or have consigned scholarly quarrels to the notes.

Lists of acknowledgement are becoming like telephone directories. On my shortlist of thanks is, first and foremost, my spouse Saskia Sassen. She has pushed me to be not too literary; I've tested particular case studies on her to see when she becomes bored. I want to thank my editor in Britain, Stuart Proffitt, and, in Germany, Elisabeth Ruge, both of whom have pushed me to be more literary. They are editors who edit, a lost craft. I owe a practical debt to my assistants Hillary Angelo and Dom Bagnato, both fiends for making things work. So, too, is Elizabeth Stratford, who copy-edited this book. I owe intellectual debts to two long-standing friends, Craig Calhoun and Bruno Latour, the first a passionate corrector of mental error, the second a laid-back suggester of it. Finally I want to thank a new friend, Archbishop Rowan Williams, whose writings span theology, philosophy and art. His religion is not mine, but his understanding of what books are for has inspired me.

Together

Frances Johnston, 'Making a Staircase', Hampton Institute, n.d., glass-plate.

Introduction

The Cooperative Frame of Mind

On a school playground in London, a chum of my grandson once blasted out a song by Lily Allen on the school's public-address system: 'Fuck you, fuck you, very much, cos we hate what you do and we hate your whole crew!' while a six-year-old girl ground her hips along with the music. The school authorities were appalled by this caper; it was 'unauthorized use'. I admit that the rebellious child in me admired the kids' seizure of the public-address system. Still, I too was appalled. The youngsters had no idea the singer meant to mock her own words; 'fuck you, fuck you' seemed to them a straightforward declaration of us-against-you.[1] It's a dangerous sentiment in the part of inner London where the school is located: the mixture of different religions, races and classes in this part of the city makes us-against-them a recipe for conflict, and indeed this part of London has regularly flared violent.

In America, whenever I'm in a masochistic mood, I listen to right-wing talk radio, which sings 'fuck you, fuck you' to Nazi-feminists, liberals, secular humanists and married homosexuals, as well as, of course, to socialists. Today the United States has become an intensely tribal society, people adverse to getting along with those who differ, but Europeans certainly can't feel smug about this: tribalism, in the form of nationalism, destroyed Europe during the first half of the twentieth century; a half-century later the Netherlands, once so inclusive, now has its version of American talk radio, where the mere mention of the word 'Muslim' triggers a Wagnerian onslaught of complaints.

Tribalism couples solidarity with others like yourself to aggression against those who differ. This is a natural impulse, since most social

3

animals are tribal; they hunt together in packs, they lay out territories to defend; the tribe is necessary for their survival. In human societies, however, tribalism can prove counter-productive. Complex societies like our own depend on workers flowing across borders; contain different ethnicities, races and religions; generate diverging ways of sexual and family life. To force all this complexity into a single cultural mould would be politically repressive and tell a lie about ourselves. The 'self' is a composite of sentiments, affiliations and behaviours which seldom fit neatly together; any call for tribal unity will reduce this personal complexity.

Aristotle was perhaps the first Western philosopher to worry about repressive unity. He thought of the city as a *synoikismos*, a coming together of people from diverse family tribes – each *oikos* having its own history, allegiances, property, family gods. For the sake of trade and mutual support during war, 'a city is composed of different kinds of men; similar people cannot bring a city into existence';[2] the city thus obliges people to think about and deal with others who have different loyalties. Obviously mutual aggression cannot hold a city together, but Aristotle made this precept more subtle. Tribalism, he said, involves thinking you know what other people are like without knowing them; lacking direct experience of others, you fall back on fearful fantasies. Brought up to date, this is the idea of the stereotype.

Will first-hand experience weaken stereotypes? That was the belief of the sociologist Samuel Stouffer, who observed during the Second World War that white soldiers who fought alongside blacks were less racially prejudiced than white soldiers who had not.[3] The political scientist Robert Putnam has stood Stouffer, and Aristotle, on their heads. Putnam has found that first-hand experience of diversity in fact leads people to withdraw from these neighbours; conversely, people who live in homogeneous local communities appear more sociably inclined towards and curious about others in the larger world.[4] The giant study on which he bases these propositions profiles attitudes more than actual behaviour. In everyday life, people may simply have to put such attitudes aside; we are constantly obliged to deal with people we fear, dislike or simply don't understand. Putnam's idea is that, confronted with these challenges, people are initially inclined to withdraw, or, as he puts it, to 'hibernate'.

Worried about the state of the world in the safe recesses of my academic office, and also, I should say, worried about the effect of 'fuck you, fuck you' on my grandson, I've wondered what could be done about tribalism. The problems of living with difference being so large, there can be no single or total solution. One of the peculiar effects of old age, though, is that we become unhappy with the observation 'what a pity . . .'; resignation doesn't seem much of a legacy.

Cooperation can be defined, drily, as an exchange in which the participants benefit from the encounter. This behaviour is instantly recognizable in chimpanzees grooming one other, children building a sandcastle, or men and women laying sandbags against an impending flood. Instantly recognizable, because mutual support is built into the genes of all social animals; they cooperate to accomplish what they can't do alone.

Cooperative exchanges come in many forms. Cooperation can combine with competition, as when children cooperate in establishing the ground rules for a game in which they then compete against one another; in adult life this same combination of cooperation and competition appears in economic markets, in electoral politics and in diplomatic negotiations. Cooperation becomes a self-standing value in rituals both sacred and secular: observing the Eucharist or a Seder together brings theology to life; rituals of civility, as small as 'please' and 'thank you', put abstract notions of mutual respect into practice. Cooperation can be informal as well as formal; people who hang out at a street corner or drink together in a bar exchange gossip and keep talk flowing without self-consciously thinking, 'I am cooperating.' The act of doing so is wrapped in the experience of mutual pleasure.

As human tribalism makes clear, cooperative exchange can produce results destructive to others; bankers practise such cooperation in the form of insider trading and buddy-deals. Theirs is legal robbery, but criminal gangs operate on the same social principle. Both bankers and bank-robbers engage in collusion, which is the dark angel of cooperation. Collusion was famously evoked in the eighteenth century in Bernard Mandeville's *Fable of the Bees*, the witty Dr Mandeville believing that some public good can come from shared vice, but only if people do not 'suffer' from religious, political or indeed any convictions.[5]

5

In this book, without invoking such cynicism, I want to focus on a small corner of what might be done about destructive cooperation of the us-against-you sort, or about cooperation degraded into collusion. The good alternative is a demanding and difficult kind of cooperation; it tries to join people who have separate or conflicting interests, who do not feel good about each other, who are unequal, or who simply do not understand one another. The challenge is to respond to others on their own terms. This is the challenge of all conflict management.

The philosopher-politician Michael Ignatieff believes that such responsiveness is an ethical disposition, a state-of-mind inside us as individuals; my view is that it emerges from practical activity.[6] One result of managing conflict well, as in a war or a political struggle, is that such cooperation sustains social groups across the misfortunes and upheavals of time. Practising cooperation of this sort can, moreover, help individuals and groups grasp the consequences of their own actions. In the spirit of generosity, let's not write off the banker as a human being: to find an ethical yardstick for his own behaviour, he would need to reckon the effects of his actions on people quite unlike himself, on small businesses, mortgage-defaulters, or otherwise struggling customers. Which is to say more largely that what we can gain from demanding sorts of cooperation is insight into ourselves.

The most important fact about hard cooperation is that it requires skill. Aristotle defined skill as *techné*, the technique of making something happen, doing it well; the Islamic philosopher Ibn Khaldūn believed that skill was the special province of craftsmen. Perhaps you, like me, dislike the phrase 'social skills', which suggests people good at cocktail party talk or adept at selling you things you don't need. Still, there are social skills of a more serious sort. These run the gamut of listening well, behaving tactfully, finding points of agreement and managing disagreement, or avoiding frustration in a difficult discussion. All these activities have a technical name: they are called 'dialogic skills'. Before explaining that label, we should ask why skilled cooperation of these sorts appears to belong more to the ideal realm of what ought to happen than to the practical realm of everyday behaviour.

DE-SKILLING

Criticisms of tribalism often contain an undertow of blame, as though the tribalist has failed to live up to the critic's own cosmopolitan standards. Moreover, it's easy to imagine that the hard work of cooperating with those who differ has always been rare. Yet modern society has weakened cooperation in distinctive ways. The most direct of these weaknesses concerns inequality.

As measured by a widely used statistical tool, the Gini co-efficient, inequality has increased dramatically in the last generation, within both developing and developed societies. In China, development has caused the Gini co-efficient to soar, as the fortunes of urbanites improve far more than those of villagers. In America, declining fortunes have increased internal inequality; loss of high-skilled manufacturing jobs has diminished wealth in the mass, while the wealth of the top 1 per cent, and within that small slice, the wealth of the top 0.1 per cent, has shot up astronomically. Economic inequalities translate in everyday experience as social distance; the elite becomes remote from the mass, the expectations and struggles of a truck-driver and a banker sharing little common ground. Distances of this sort quite rightly make ordinary people angry; us-against-them thinking and behaviour is a rational result.

Changes in modern labour have in another way weakened both the desire and the capacity to cooperate with those who differ. In principle, every modern organization is in favour of cooperation; in practice, the structure of modern organizations inhibits it – a fact recognized in managerial discussions of the 'silo effect', the isolation of individuals and departments in different units, people and groups who share little and who indeed hoard information valuable to others. Changes in the time people spend working together increase this isolation.

Modern labour is increasingly short-term in character, as short-term or temporary part-time jobs replace long-term careers within a single institution. By one estimate, a young person entering the workforce in 2000 will change employers twelve to fifteen times in the course of his or her working life.[7] Within organizations, social

7

relations are also short-term, managerial practice recommending that teams of workers be kept together no more than nine to twelve months so that employees do not become 'ingrown', that is, personally attached to each other. Superficial social relations are one product of short-term time; when people do not stay long in an institution, both their knowledge of and commitment to the organization weakens. Superficial relations and short institutional bonds together reinforce the silo effect: people keep to themselves, do not get involved in problems which are none of their immediate business, particularly with those in the institution who do something different.

In addition to material and institutional reasons, cultural forces today work against the practice of demanding cooperation. Modern society is producing a new character type. This is the sort of person bent on reducing the anxieties which differences can inspire, whether these be political, racial, religious, ethnic or erotic in character. The person's goal is to avoid arousal, to feel as little stimulated by deep differences as possible. The withdrawal of which Putnam speaks is one way to reduce these provocations. But so is the homogenization of taste. Cultural homogenization is apparent in modern architecture, clothing, fast food, popular music, hotels . . . an endless, globalized list.[8] 'Everybody is basically the same' expresses a neutrality-seeking view of the world. The desire to neutralize difference, to domesticate it, arises (or so I will try to show) from an anxiety about difference, which intersects with the economics of global consumer culture. One result is to weaken the impulse to cooperate with those who remain intractably Other.

For such material, institutional and cultural reasons, modern times are ill-equipped to meet the challenges posed by the demanding sort of cooperation. I'll frame this weakness in a way which might seem initially odd: modern society is 'de-skilling' people in practising cooperation. The term 'de-skilling' derives from the replacement of men by machines in industrial production, as complex machines replaced skilled craft-labour. In the nineteenth century this replacement occurred, for instance, in steel-making, leaving the craft-workers only more simple, brutal tasks to perform; today it is the logic of robotics, whose aim is to replace expensive human labour in providing services as well as in making things. De-skilling is occurring in the social realm in equal measure: people are losing the skills to deal with intractable differences as material inequality isolates them, short-term labour makes their social contacts more superficial and activates anxiety about the Other. We are losing the skills of cooperation needed to make a complex society work.

My argument is not grounded in nostalgia for that magical past in which things seemed inevitably better. Rather, the capacity to co-operate in complex ways is rooted in the earliest stages of human development; these capacities do not disappear in adult life. These developmental resources risk being wasted by modern society.

COOPERATIVENESS IN INFANCY

The child psychologist Alison Gopnik observes that the human infant lives in a very fluid state of becoming; astonishingly rapid changes in perception and sensation occur in the early years of human development, and these shape our capacity to cooperate.[9] Buried in all of us is the infantile experience of relating and connecting to the adults who took care of us; as babies we had to learn how to work with them in order to survive. These infant experiments with cooperation are akin to a rehearsal, as infants try out various possibilities about getting along with parents and peers. Genetic patterning provides a guide, but human infants (like all young primates) also investigate, experiment with and improve their own behaviour.

Cooperation becomes a conscious activity in the fourth and fifth months of life, as babies begin to work with their mothers in breast-feeding; the infant starts to respond to verbal cues about how it should behave, even if it does not understand the words, for instance responding to certain tones of voice by snuggling into position to help. Thanks to verbal cueing, anticipation enters the repertoire of the infant's behaviour. By the second year of life infants become responsive to each other in a kindred way, anticipating each other's movements. We now know that such cued behaviour – the stimulations of antici-pating and responding – helps the brain activate previously dormant neural pathways, so that collaboration enables the human infant's mental development.[10]

The cues non-primate social animals give are static in the sense of being instantly readable; when bees 'dance' to each other they send precise signals, for instance, that pollen can be found 400 metres to the north-west; other bees know instantly how to read these cues. In infant human experience, cueing becomes increasingly un-beelike. The human infant tries out hand gestures, facial expressions, grips or touches which prove puzzling to adults rather than being instantly read and understood.

The psychologist Jerome Bruner has emphasized the importance of such enigmatic messages as signs of cognitive development. The infant increasingly intends a meaning on his or her own terms, as in crying. An infant crying at two months is simply reporting pain; in time, crying takes more varied forms because the infant is trying to say something more complicated, something the parent has more trouble interpreting. This gap is established by the second year of life, and changes the meaning of 'mutual'; infant and adult continue to bond through give and take, but are not quite sure what they are exchanging, since the cueing process has become more complex. The gap between transmission and reception, Bruner says, constitutes a 'new chapter' in the bond between infant and parent.[11] But the new chapter is not a disaster. Both infants and parents learn to adjust to it, indeed are stimulated by it to pay more attention to one another; communication has become more complex rather than broken down.

Still, for parents it's easy to imagine babies have left the Garden of Eden when entering what Benjamin Spock famously called 'the terrible twos'.[12] The common explanation for a surfeit of anger at this stage is that the infant becomes surly as it separates physically from its mother. The child psychologists D. W. Winnicott and John Bowlby were the first to draw a more refined picture. In his studies, Winnicott built on the common parental observation that an infant, in working with the mother during breastfeeding, comes to recognize that the mother's nipple is not part of his or her own body; Winnicott showed that the more freedom an infant is given to touch, lick and suck the nipple, the more aware he or she is of it as an outside, separated thing, belonging only to the mother. Bowlby made the same observation about tactile freedom in the child's play after the second year of life; the more freely children interact with toys, the more they become aware of physical things as having an existence all their own.[13] This physical awareness of separateness also appears in dealings with other children, in freely punching, kicking and licking them. It's a discovery that other kids do not respond as the child expected, that others are separate beings.

Toddler life thus provides an early grounding in the experience of complexity and of difference. Children hardly 'hibernate' from each other, to invoke Robert Putnam's image, as a result. If anything, separated and at cross purposes as they may be, they are ever more interactive. In this regard we want to put parents into the picture. On one account, parents who talk constantly to their babies produce two-year-olds who are more sociable with other infants, less anger-triggered against care-givers, than silent parents whose infants are more likely to be social isolates; the difference parental stimulation makes is detectable in greater or lesser activation of the infant's neural circuits in the brain.[14] But even if parental stimulation is inhibited, the baby's physical drive to exchange cannot be extinguished. By the second year of life, all infants begin noticing and imitating what others do; learning about physical objects also speeds up, particularly about the size and weight of things, as well as their physical dangers. The social capacity to cooperate together on a common project, like building a snowman, becomes well established in toddlers by the third year of life: young children will do it, even if parental behaviour does not encourage it.

One virtue of understanding early experiences of cooperation as a rehearsal is that this concept explains how infants deal with frustration. Inability to communicate produces the frustration evinced by wailing, and trying out different wails is something infants learn to do – with a surprising result. Bowlby found infants are inclined to wail more as their vocal repertoire expands, since they now focus on, and are more curious about, the vocalization itself; they are no longer simply sending a sheer report of pain.

Equally important is the matter of structure and discipline. In a rehearsal, repetition provides a disciplining structure; you go over things again and again, seeking to make them better. Sheer mechanical repetitiveness is, to be sure, an element of play in childhood, just as hearing the same story over and over exactly in the same form is a pleasure. But mechanical repetition is only one element. Round about the age of four, children become capable of practising in the sense we understand it, either in playing a sport or a musical instrument; through repetition they try to get better at what they are doing.

Social consequences follow. In the nursery, Bowlby found, repetition begins to bond infants to one another when they experiment together and repeatedly; in performing a gesture together, the frustration of singing in coordinated time, for instance, becomes what he called a 'transitional affect', that is, no absolute bar to trying to get the coordination right the next time. Much other research has found that rehearsing, in the sense of working over a routine to improve it, is harder when done alone. Put more formally, repetition in time makes cooperation both sustainable and improvable.

The developmental origins of cooperation advance a further step by the age of four. Of course, sign-posting by years is arbitrary; development is elastic, varying from child to child. Still, by this age, the psychologist Erik Erikson has shown, young children become capable of studying their own behaviour reflexively, self-consciously, the act detachable from the self.[15] In practical terms, he means that children have become more capable of self-criticism without the need of cueing or correction from parents or peers; when a child can do this, he or she has become, in Erikson's framework, 'individuated'. Around the age of five, children become avid revisionists, editing behaviour which has served them before but which no longer suffices.

Reflexive, self-critical thinking doesn't imply withdrawal from other kids; children can be reflexive together. One piece of evidence Erikson provides for this process is game-playing. At the age of five to six, children begin to negotiate the rules for games, rather than, as at the age of two to three, take the rules as givens; the more negotiation occurs, the more strongly do children become bonded to one another in game-playing.

A century ago, in his study of play, *Homo Ludens*, the historian Johann Huizinga noted the difference between observing the rules of a game and discussing what these rules should be. To Huizinga, these seemed just alternatives children could choose at any time; modern psychology instead sees them as a sequence in the process of human development. As a recent study put it, sheer obedience comes first in the developmental process, the powers of negotiation later.[16] A profound consequence ensues: development makes us capable of choosing the kind of cooperation we want, what its terms of exchange are, how we will cooperate. Freedom enters the experience of cooperation as a consequence.

Erikson's sweeping point about this passage is that cooperation precedes individuation: cooperation is the foundation of human development, in that we learn how to be together before we learn how to stand apart.[17] Erikson may seem to declare the obvious: we could not develop as individuals in isolation. Which means, though, that the very misunderstandings, separations, transitional objects and self-criticism which appear in the course of development are tests of how to relate to other people rather than how to hibernate; if the social bond is primary, its terms change up to the time children enter formal schooling.

This is one way cooperation begins to develop. I'm sure every parent could tell a distinctive story about how their children grew. Mine emphasizes that connection to others involves skill; as children cooperate better, social and cognitive skills entwine. The two skills I've highlighted are experiment and communication. Experiment entails doing new things, and more, structuring these changes over time. Young people learn to do this by the repetitive, expansive process of practising. Early communication is ambiguous, as when the infant sends out ambiguous cues; by the time children can negotiate the rules for a game, they are able to negotiate ambiguities and resolve them. Erik Erikson's large idea certainly makes sense to me, that self-awareness emerges within the context of experimenting and communicating to others. I also follow Alison Gopnik in stressing that early development consists of a rehearsal of possibilities.

You might well observe, whatever your own views about children, that learning to cooperate on these terms is not easy. That very difficulty is, in a way, positive; cooperation becomes an earned experience rather than just thoughtless sharing. As in any other realm of life, we prize what we have struggled to achieve. How then might the rehearsal process lay the groundwork for complex cooperation later in life?

DIALOGICS

'People who do not observe, cannot converse.'[18] This wisdom-nugget from an English barrister evokes the essence of 'dialogics'. This technical word names attention and responsiveness to other people. The barrister's bon mot particularly calls attention to the listener's share in a discussion. Usually, when we speak about communication skills, we focus on how to make a clear presentation, to present what we think or feel. Skills are indeed required to do so, but these are declarative in character. Listening well requires a different set of skills, those of closely attending to and interpreting what others say before responding, making sense of their gestures and silences as well as declarations. Though we may have to hold ourselves back to observe well, the resulting conversation will become a richer exchange for it, more cooperative in character, more dialogic.

Rehearsals

A common vice consists of believing that our own experience has great symbolic value, and for a few pages I'm going to indulge in this vice. One model for listening skills appears in adult rehearsals of a professional sort, the kind necessary in the performing arts. This is a model I know well. As a young man, I worked professionally as a musician, both as cellist and conductor. Rehearsals are the foundation for making music; when rehearsing music, listening skills become vitally important, and in listening well, the musician becomes a more cooperative creature.

In the performing arts, the sheer need of others can often prove a shock. Young musical hotshots are often brought up short when they begin playing chamber music; nothing has prepared them to attend to others. (I was like that, aged ten.) Though they may know their own part perfectly, in rehearsal they have to learn the ego-busting art of listening, turning outward. It's sometimes thought that the result moves to the opposite extreme, the musician blending in, submerging his or her ego in a larger whole. But sheer homogeneity is no recipe for making music together – or rather, a very dull recipe. Musical character appears instead through little dramas of deference and assertion; in chamber music, particularly, we need to hear individuals speaking in different voices which sometimes conflict, as in bowings or string colour. Weaving together these differences is like to conducting a rich conversation.

In classical music we are working with a printed score, and the score might seem to rule the conversation. Those blobs of ink on the printed score are not enough, however, to tell us how the music will actually sound. As the cellist Robert Winter has written about rehearsing a Beethoven quartet, the difference between page and act is composed by the particular character of the instruments the musicians are playing, by the differing character of the players and of course by textual puzzles.[19] The most maddening musical instruction in music is *espressivo*, expressively; to translate this instruction into sound we have to intuit the composer's intent; individual players may send out cues for how to play *espressivo* which other players cannot interpret – a sort of return to cries from the crib.

Apart from puzzling instructions, the conversation which occurs in rehearsal seeks to fathom the sound the composer heard when he or she set ink to page. In the Schubert Octet, for instance, the composer breaks into fragments melodies which initially all eight players share. It's quite subtle: when a break occurs, each player has to convey something like 'I'm getting off the train here' without making a big deal about his or her departure. That's what I imagine Schubert wanted, but I can only justify it by working with the other players, my sound uniting with then diverging from theirs. Because of the gap between score and sound, my conducting teacher, the great Pierre Monteux, used to command students, 'Hear, don't read!' This has to happen in rehearsals.

In making music, there's a basic distinction between practising and rehearsing; the one is a solitary experience, the other is collective. Common to both is the standard procedure of attending initially to a whole score, then focusing on particular testing passages. The two forms of work on music divide, first, because rehearsing drags musical habits into shared consciousness. When practising alone, the musician goes over his or her part again and again so that passages become ingrained routines; this is especially necessary for the musician preparing his or her part for public performance – only a very few performers, like the violinist Fritz Kreisler, or Pierre Monteux, can commit a score to memory after a couple of run-throughs. The danger for the rest of us lies in losing sight of how ingrained passages sound to others. In rehearsing, one player can jolt another into this awareness.

Children discussing the rules of a game have to arrive at a consensus in order to play together. Musicians do not, or not quite. When I once rehearsed the Schubert Octet with the clarinettist Alan Rusbridger, he remarked to me at one point: 'Professor' – he is a journalist by trade so this form of address is not entirely a compliment – 'your top note sounds harsh.' In practising alone, I'd forgotten how it might sound to him and he made me hear it. But I didn't soften the sound; I pondered whether it should sound harsh, decided it should, and made it even more so. Our exchange produced, in me, a more conscious valuing of the note he disliked. As in a good discussion: its richness is textured as disagreements that do not, however, keep people from continuing to talk.

A rehearsal will not progress if one player comes in with an explanation of the 'Meaning of the Schubert Octet' or if all the players discuss its cultural significance; the rehearsal itself would then become like a seminar. But in fact few rehearsals run like philosophy seminars. Musicians with good rehearsal skills work forensically, investigating concrete problems. True, many musicians are highly opinionated (I certainly am), but these opinions will sway others only if they shape a particular moment of collective sound. This empiricism is perhaps the most resonant point about artistic cooperation in a rehearsal: cooperation is built from the ground up. Performers need to find and work on telling, significant specifics.

Differences in time also divide practising and rehearsing. Professional musicians practising alone can go eight or more hours at a stretch; they have learned how to structure the process of 'investigative repetition' so that they can pay attention for long periods. The violinist Isaac Stern was a champion of such sessions, once remarking to me, 'I didn't sleep the whole night, I finally got the opening bars of the Brahms Concerto right.' Rehearsals for groups of professional musicians seldom stretch beyond three hours at any one time, in part due to union rules about overtime and other economic constraints. If a group is lucky, they will have five or more rehearsals of a particular piece before they first perform it, though the reality is more likely to be two or three. A lot of collective labour has to be crammed into a short amount of time. Performers need to be economical in the telling, significant specifics they explore.

The conversation during professional musical rehearsals is distinctive socially in that it is so often a conversation with strangers. The professional musician is a migrant. If the musician is a star performer, he or she will be constantly on the road working with unknown orchestras or pick-up groups. Even for more settled musicians rooted inside orchestras, extra hours get filled up by grabbing chance gigs, opportunities which often arise out of town in churches or at weddings, as well as in other concert halls. The challenge of communicating with strangers sharpens the quest for specifics, since you have only a few hours together.

One solution to this problem lies in a set of portable rituals. Each musician will have developed a set of expressive habits which he or she wants to apply right away to key passages; when I was on the road playing the Schubert Octet, I had flagged in my printed score key places I knew I wanted to subject to retards in tempo, passages where I wanted to get off the melodic train. The ritual in rehearsal lies in sharing these flags; if others have similarly marked them, we can deal immediately with just how much to slow down; if others have not flagged them, we will negotiate about whether or not to slow down. The ritual of the flagged passage has a kind of symbolic force, since it conveys to other musicians what kind of player you are, how you tend to bow phrases or shape dynamics; colleagues will intuit what you are likely to do in other, unflagged passages, which can remain unrehearsed.

Ritual makes expressive cooperation work – and this is a large point. As will appear, ritual enables expressive cooperation in religion, in the workplace, in politics and in community life. It's certainly true that nights devoted to the mysteries of the Schubert Octet are not what is now called a 'mainstream activity'; this is an arcane way of life. Nor have I discussed here the straightforward comparison between the rehearsal process among musicians and our near cousins, professional athletes, another highly specialized form of cooperation. Yet the experience I'd had as a young professional is built on an elemental human foundation. The points of contact with early childhood lie in communications which address ambiguity; practices which become structured and focused in time; conversations about differences; practices subject to reflexive self-criticism.[20] Musicians in rehearsal are adult Eriksonians; they need to interact, to exchange for mutual benefit. They need to cooperate to make art.

Dialectic and dialogic conversations

There is an analogy between the musical rehearsal and the verbal conversation, but it conceals a puzzle. Much of the actual communication between musicians consists of raised eyebrows, grunts, momentary glances and other non-verbal gestures. Again, when musicians want to explain something, they more frequently show than tell, that is, they play a particular passage to others, leaving the others to interpret what they are doing. I'd be hard pressed to explicate in words exactly what I mean when I say 'perhaps more *espressivo*'. Whereas, in a conversation, we need to find the words.

Still, the musical rehearsal resembles those discussions, in which the skills of listening to others become as important as making clear statements. The philosopher Bernard Williams writes scathingly about the 'fetish of assertion', that impulse to ram home your case as though its content is all that counts.[21] Listening skills don't figure much in this kind of verbal joust; the interlocutor is meant to admire and so to agree, or to counter with equal assertiveness – the familiar dialogue of the deaf in most political debate.

And, though a speaker may express him- or herself awkwardly, the good listener cannot dwell on the sheer fact of that insufficiency. The good listener has to respond to intent, to suggestion, for the conversation to keep moving forward.

Listening carefully produces conversations of two sorts, the dialectic and the dialogic. In dialectic, as we learned in school, the verbal play of opposites should gradually build up to a synthesis; dialectic starts in Aristotle's observation in the *Politics* that 'though we may use the same words, we cannot say we are speaking of the same things'; the aim is to come eventually to a common understanding.[22] Skill in practising dialectic lies in detecting what might establish that common ground.

About this skill, Theodore Zeldin writes, in a small, wise book on conversation, that the good listener detects common ground more in what another person assumes than says.[23] The listener elaborates that assumption by putting it into words. You pick up on the intention, the context, make it explicit, and talk about it. Another kind of skill appears in the Platonic dialogues, where Socrates proves a very good listener by re-stating 'in other words' what his discussants declare – but the re-statement is not exactly what they have actually said, or indeed intended. The echo is actually a displacement. This is why dialectic in Plato's dialogues does not resemble an argument, a verbal duel. The antithesis of a thesis is not 'you dumb bastard, you are wrong!' Rather, misunderstandings and cross purposes come into play, doubt is put on the table; people then have to listen harder to one another.

Something akin occurs in a musical rehearsal when a player observes, 'I don't get what you are doing, does it go like this?' The re-statement makes you think again about the sound and you may adjust as a result but not copy what you heard. In everyday conversation, this is the sense of the common phrase 'bouncing ideas off other people'; where these verbal balls land may surprise everyone.

'Dialogic' is a word coined by the Russian literary critic Mikhail Bakhtin to name a discussion which does not resolve itself by finding common ground. Though no shared agreements may be reached, through the process of exchange people may become more aware of their own views and expand their understanding of one another. 'Professor, your top note sounds harsh' inaugurated a dialogic exchange in rehearsing the Schubert Octet. Bakhtin applied the concept of knitted-together but divergent exchange to writers like Rabelais and Cervantes, whose dialogues are just the opposite of the converging agreement in dialectic. Rabelais's characters shoot off in seemingly irrelevant directions which other characters pick up on; the discussion then thickens, the characters spurred on by one another.[24] Sometimes great performances of chamber music convey something akin. The players do not sound entirely on the same page, the performance has more texture, more complexity, but still the players are sparking off one another – as true in classic chamber music as in jazz.

Of course, the difference between dialectic and dialogic conversation is not a matter of either/or. As in Zeldin's version of a dialectical conversation, the forward movement in dialogic conversation comes from paying attention to what another person implies but does not say; as in Socrates' cunning 'in other words', in a dialogic conversation misunderstandings can eventually clarify mutual understanding. The heart of all listening skills, though, lies in picking up on concrete details, on specifics, to drive a conversation forward. Bad listeners bounce back in generalities when they respond; they're not attending to those small phrases, facial gestures or silences which open up a discussion. In verbal conversation, as in musical rehearsal, exchanging is built from the ground up.

Inexperienced anthropologists and sociologists can suffer a peculiar challenge in conducting discussions. They are sometimes too eager to respond, going wherever their subjects lead; they do not argue, they went to show that they are responsive, that they care. A big issue lurks here. A dialogic conversation can be ruined by too much identification with the other person.

Sympathy and empathy

We imagine awareness of others most commonly as a matter of sympathy, which means identification with them. In the classic words of the American President Bill Clinton, 'I feel your pain.' In *The Theory of Moral Sentiments*, Adam Smith portrays it as a person's 'endeavour . . . to put himself in the situation of the other, and to bring home to himself every little circumstance of distress which can possibly occur to the sufferer . . . in its minutest incidents'.[25] Smith puts a particular gloss on the biblical injunction to do unto others as you would have them do to you. A person must see him- or herself in the other, not just as a fellow human being, but in those 'minutest incidents', which in fact often diverge greatly from one's own concrete experience. In Smith's view, imagination can overcome these barriers; it can make a magic leap from difference to likeness so that strange or foreign experience seems our own. Then we can identify with them and will sympathize with their trials.

Instant, generalized sympathy of the Clintonian sort animates many inexperienced social-science interviewers, with bad consequences. The hard work Adam Smith recommends of imagining the specifics of another human being's experience does not occur. Nor does 'I feel your pain' help musicians play together better. Of more use to both interviewer and musician is another form of engagement: empathy.

In a musical rehearsal, a string player may realize that his or her fellow musicians hear a musical phrase in an entirely different way and so phrase differently with their bows; he or she registers the difference. The sympathetic response would be to identify with and so imitate them. The empathic response is cooler: 'You do an up-bow, I do a down-bow . . .'; the difference may be left hanging in the air but a sign of recognizing what you are doing has been given. In an interview, the listener's empathy can be expressed by maintaining eye-contact even while keeping silent, conveying 'I am attending intently to you' rather than 'I know just what you feel'.* Curiosity figures more strongly in empathy than in sympathy.

Both sympathy and empathy convey recognition, and both forge a bond, but the one is an embrace, the other an encounter. Sympathy overcomes differences through imaginative acts of identification; empathy attends to another person on his or her own terms. Sympathy has usually been thought a stronger sentiment than empathy, because 'I feel your pain' puts the stress on what I feel; it activates one's own ego. Empathy is a more demanding exercise, at least in listening; the listener has to get outside him- or herself.

Both these recognitions are necessary at different times and in different ways to practise cooperation. If a group of miners is trapped below ground, 'I feel your pain' activates our desire to help them out; it doesn't matter that we may never have been down a mineshaft; we leap over that difference. But there are situations in which we help other people precisely when we do not imagine ourselves like them, as in letting someone in mourning talk, not presuming to intrude on what they are going through. Empathy has a particular political application; by practising it a legislator or union leader could – certainly

---

* This is why, in training young ethnographers, I work as much with bodily gestures and the use of the eyes as with their questionnaires.

it's a distant possibility – learn from his or her constituents rather than simply speak in their name. More realistically, empathic listening can assist the community worker, priest or teacher mediate in communities where people do not share the same race or ethnicity.

As a philosophic matter, sympathy can be understood as one emotional reward for the thesis-antithesis-synthesis play of dialectic: 'Finally, we understand each other,' and that feels good. Empathy is more linked to dialogic exchange; though curiosity sustains the exchange, we don't experience the same satisfaction of closure, of wrapping things up. But empathy does contain its own emotional reward.

Indirection

'Fuck you, fuck you' is more than an outburst of sheer aggression; it is paralysing. Confronted with this outburst the most likely response is, 'Well, fuck you too.' The antagonists are now locked in. When I first came to live in Britain, I thought Prime Minister's Question Time in Parliament was an example like this, a verbal combat in which the Prime Minister and the Leader of the Opposition do not give an inch, and seem on the verge of coming to blows. Of course, they don't; today this seemingly mortal combat, like professional wrestling in America, is made for television. But in real life rigid verbal aggression frequently crosses the line.

More youthful experience of Brits revealed to me one way out of this danger. As a young music student, fresh from the competitive pressure cooker of the Juilliard School in New York, I was amazed when I first began to rehearse with young musicians in London; discussions were couched in terms of 'possibly' and 'perhaps' and 'I would have thought'. So too in other conversations, whether in a local pub or a patron-grandee's drawing room, the Brits proved themselves skilled masters in the use of the subjunctive mood.

Only courtesy? It is that, yet not just politeness. Rehearsals went more effectively because this subjunctive mood opened up a space for experiment; tentativeness issued an invitation to others to join in. It's certainly true that diffidence, like embarrassment, can be an inverted form of narcissism, a person being intensely – too intensely – aware of her- or himself. It's also true that the British like to see themselves as less competitively driven than Americans; in my experience they were every bit as ambitious, but didn't let it show as much. This made for good cooperation in the rehearsal studio, and eased conversation in the pub.

When I became a social researcher, the subjunctive mood loomed larger for me in thinking about human relations. Diplomats need to master this mood in negotiating with each another when trying to avoid war; so too in business dealings and in everyday sociability, 'perhaps' and 'I would have thought' are antidotes to paralysed positions. The subjunctive mood counters Bernard Williams's fear of the fetish of assertiveness by opening up instead an indeterminate mutual space, the space in which strangers dwell with one another, whether these strangers be immigrants and natives thrown together in a city or gays and straights living in the same street. The social engine is oiled when people do not behave too emphatically.

The subjunctive mood is most at home in the dialogical domain, that world of talk which makes an open social space, where discussion can take an unforeseen direction. The dialogic conversation, as noted, prospers through empathy, the sentiment of curiosity about who other people are in themselves. This is a cooler sentiment than sympathy's often instant identifications, yet empathy's rewards are not stone-cold. By practising indirection, speaking to one another in the subjunctive mood, we can experience a certain kind of sociable pleasure: being with other people, focusing on and learning about them, without forcing ourselves into the mould of being like them.

Certainly for me this is the pleasure which comes from ethnographic fieldwork: you get out and about, meeting people unlike yourself. The pleasures of relaxed chat, of casual conversation, like a stroll down an unfamiliar street, encourage the ethnographer in everyone. There's a dose of voyeurism in this, but perhaps voyeurism has too bad a name; life would be intolerably cramped if we only knew about people we knew intimately. As in looking carefully, so a casual conversation requires skill to become a meaningful encounter; refraining from assertiveness is a discipline that makes a space for looking into another person's life, and for them, equally, to look into yours.

The conversation is like the rehearsal in which listening skills come to the fore. Listening well is an interpretative activity which works best by focusing on the specifics of what one hears, as when we seek to fathom from those particulars what another person has taken for granted but not said. Dialectic and dialogic procedures offer two ways of practising a conversation, the one by a play of contraries leading to agreement, the other by bouncing off views and experiences in an open-ended way. In listening well, we can feel either sympathy or empathy; both are cooperative impulses. Sympathy is the more arousing, empathy the cooler, and the more demanding, since it requires us to focus outside ourselves. In dialogics, while people do not neatly fit together like pieces in a jigsaw puzzle, yet they can get both knowledge and pleasure from their exchanges. 'Perhaps' makes it easier to cooperate in talking. These conversational skills may seem very far from the sandbox in which toddlers play with one another. There is, however, a connection. In the earliest stages of life, human beings learn how to rehearse cooperation, exploring its different, shifting forms. Eventually, conversations among adults sort out these possibilities into two tracks.

Modern society is much better at organizing the first sort of exchange than the second, better at communicating through dialectical argument than through dialogic discussion. That contrast appears strikingly in the technological frontier for cooperation.

COOPERATION ONLINE

Like many people my age, online communication does not come naturally to me. When I write letters, I take time and care over the writing, and so I write few; the avalanche of emails I get every day is disheartening in its sheer number. Conversely, conducting a written conversation online seems painfully slow, compared with speaking to someone on the phone or face to face. New communications technologies have, however, irreversibly transformed the landscape of communication.

Their most potent political effect occurs when they stimulate and arouse people to act off-line, rather than containing them to experience on-screen. Ironically, compressed tweets and text messages can have this effect, as in the Tunisian and Egyptian uprisings of 2011; compressed messages told people where a significant event was happening, or who was involved; people went to the town square, government building or barracks to work out what they should do next; the compressed message is too fragmentary or brief to perform a political analysis. Facebook images have this same compressed effect: they show the significant action happening, and issue the urgent invitation, 'Be there!' When communication works this way, compressed communication is released physically, by massing the presence of people; cooperation online translates into cooperation in the flesh.

What of online communication? Do these exchanges have the same arousing power? To find out, I agreed to become part of a beta-testing group working with GoogleWave, a program designed specifically for serious online cooperation. Fresh out of the box, GoogleWave looked good. It aimed to make ideas and contributions appear on-screen in crisp and clear form; it tried to be open, so that participants could add to it freely, or alter the project itself in the course of time. An old Renaissance idea of the experimental workshop seemed to have found in GoogleWave a new site in cyberspace. But this effort didn't succeed; GoogleWave was up and running for just one year, from 2009 to 2010, before the company declared it a failure and shut it down.

The GoogleWave group I joined sought to assemble information and create policy about migration to London. The data our group had to interpret consisted of statistics, transcribed interviews, photographs and film of immigrant communities, maps of where people came from and where they settled in London. The participants were scattered across London, Britain and the Continent; we posted, read and chatted every few days.

Our project puzzled particularly about why, among Muslim families, the second generation of immigrants to Britain tends to be more disaffected with the country than the beachhead, first generation. But we also faced a technical challenge. Statisticians and ethnographers have different kinds of evidence for disaffection: the statisticians chart paths of mobility in education and in work that were blocked; the ethnographers find the young idealizing culturally the places and ways of life their parents left, no matter their present circumstances.

Just to make matters more complicated, the government sponsor, worried about 'alienated' Muslim youth, wanted to know what policies it should put in place. Could online cooperation sort all this out?

The aim of the project was very different than that of social networking online, though both use the same basic technology. We didn't want to engage in 'friending', and we didn't have to worry about Facebook's violations of privacy. Many social networking sites aren't, indeed, very socially interactive. In cyberspace, the writer Sarah Bakewell ruefully observes, 'the twenty-first century is full of people who are full of themselves' online; 'a half-hour's trawl through the online ocean of blogs, tweets . . . brings up thousands of individuals, fascinated by their own personalities and shouting for attention.'[26] Her observation is just but incomplete. The same technology can enable more consequent conversation, as in the online chat room for breast cancer patients studied by Shani Orgad. On this site, women share with one another vital information and experience to supplement their communication with doctors; Orgad found the chat room often proves more helpful in coping with the disease than face-to-face exchanges in hospital.[27]

Of more immediate concern to us were the mental habits which discolour the political blogosphere, filled as it is with aggressive opinion-pushing rather than real give-and-take discussion – a huge archipelago, Cass Sunstein fears, of us-against-them expression.[28] We had to break these online habits which exemplify the fetish of assertion; only a dialogical, exploratory conversation could help us gain insight into the complex issues we faced.

I had imagined when we started that the GoogleWave technology would enable that sort of conversation, but the program worked against it. The program's engineers had a definite idea about what cooperation entails; theirs was the dialectical model of conversation, one conducted in visual form. GoogleWave makes use of coloured text, hypertext links and side-windows to shape a converging narrative appearing in the largest box on-screen. The big box shows a straight-line account of how the play of views can arrive at consensus, from inception to consummation of a project. The program preserves what has come up before in a discussion, and makes the past immediately accessible with a click of the mouse; the visual set-up at a given moment, though, side-windows or suppresses what have come to seem irrelevancies and dead ends.

The instructions given to us for using GoogleWave claimed this set-up was an efficient way to cooperate, since irrelevancies fall to the wayside, but the program proved too simple. Its dialectical, linear structure failed to account for the complexities which develop through cooperation. One feature of all true experiment is finding something you didn't expect. Discovery of this sort obliges people, as we commonly say, to 'think outside the box', that new way of making associations and comparison the historian of science Thomas Kuhn labels a 'paradigm shift'. The structure GoogleWave provided for cooperative conversation visually inhibited thinking outside the box; it discarded just those seeming irrelevancies which later on proved pregnant.

In our group, as give and take focused ever more on the one issue of religion, interjections like 'What about young women moving to London from the North?' registered less, seeming irrelevant, and so were side-barred or side-screened. Someone queried the researcher who had earlier interjected the issue of young women migrants, 'We haven't heard from you in a while.' She responded, 'No, the work has moved on.' Her time had passed, but, as we were ultimately to find, gender was a key variable for unlocking who in the second generation becomes alienated and who does not. Hers was a dialogic response, introducing a seemingly extraneous element, and that response was suppressed by side-screening it.

Side-screening has a profound social consequence within an online group: if dialogic reactions are eliminated step by step, the contributors of stray thoughts can feel left out as the project becomes increasingly defined. Because complex layers of meaning did not seem to build up, dealing with neither our social nor technical issues, enthusiasm in our group began to wane as we followed the dialectical narrative envisaged by the program.

GoogleWave is not, I should emphasize, a dictator. It can be rejigged, for instance, by making the main screen smaller than all the side-bars surrounding it. Instead of the 'moderator' recommended by

GoogleWave – who could become a mental traffic-cop winnowing out supposedly irrelevant ideas – we gave each participant a distinctively coloured, dotted or dashed line to draw arrows between windows, suggesting further connections. But the screen looked increasingly a mess, becoming harder to use. So instead of working online, we increasingly started to board aeroplanes – the hideous torture-tools of modern society – meeting face to face to practise more effective lateral thinking, including everyone fully in the conversation.

'I can't see why people wouldn't want it,' said Lars Rasmussen, one of its designers (with his brother also the programmer behind Google-Maps). The program was proving a fiasco for other users, and in the summer of 2010 Google cancelled the service it had begun a year before. 'It's a very clever product. You never know why it didn't work,' declared Google chief executive Eric Schmidt.[29] Perhaps it is not such a mystery. We wanted a more dialogic kind of cooperation.

One large reason for failure may be that the program mistook information-sharing for communication. Information-sharing is an exercise in definition and precision, whereas communication is as much about what is left unsaid as said; communication mines the realm of suggestion and connotation. In the hurry which attends emailing, responses tend to get stripped down to the bare minimum; in online exchanges like GoogleWave, where the visual dominates, it's hard to convey irony or doubt; simple information-sharing subtracts expression.

The divide between information and communication affects the institutional practice of cooperation. Studies of corporations, hospitals and schools that run on email or email-like technologies show that shedding context often means shedding sense; understanding between people shrinks. Online commands enacted through denotative language produce abstract guidelines; people below have constantly to read between the lines coming from employers – who are seldom gifted writers. Interaction about concrete problems slows, requiring ever more emails to deal with particular cases. These reductions of sense worry Jaron Lanier, the technologist who built the first programs to simulate reality in three dimensions on-screen: 'when my friends and I built the first virtual reality machines, the whole point was to make this world more creative, expressive, empathic, and interesting . . . not to escape it.'[30]

The defect in this program is not uniquely Google-ish; many other programs (some still standing and freely available in Linux) imagine cooperation in dialectical rather than dialogical terms; the result is again constrained experiment and inhibited cooperation. It could be said that the programmers did not allow users to rehearse via their machines, testing out possibilities for interaction with one another. 'Rehearsal', as I've tried to show in these pages, is a category of experience, rooted in infant and child development, which expands the capacity to communicate. This is the paradoxical thing about Google-Wave: it showed that, in undertaking cooperation, users are capable of handling more complexity than the programmers provided for; the programmers' imaginations were insufficient to the conversation people needed to conduct.

The fault, I want to emphasize, is in the software rather than in the hardware, software written by engineers with an inadequate understanding of social exchange. The failure of GoogleWave highlights the contrasting virtue of the same hardware to ends, like political revolt, which the engineers did not envision when the programs were written. Lanier's caution is that in ordinary usage the technology is more likely to bend human will than to bend in response to it; put another way, you have to struggle with or deform an engineered social programme to practise complex social exchange.

Failure to enable complexity is a sweeping theme in the work of the philosophers Amartya Sen and Martha Nussbaum. Their 'capabilities theory' argues that our emotional and cognitive capacities are erratically realized in modern society; human beings are capable of doing more than schools, workplaces, civil organizations and political regimes allow for.[31] Sen and Nussbaum's views have been an inspiration for me, and provide the orienting theme for this book: people's capacities for cooperation are far greater and more complex than institutions allow them to be. In this Introduction I've tried to show how rich can be the experience of responding to others. What then follows?

THIS BOOK

This book is divided into three parts, exploring how cooperation can be shaped, weakened and strengthened. Each part explores cooperation in the round, drawing on research in anthropology, history, sociology and politics. The book proceeds through a series of concrete case studies. I've framed these for a dialogical discussion rather than cut-and-thrust dialectical argument; I'll try to enlist your critical engagement rather than to score points or wrestle you into a particular position. I want to practise cooperation on the page.

Part One begins with how cooperation is shaped in politics. The focus here is on solidarity, since us-against-them is writ large in the modern political landscape. Is there a sort of politics of cooperation which can contest it? Chapter 2 takes up the relation of competition and cooperation. They are related in complex ways which I'll try to plumb anthropologically. Chapter 3 provides one particular framework for how cooperation has been shaped historically. How to cooperate became a question at the dawn of the modern era, as science began to separate from religion, and in Europe religion itself divided.

The second part of the book, on how cooperation can be weakened, is sociological in character, and zeroes in on the present. Here I engage with the critical viewpoint of Sen and Nussbaum. To do so, Chapter 4 probes how the inequalities children experience affect their cooperative experience. Chapter 5 explores the erosion of cooperation in adult work; here I pay particular attention to the diminished relations, on the job, of cooperation, authority and trust. Chapter 6 contemplates a new character type emerging in modern society, an uncooperative self, ill-disposed for dealing with complexity and difference. All social critique risks the dangers of drawing a cartoon; mindful of this, I've tried to give as nuanced an account as I can of these social ills.

Part Three considers ways in which cooperation might be strengthened, and my focus throughout is on the skills which could make it so. In the Preface I invoked rather casually the phrase 'cooperation as a craft'. Now I dig deeper into it, trying to show in Chapter 7 what can be learned about social life from the craft of making and repairing physical things. Chapter 8 proceeds to one application in what I'll dub 'everyday diplomacy', the craft of working with people we disagree with, perhaps don't like, or don't understand; the techniques for doing this relate to performance practices. Part Three concludes in Chapter 9 with an exploration of commitment. Responsiveness to others, cooperation with them, obviously requires some kind of commitment, but commitment comes in many forms: which should we choose?

This is how I've sought to see cooperation in the round, from many different angles. The world I've come to inhabit as a sociologist is infested with policy wonks, people who make a career of telling other people how to behave. At the book's end, I can't offer the wisdom of policy-wonkery. Instead, I've sought to relate this journey to the most dialogical of all writers, the essayist Michel de Montaigne.

PART ONE

Cooperation Shaped

I

'The Social Question'

Reformers in Paris Explore a Puzzle

A visitor to the Paris Universal Exposition in 1900 searched hard to find its most explosive exhibit. Out in the open, the Exposition sprawled over the vast *Champ de Mars* fairground in the shadow of the Eiffel Tower, the tower painted a beckoning bright yellow; beneath it, stands displayed the very latest in flush toilets, machine guns and industrial cotton-looms. In the open air, officialdom celebrated 'The Triumph of Industry and Empire', but tucked away on a side street were cramped rooms devoted to reckoning the human issues raised by this triumph. The fair's organizers dubbed the side-space a *musée social*, a social museum, a Louvre of labour meant to show how capitalism gets its work done. The exhibitors described their rooms quite differently, naming the space *La Question sociale* – 'The Social Question'.[1]

No modern museum curator would ever have mounted a show as these exhibitors did. A modern curator will pay a fortune for a canvas of dried human blood, this 'transgressive' object presented as somehow making a social 'statement'. The statements made in the Paris rooms came mostly in the form of documents and maps tacked up on the walls. One wall displayed Charles Booth's maps of poverty in London, 'the class relations of the city outlined, street by street, in bright washes of wealth and dark masses of poverty'.[2] The Germans posted documents on the history-making coalition of labour unions and political parties represented by Ferdinand Lassalle's *Allgemeiner Deutscher Arbeiterverein* (General German Workers Association, including both skilled and semi-skilled workers); the French hung up various pamphlets on social policy; mixed among government reports was testimony from various voluntary associations in local communities, most notably documents from the nascent Catholic Worker movement.

The American exhibit was the smallest. Much of it dwelt on race, a novelty of sorts for Europeans, who generally focused on class. In one corner of the exhibit visitors found pinned up a daunting statistical study by W. E. B. Dubois on the fate of African-Americans in the state of Georgia since the end of slavery. In another corner, the American room contained a tangible display of handiwork from the Hampton and Tuskegee Institutes, institutions training African-American ex-slaves to become artisans – artisans whose work together was no longed enforced by the lash of a master.[3]

Though couched in dry language, all the exhibits in these rooms were meant to be provoking, and succeeded, at least in terms of visitor numbers. After the inauguration, tourists to the Universal Exposition wandered rather aimlessly among the flush toilets and industrial drills; but as attendance thinned out on the *Champ de Mars*, the alternative rooms swarmed with people packed together discussing and arguing.

The contributors to the 'Social Question' rooms and their arguing visitors shared a common enemy: the surging capitalism of their era, its inequalities and oppressions. They were convinced that raw capitalism could not produce a good quality of life for the masses. Yet the exhibits on the edge of the *Champ de Mars* did not dwell on this enemy in itself; this was a more adult forum than the modern curator's transgressive exhibit meant to elicit howls of shock, horror and rage. The Parisians had aptly named their project 'The Social Question'. How should society be made different? Socialist kitsch – happy workers singing while working for the revolution – did not figure among the answers; nor had proposals for reform degraded into simple media labels like 'fairness' or 'the big society' (as the British Left and Right have recently branded their politics).

The exhibitors did agree on a common theme. 'Solidarity' was the buzzword in these rooms; people debated what it meant. Solidarity named generally the connection between everyday social bonds and political organization. Cooperation made sense of this connection: the German's united labour union, the French Catholic voluntary organization and the American workshop exhibited three ways to practise face-to-face cooperation in order to bring about solidarity. The more radical among the Parisian exhibitors took these examples of cooperative activity as an invitation to think about the social in socialism.

We should dwell for a moment on that word 'social', for it was at this time undergoing a sea change in social thought.

Migrants at the end of the nineteenth century flooded into European cities, and immigrants to America left the Continent altogether. Industrialization created a geography of isolation wherever it took hold, so that vast numbers of workers knew little, inside the factory or at home, about people unlike themselves. Industrial cities were becoming internally more dense; the isolated classes were compacted ever more tightly. What could arouse mutual understanding among these people, who knew one another not even though they were pressed together?

Answering that question preoccupied Georg Simmel (1858–1918), who did not attend the *musée social* but avidly followed debates about the social question. His work was a radical enterprise that connected history, sociology and philosophy; his life exemplified a particular struggle with social relatedness. Jewish origins kept him out of German academic life until well into middle age; marriage to a Lutheran estranged him from his Jewish roots. He had good cause to see himself as marginal, though as a German bourgeois his marginality was not life-threatening. Still, he did not stew in this estranged state. He thought it to be the condition of modern man, and believed it contained a certain promise.

Modern social life went beyond the sheer pleasure people take in one another's company, which Germans call *Geselligkeit*. In a talk given in 1910 in Frankfurt, Simmel argued that this pleasure is universal, occurring in all human development, as the physical body-sports and rough-housing of children gradually modulate into friendly words shared in a bar or café.[4] As he contemplated the arrival of ethnic immigrants, mostly very poor Jews from Eastern Europe, in Germany's midst, Simmel wondered what the intrusion of strangers would do to this playful, sociable pleasure. If living amid foreign bodies tamps down *Geselligkeit*, he thought, their presence can also deepen social awareness; the arrival of a stranger can make others think about values they take for granted.[5]

Stranger-shock Simmel found strongest in big, expanding cities like Berlin. New stimulation constantly occurs in a city's streets, particularly in places like the Potsdamer Platz of his day where streets emptied their differing human contents into a concentrated centre. A celebrant of difference, Simmel thought his contemporary Ferdinand Tönnies – who equated 'the social' with intimate, small-scale community (*Gemeinschaft*) – wore blinkers; life with others is bigger, richer.[6]

Yet awareness of others occurs inside the urbanite's head. The man or woman of the city, Simmel said, dons a cold, rational mask in public to protect him- or herself against the waves of stimulation coming from outside; if the presence of others is felt, the urbanite seldom shows what he or she feels. Packed densely together with strangers, seeing but not speaking to them, masked, modern man has taken a journey in the city from the universal, sociable pleasures of *Geselligkeit* to a subjective condition Simmel called 'sociality'.

Though this word is not ordinarily used in English, it has long existed in French, as *socialité*. In French usage, *socialité* includes the assurance people possess to deal with difficult or hostile situations, as when diplomats sit down at the negotiating table; they don an imperturbable mask, open to what others say but cool and calm, not instantly responsive. In this, *socialité* is a cousin to empathy, as described in the Introduction to this book. It too requires skill; the French link capable behaviour in difficult situations to *savoir faire*, a word with a larger compass than knowing which wines to order in a restaurant. To Simmel, the virtue of sociality is that it can run deep, rather than consisting just of casual impressions. He explains this by contrasting sociality to *Verbindung*, the German word for tying together, making whole again, healing. Sociality can have a tragic scope in recognizing those wounds of mutual experience that do not heal. What Simmel had in mind was brought home to me by a Vietnamese taxi driver who addressed a group of Americans returning to Hanoi twenty years after America's ill-fated war: 'We have not forgotten you.' He said nothing more and nothing less, he offered simply the acknowledgement of a painful connection rather than healing words. My companions, admirably, said nothing in return.

For all this, sociality is not an active reaching out to others; it is mutual awareness instead of action together. Sociality thus contrasts to solidarity. In Paris, the radicals debating the 'Social Question' took an opposing course to Simmel's thinking: they wanted to heal the cracks and separations in society through concerted action, they wanted *Verbindung*. A particular call to arms arose from the Dreyfus Affair in France, which began in 1894 with the trumped-up conviction for treason of a Jewish military officer, and from the election of the anti-Semitic Karl Luegar as Vienna's mayor in 1895. Many ordinary workers in both places turned against poor Jewish neighbours as well as against Jews higher up the social scale. Some radicals addressed this eruption by preaching toleration, which is a very Simmelian virtue; sociality asks you to accept the stranger as a valued presence in your midst. Others said toleration alone could not suffice; the working classes needed a more engaging, bonding experience, such as going on strike together for higher wages, to heal the ethnic breach.

The more vigorous meaning participants and visitors to the *museé social* gave to 'the social' did not, however, unify them. Their debates about solidarity raised two big issues. The Left divided between those who sought to establish solidarity top-down and those who sought to create it bottom-up; the centralized German labour union represented the one approach, the local American workshop the other. This divide led to a question about cooperation. The top-down activists thought about cooperation as a tool, a means, for realizing their political goals; to achieve political ends, discipline has to be imposed on face-to-face exchanges. Local activists working from the ground up worried about the power-games within their small organizations: who rules the group, who is accepted or excluded? The local activists wanted as much free participation as possible within the parish hall or on the street, even if this meant sacrificing a certain amount of discipline.

There were thus two versions of solidarity in these discussions, the one emphasizing unity, the other inclusion. These contrasts were not unique to the Left, nor do they belong just to the past. Movements of all political stripes have to decide whether to emphasize unity or more diverse inclusion, they have to cope with intra-group politics, they have to define the kind of solidarity they want. In the course of the twentieth century, the two versions of solidarity came to mark off what could be called the political Left from the social Left.

THE DIVIDED PATH

In Paris, activists on the political Left argued that you have to counter big power with big power; large political parties and labour unions are the only way to transform the capitalist beast.

Military organization served as one model for this radical politics. The very word 'militant' has, from the twelfth century, been used as a synonym for soldier of all sorts; during the Counter-Reformation the Catholic Church began to speak of itself as a militant organization at war with Protestants; in the early twentieth century the word came into colloquial use, in both England and France, to apply specifically to radical politics. Saint-Just's *Institutes* and Lenin's *What is to be Done?* are equally bloodthirsty radical tracts, but, at the end of the eighteenth century, Saint-Just likens the revolutionary most often to the policeman, whereas in the early twentieth century Lenin's language moves seamlessly between organized politics and warfare. As in an army, Lenin writes, radical discipline has to come from the top; solidarity requires surrender of self among the troops. Verbally, militant activism of Lenin's sort made the 'fetish of assertion' (discussed in the Introduction) into a virtue.

Because Marxism-Leninism so dominated the later history of state socialism, it might be imagined as identical with top-down politics on the Left, but that was not the case a century ago; in fact, top-down politics pitted many radicals against Marxism. They sensed, correctly, that Marxism would dwell on warfare against other Left parties rather than seek to cooperate with them. The publication of Karl Marx's *Critique of the Gotha Programme*, a pamphlet written in 1875, encapsulated this refusal to cooperate; the pamphlet attacked the nascent Social Democratic Party in Germany – the strongest Left organization in Europe – for being insufficiently revolutionary; the pamphlet managed to turn most friends into enemies, and remains a foundational text of fratricide on the Left.

For the German Social Democrats, as for French radicals rebuilding their political fortunes after Germany's invasion of France in 1870, solidarity required absorbing factions and splinter groups on the Left into a single whole. Collective bargaining on a national scale, seeking strength in numbers, was an invention of the later nineteenth century. It was intended to establish a common thread between people who did very different kinds of industrial and craft labour; however, many workers clung to the old guild ideal of a trade as something special, each trade having its own political interests. To overcome that disposition needed a measure of accommodation and compromise between groups; still, action on the national or European level sought to establish the main themes of struggle, leaving relatively minor variations of practice and belief to particular trades or local communities. Strength dictated organizational hierarchy. As Hannah Arendt has observed about German Left political parties based on union membership, equality of views within the organization was seen more as a threat than as a bond.[7]

It's important not to make a cartoon of firm rule from the top. Ferdinand Lassalle and his followers were willing to engage in ferocious debate, but wanted to keep turf, strategic and ideological quarrels private so that in public they could present a united front. Any dialogic bouncing-off of views and lateral thinking, in public, seemed to spell political weakness to the national leaders, effectiveness in fighting the capitalist bosses requiring unity top-down. So they feared and suppressed people like Gustav Kessler (1832–1904), who argued for the primacy of local unions and political parties, each going its own, sometimes erratic, way.

The conditions of struggle made theirs an urgent view, as Samuel Gompers in America and the Fabian socialist Edward Coulson in Britain, both leading lights of labour organizing at the time of the Universal Exposition, knew only too well. These labour organizers were in the position of outnumbered soldiers, their right to protest unprotected by government, their strikers often violently menaced by employers and hired security forces, their unions occasionally betrayed by informers from within. Internally, wildcat strikes in Europe and America proved equally destabilizing to the movement, spontaneous rebellions lacking discipline and so fizzling out. In this climate of menace and disorder, solidarity had to entail both rigidity and fixed hierarchy; were the leadership to change constantly, acquired knowledge and experience would disappear; new officials would have to learn the enemy's ways all over again. This is one reason why union elections in the early decades of the twentieth century in America, Britain and France tended to return the same veteran cast of characters.

Most people in the rooms dedicated to the 'Social Question' could also draw on a memory which argued for clarity of purpose and disciplined action. This was the short-lived Paris Commune of 1871, which existed for a period of months after the fall of the empire of Napoleon III when the city was surrounded by the German army. During this siege, Parisians, with a shifting and weak cast of leaders, argued and voted about every aspect of daily life. Reports from within the siege speak of everyday acts of mutual help and support, as when the citizens peacefully shared out the animals in the Paris zoo for food; improvised acts of cooperation were no strategy for survival, however, and the German army, cheered on by the provincial bourgeoisie, soon brought an end to it. The Commune thereafter haunted the imagination of the European Left: its individual acts of generosity, its spontaneous mutual support, but also its inevitable doom.

The other side of the divide seemed to inhabit a different world; reformers were concerned with such social questions as lack of education, the management of family life, housing or the isolation of newcomers to cities. Community and labour organizers on the social Left believed that dealing with these conditions meant change built from the ground up. In this, they drew upon a long-standing nineteenth-century movement called 'associationism', the origins of modern grass-roots organizing. This movement emphasized the sheer act of cooperation with others as an end in itself rather than as a strategic tool. Associationism did not at its beginnings belong to any political ideology. Local American Church organizations practised under its banner as did nineteenth-century British Masonic lodges; associationism justified, in France, the revival of *confréries*, old guilds made new as charitable bodies; in nineteenth-century France, consumer cooperatives were formed as adjuncts to *confréries*; in

Britain, building societies provided workers with loans for homes. Association as an end in itself was invoked by the anarchist Peter Kropotkin, who believed unions should function like communities rather than become the base for political parties, a view of unionism that held sway in places as widely separated as Barcelona, Moscow and the American Northwest.

The divide between the political and social Left is sometimes drawn as a contrast between Europe and America, European radicals focusing top-down on the state, Americans bottom-up on civil society. As the instances cited above make clear, this stark contrast won't do. Moreover, after the Civil War, as the social analyst Theda Skocpol has shown, America developed the rudiments of a welfare state, and by 1900 a good deal of political activity on the American Left was devoted to strengthening it.[8] Rather than nationality, the difference between the political and social Left lay in the contrast between national and local solidarities.

The star exhibit in Paris for solidarity built from the ground up was the settlement house. In form the settlement house was a voluntary association, located in a poor urban community, where poorly skilled workers could receive education, get advice on everyday problems or simply find a warm, clean place to hang out. The providers of services were mostly middle-class women, usually working for nothing; middle-class donors bought or underwrote the buildings, though in some settlement houses the poor contributed what they could by cleaning, repairs and cooking for the community. Settlement houses were small, usually one or two full-time workers supplemented by a dozen or so part-time visitors serving a community of 600–800 people who came to the settlement houses at night (infant care was minimal, and older children usually had to go out to work during the day). The settlement-house movement gathered steam in the later decades of the nineteenth century, spreading in Europe from the East End of London to Moscow, where worker-houses were founded by Alexander Zelenko; they reached across the Atlantic to shelters in New York and to the Hull House settlement founded by Jane Addams in Chicago.

The small display of the Hampton and Tuskegee Institutes also fell on the social side of the divide. These local institutions meant to build up the skills and the morale of ex-slaves through cooperative work. The Institutes were small, like the settlement houses, and they relied on wealthy white donors for cash. They differed from the settlement houses in that many African-Americans had, as slaves on plantations, developed sophisticated skills in farming, carpentering, house building and domestic management. Older ex-slaves now taught these skills to a younger generation; there were few white teachers.

The European roots of the American workshops can be traced in part to Robert Owen. Born in 1771 to a moderately prosperous Welsh family, Owen had already in his teens proved an adept manager of new industrial enterprises springing up in Britain. But he was also an unhappy manager. The workplaces he knew and hated first-hand were British textile mills spinning cloth out of cotton from the colonies, and industrialized mines. These were both scenes of the blind, soulless division of labour. In their stead he imagined cooperative communities which would create a 'new moral world' leading ultimately to socialist society. An idealist? Certainly, though one of the workshop communities he founded, New Harmony, Indiana, did survive in modified form for a long time.

More important for the social Left were Owen's differences from Marx. In 1844 Owen formulated a set of precepts, the Rochdale Principles, which have served as a beacon to Leftists of a less combative stripe than Marx's followers. Six in number, these principles are: workshops open to anyone (equality of employment); one person one vote (democracy in the workplace); distribution of surplus in relation to trade (profit-sharing); cash trading (he hated 'abstract debt' and would have eschewed the modern credit card); political and religious neutrality (and so, toleration of differences at work); and promotion of education (job training tied to employment). In the 'Gotha Programme' Marx bitterly attacked principle five: there is no such thing as political neutrality, and religion, that 'opiate of the masses', should be demystified. Still, Owen's version of socialism built from the ground up in a workshop became a founding text for social democracy; when we think about the rights of labour today, we generally revert to one or more of these principles.

*

By 1900, then, the political and social Left had roughly divided along these enduring lines. In principle the two should have combined since they were addressing the same injustices. In practice, they did not. The difference between top-down and ground-up may be a matter of temperament, at least as the divide has come down to us in modern times, a difference in temperament that has a wider compass than the Left's own inner struggles. Liberal and conservative reformers also experience this divide in outlook: any think tank filled with policy wonks who speak in bullet-points is heir to the spirit of the old political Left; any grass-roots organization which embraces different, sometimes conflicting, sometimes incoherent voices is heir to the spirit of the old social Left. The one path emphasizes coming to shared conclusions, which is dialectic's goal; the other path emphasizes the dialogic process, in which mutual exchange may lead to no result. Along the one path, cooperation is a tool, a means; along the other, more of an end in itself.

But the divide is as much about practice as temperament. Men like Lassalle, Gompers and Coulson spoke in the name of tough-minded realism. They shared the memory of the Commune; some, like Samuel Gompers, thought the settlement houses did little to improve the material lot of the poor; Owen's workshops seemed to many of these realists a dream seducing people from more immediate and urgent problems. Yet equally, the realists rejected the fratricidal militancy of Marx's sort. The political Left wanted to become stronger through forging coalitions, yet found that practising cooperation could compromise them – this lesson, too, is part of their legacy.

COALITIONS

In Paris the distillation of this problem appeared in the German exhibit. That exhibit was big because by 1900 Germany had developed a full-blown welfare state. In the 1870s the German chancellor Otto von Bismarck had understood, in the wake of widespread unrest, that the social question needed to be solved for capitalism to survive. In the 1880s his government devised insurance plans for the sick and the aged; in the 1890s he improved German schools serving the poor.

Charity did not move Bismarck; his aim was to crush the Left politically by colonizing its social programme. And the welfare his government provided was real.

Though German universities were the envy of the scholarly world,* for the working classes the *Realschule* was a more important institution; these six-year secondary schools provided thorough training in a craft, in writing a business letter, in understanding accounting; a pupil who passed through the *Realschule* was fully prepared to serve as an apprentice in a shop or an office; during Germany's imperial age government began also to smooth the transition from education to employment. In the Paris Exposition, the fruits of that system were put up on the walls: photographs showed spotlessly clean classrooms or children proudly holding up machines they'd made in shop class; copies were displayed of concise letters written to prospective employers.

German political parties such as Lassalle's Social Democratic Party early on pressed for these gains, which were achieved through backroom negotiations with the conservative chancellor. But the reformers could not boast easily. The more the Left cooperated in reform, the more it risked losing its own distinct identity, because these negotiations behind the scenes involved bureaucratic complexities never explained to the public. Increasingly, the political Left was sucked into the opaque machinery of the state; reform became increasingly difficult to distinguish from co-optation.

This was not just a German problem, then or now. In the Britain of 2011, the Liberal Democrat Party is losing its identity in coalition with the Conservatives. As between parties, so within them, compromise dilutes identity: right-wing Tea Party legislators in America fear becoming less distinct as they are absorbed into the machinery of the Republican Party. Critics may decry every back-room accommodation itself as a sell-out, the united front presented in public may be dismissed as a cover-up. While armchair cynicism may be just that – an armchair exercise – cooperation at the apex of power produces a structural problem for all coalitions: the loss of connection of the apex to its base.

---

* The German research university inspired, in America, the creation of the University of Chicago and Johns Hopkins University.

This can be no more and no less than a dull matter of bureaucracy. In the late nineteenth century the Left's drive for power took a new turn when political parties began to base their fortunes on labour unions, a combination we now take for granted. The fusion of party politics and unions did grow European socialist groups to a big size, but growth produced a forest of bureaux and directorates within the organizations; as a result, face-to-face relations with the movement's base counted for less and less. Whatever their politics, this price is paid by most political movements when they become big.

This gap is made worse when there are many different groups in the back-room. As more interests have to be resolved through back-room negotiation, the resultant agreements become more convoluted and complicated, making it harder for the people represented by each of the contending parties to see themselves represented. In Europe today, the contrast between environmental coalitions in Germany and Italy is a good example. Coalition government in Germany, involving only two parties, has produced clear agreements which reflect the interests of at least some large slice of the Green base; the coalitions in Italian politics are so Byzantine that few members of its varied environmental parties involved feel their interests have been served.

Close students of top-down coalitions point to a delicate social process occurring within the back-room which may make its public face a sham. This is, indeed, a matter of face, particularly face-saving. Coalitions arise in the first place only because each party is too weak to alone get its own way; 'face' means acknowledging the value of a partner, and particularly a junior or weaker partner; seeking to bully them into submission too often proves counter-productive. Coalitions of all sorts often stand or fall due to seemingly small matters of face-etiquette. Did you call your junior partner before going in front of the press? What exact words did you use to address weaker colleagues at the table? Even, what was the seating plan at the meeting? Failing to honour face-codes can pull an alliance down, even though it might be in the interests of all parties to stay together.

Face-saving is a ritual of cooperation. The anthropologist Frank Henderson Stewart believes that all societies form such rituals so that the strong and the weak can participate in a common code of honour.[9] In politics, however, these codes of honour can prove weak.

The Labour Party in Britain failed to practise face-saving rituals in its 2010, post-election dealings with the Liberal Democrats: Labour, with the larger share of votes, treated the smaller party with scant respect, lecturing them about what they could and could not expect as the minor party, and so driving them into Conservative arms, where they were treated with respect.[10] Compromised in public, the Liberal Democrats were honoured in the back-room.

The problem of face-rituals in politics, then, is that they are not transparent to people who are not in the room. Inclusive within, invisible without – or worse, the camaraderie and smiles evident when people emerge from meetings seem signs of sell-out to people who were not there.

The alienation of the top-guns from the base has another dimension, in the coalition forged between politics and the media.

A big slice of the political leaders attending the *musée social* had at some time been working journalists; Karl Kautsky, one of the luminaries of 1900, had made such a career move; earlier Karl Marx had shown himself a master journalist. The intersection has an older history. In the eighteenth century, a stunning pamphlet could launch someone like Cesare Beccaria, the reformer of prisons, into political office; pamphleteer-politicians crowded the French and British political stages. The alliance between politics and journalism became more professionalized in the nineteenth century as printing costs came down, literacy among workers went up and the habit of newspaper-reading became truly widespread; now the radical journalist could reach a mass audience. Explicitly opinionated journalism began to appear in very large newspapers in their *feuilleton* sections – the origins of today's opinion pages. The professional commentator became a public figure.

Even if the commentator remained a journalist, the knot between politics and media tightened. On the Left, this was in part that 'speaking truth to power' meant grabbing the attention of the powerful. But more than just attracting notice, a symbiosis of rhetoric occurred. Professional commentators, speaking truth to the powerful, spoke, they claimed, in the name of ordinary people, representing their sufferings, outrage, etc. Conversely, they addressed the mass public as insiders, lifting the curtain on that back-room scene to which they were privy thanks to contacts and insider gossip. The people were spoken to, rather than spoken with.

Online blogs are now supposed to counter this trend, since everyone can comment, but the most influential blogs are those animated by people closest to power.[11] It may seem odd to think of the symbiosis between politics and journalism as a coalition, and an alienating one at that, but it helps to explain the continuing drama in which leaders are accused of being out of touch, of not getting it, of speaking the condescending rhetoric of insiders.

For much of my sociological life I've studied what our trade calls *ressentiment*, the feeling of ordinary people that the elite does not know much about their own problems first-hand, even though presuming to speak on their behalf. In the families of white, working-class Americans I studied in Boston, *ressentiment* appeared to cross class with race. The liberal elite identified with poor blacks but not with these white workers, many of whom were indeed racially prejudiced at the time. The liberal elite presumed to explain why these policemen, factory workers and sales clerks felt prejudices without much face-to-face contact, certainly without recognizing them as peers.[12] Many other researchers have documented the *ressentiment* aroused, in the United States, by the discourse of white elites about immigrants; in Europe, *ressentiment* appears particularly in attitudes of native workers to Islamic immigrants.[13] The elite seems on the side of the oppressed, but not on the side of the ordinary.

One thing that has struck me particularly about *ressentiment* is the aura of conspiracy which shapes it. In one way this aura is irrational, particularly in the United States; the liberal elites are seen as in cahoots with one another – politicians, media, Left-leaning foundations, Ivy League universities with their bearded radicals, union leaders appear to have sworn a secret pact. Irrational it may be, but conspiracy is one way of making sense on the ground of everyday impotence. Reforms in the name of the people done through back-room deals translate into conspiracies that deprive ordinary people both of their rights and of their respect.

Political movements of all colours face this dilemma. Coalitions in political practice, alliances between politics and the media, have opened an ever-widening gap between leadership and base, a structural and a symbolic distance represented by the equation of coalition and conspiracy. This equation is the modern appearance of that nefarious conniving which long ago appeared in the pages of Mandeville's *Fable of the Bees*. So too the rituals of face which are not transparent to people outside. Both are a particular worry for the Left, as was evident a century ago to critics of the German socialists who participated in Bismarck's social coalition. When reform is conducted top-down, what goes missing is equality. Because equality is weakened, solidarity becomes an abstraction.

The contrary emphasis on cooperative politics practised in a local community has intended to remedy these defects of coalitions at the top.

COMMUNITY

Saul Alinsky (1909–1972) was probably the most effective American community organizer of the last century (my family knew him well, so perhaps I'm biased). Based in Chicago, Alinsky fought for the rights of local African-Americans against the 'Daley machine', the Chicago mayor's political organization which enacted rigid segregation in that city; he also helped local whites and blacks combat the sometimes oppressive grip of national labour organizations. His 'method' of organizing was to learn the streets of a community, gossip with people, get them together, and hope for the best; he never told people what to do, instead encouraging the shy to speak up, himself providing information in a neutral manner whenever it was requested. Funny as well as feisty – 'booze', he once told my mother, 'is the organizer's most important tool' – he cast a spell over young followers, who have included Barack Obama and Hillary Rodham Clinton, both of whom later strayed from the master's path.[14]

One of Alinsky's own big preoccupations was the difference between how labour unions and community activists engage with the oppressed. He puts this difference bluntly: 'Labor union organizers turned out to be poor community organizers.' The habits of back-room coalition, intended to produce a united front, fail to forge strong bonds in urban neighbourhoods; unite-and-fight has to be rethought, because clarity and precision do not animate local communities. In Alinsky's struggles in Chicago, union officials'

> experience was tied to a pattern of fixed points, whether it was definite demands on wages, pensions, vacation periods, or other working conditions. . . . Mass [community] organization is a different animal, it is not housebroken. There are no fixed chronological points or definite issues. The demands are always changing; the situation is fluid and ever-shifting; and many of the goals are not in concrete terms of dollars and hours . . .[15]

This is dialogical exchange with a vengeance. Put a bit differently, the social process of back-room negotiating, both its conflicts and its face-rituals, is put on public view in community organizing. Alinsky focused on the informality of that process, a looseness which the labour organizer abjures but the community organizer makes use of. By getting together people who have never really talked, providing them with facts they did not know and suggesting further contacts the Alinsky-style community organizer hopes to sustain dialogical talk.

This was a challenge which settlement houses took up earlier. Leftists today tend to condemn charity work, seeing it as demeaning to the poor, but without the volunteers who manned institutions like Jane Addams's Hull House, the lives of the poor would have been immeasurably worse. At the beginning of the twentieth century the challenge was special because many of the people in its local urban neighbourhoods literally could not speak to one another. The settlement house aimed to make peaceable if imperfect verbal connections in the immigrant ghettos.

With the rosy spectacles of hindsight, immigrant communities appear tight-knit. In fact, within the cramped tenements and in the streets, immigrants in Chicago and other American cities fought violently with one another for turf. The proletariat who had abandoned Europe were disoriented by their uprooting. In Chicago, Addams was much struck by the fact that, though immigrants indeed only felt comfortable by associating with people they knew – which locked them into marginality – even then they did not bond strongly. And the foreign city in time leached away old ties; the mass of immigrants who did not live out the American Dream, who remained poor, became increasingly resigned and passive. Addams said she could instantly identify such people on the streets; they were the silent ones sitting on stoops, withdrawn into themselves, disconsolates who rarely appeared in churches or union halls.

The social question in the settlement houses thus became twofold: how to encourage cooperation with others who differ, and how to stimulate the desire to associate at all. Concretely, this meant a century ago that settlement-house workers were trying to figure out how the Jewish immigrant from Poland might talk, and want to talk, with his Italian neighbour – a challenge that resonates in different form in European cities today in relations between Muslims and non-Muslims. In her own thinking, Addams recast the social question as what we now call multi-culturalism. To her, multi-culturalism posed a problem; the word in itself does not suggest how to live together.[16]

Addams responded to the problems of difference and participation in a stunningly simple way: she focused on everyday experience – parenting, schooling, shopping. Ordinary experience, not policy formulas, is what counts, she thought, in social relations. In this, she foreshadowed Saul Alinsky; the test of joint action should be its concrete effect on daily life, not an eventual effect such as policy promises. What role should cooperation face to face play in shaping everyday experience? Addams's answer here was equally a mother to Alinsky's: Hull House emphasized loose rather than rigid exchanges, and made a virtue of informality.

With her fellow organizer Ellen Gates Starr, Addams found a rather grand Italianate building on the Near West Side of Chicago to set up, in 1889, a community centre in the midst of a tightly packed slum. Inside its doors, people could pursue organized activities – or none. The exterior grandeur of Hull House might have put off the poor, but its interior of chopped-up rooms and crowded corridors was more welcoming. Informality marked life at Toynbee Hall, London's East End equivalent to Hull House, as well; there was space just to sit and hang out as well as programmed activities, people mixing with others or not, away from the pressures of the street. The organizers of both settlement houses thought the value of them first and foremost to be places of refuge; a strict schedule of social activities modelled on those of a cruise liner was to be avoided.

Hull House contained a floating residential population of people from the streets, combined with more permanent, university-trained tenants; the latter, influenced by Ruskin's beliefs in the unity of hand and head, taught courses in crafts such as bookbinding, or they stage-managed plays, or ran the youth-club (I once found in the Hull House archives the photograph of a rather dandified young man looking a bit worried as he oversees a game of stick-ball among some very tough-looking neighbourhood kids).[17] Cooperation most shaped the ways Hull House taught English. The classrooms mixed foreigners from different places who could use only English to communicate with one another; there were no segregated classes for Italians, Greeks or Jews only, no bilingual education. The mixture produced a classroom locked in the same linguistic struggle, playing with words, discussing and sometimes arguing their meaning, as they rehearsed the English language.

The community organizer had, and has, to engage poor people who feel paralysed, whether as foreigners or simply losers in the capitalist game. To rouse people from passivity, the organizer has to focus on immediate experience, rather than dramatizing, say, the evils of capitalism; that big picture is likely to root even more deeply someone's sense that it is hopeless to get involved. To enable participation, the organizer may establish tacit ground rules, the conventions and rituals for exchange, as in the Hull House English classes, but must then leave people free to interact. The Chicago social worker Charlotte Towle, a protégée of Jane Addams, once put the logic of informality as a staff instruction: assist, don't direct, a view summarizing the tradition of community organizing which stretches from Jane Addams to Saul Alinsky. To practise Towle's Rule, moreover, the organizer will have, him- or herself, to enjoy informality. Solidarity will then morph – so this tradition of community organizing hopes – into an experience of sociability.

In my own childhood, I might add, I experienced these precepts close up. The public housing project in which I lived, Cabrini Green, lay close to Hull House in Chicago, though the settlement house more familiar to me was a Hull House spin-off on the very edge of the project. Multi-culturalism had shifted its ground from ethnicity to race within the project's confines; Cabrini Green, in the 1950s still containing some white families, had become a daily, violent battle-ground between black and white children.

One escape was the school that many children attended, a Catholic institution run by nuns of the Blessed Virgin Mary order; these nuns taught us hard and well and were not much interested in whether we were black or white; they taught us equally and strictly. The Hull House spin-off addressed our social differences, after school. Toll's Rule was applied to race. The games and projects we pursued mixed white and black; the activities themselves, whether carpentering or playing music, were left to us to run without too much supervision. To the outsider, the settlement house seemed anarchic; the nuns believed that in the secular settlement house children were neglected. The settlement workers countered by pointing to the fact that they were working out how to cooperate across racial lines, in sharp contrast to the violent anarchy which ruled the streets of poor Chicago after the Second World War as much as it did at the end of the nineteenth century.[18]

'Toll's Rule' symbolizes the parting of the ways between the polit-ical and the social Left, with consequences for working-class struggle. A century ago, the political Left began to dream that disaffected immigrants would become a new proletariat. Settlement houses resisted becoming centres of revolt because political protest alone seemed not to be the way to heal the personal damage caused by dis-placement. Which is not to say that the settlement-house workers were apolitical in the sense of being disengaged from the electoral process; indeed, in America most of the support for the minute Social-ist Party of America came from community organizers. But in their direct work, the settlement-house workers knew that sheer anger at the system would do little to help their members manage daily life. Working-class struggle, as the community organizers have under-stood, is first and foremost the matter of nurturing the tissues of community. This social foundation might or might not lead to a larger movement; the emphasis of community organizing is simply and clearly that the base comes first.

For all this, informality always risks disorganization. And even if it does rouse people inside its hallways and rooms, the settlement house risks becoming just a good experience they have occasionally, rather than a guide to life outside. That may be true more largely of communal cooperation: it offers good experiences but is not a way of life. You felt good; so what? Manuel Castells, today's leading expert on community organizing, faults Saul Alinsky and his school precisely for these reasons. The results of bonding in the community have to lead somewhere; action needs a structure, it has to become sustainable.[19]

The smallest exhibition on display in Paris at the *museé social* addressed this concern. It envisioned a mixture of formal and informal cooperation which would be pointed and lifelong.

THE WORKSHOP

After the American Civil War, freed slaves faced the prospect of becoming impoverished farm labourers still under the thumb of their former owners; legal freedom did little to lessen their economic and social miseries. They were caught in the same trap as Russian serfs, who were emancipated in 1861. On the plantation, however, many slaves developed artisan skills, just as had Russian serfs; the 'ex' in the ex-slave condition meant exercising these skills without a master. An ex-slave, Booker T. Washington, conceived a project in which African-Americans recovering from slavery should leave home, go to train at two model institutions, the Hampton and Tuskegee Institutes, then return to their home communities. During this temporary relocation, he hoped, cooperation would be regenerated, forged by direct experience and daily contact with others as equals. Like the settlement houses, Washington's project emphasized a local institution, but sought to make a lasting impact on the lives of those it housed by shaping their technical skills. The objects in the American exhibit embodied this huge aspiration.

The Tuskegee Institute, located in Alabama, opened in 1881; its sister institution, the Hampton Normal and Agriculture Institute, located in Hampton, Virginia, had been founded in 1866, just after the Civil War ended. Washington had been a student at Hampton, later in life its leader; he founded Tuskegee to accommodate more young ex-slaves. Both institutions taught students animal husbandry, horticulture, carpentry and metal working; to graduate, the students had also to learn how to teach, so that they could spread these technical skills when they returned home. In a way, Washington was preaching to the converted. The work was not easy in either place, Washington wrote in his autobiography, but the students 'were so much in earnest that only the ringing of the retiring-bell would make them stop studying'.[20] Certainly a hard kernel of shared strength had kept slaves together as communities before the Civil War, but Washington knew from his own slave past that the master's humiliations could be internalized as mutual fear and suspicion among the oppressed; he was a realist in recognizing that people are bruised by their chains.

But he was an idealist as well, of a sort recognizable in his own time and to the modern observer. Gender equality was inscribed within racial recovery. The organizers rethought craft labour to accomplish this; cheese-making, for instance, was a traditionally arduous and male pursuit on the slave plantations; the Institutes reconfigured the tools used for making cheese so women could as easily practise it. In a similar vein the workshops taught men how to use and repair sewing machines, bringing them into a traditional female sphere. Each workshop was in part self-governing, involving special meetings where the student-labourers discussed their work without the presence of a teacher. The Rochdale Principles thus appeared in these ground rules: work open to all, active participation, the work in which people cooperated rethought. But the Institutes were not free-form processes; each workshop had fixed productive targets, and the overall design of the Institutes was set by Booker T. Washington alone.

The workshop has been since ancient times a model for sustained cooperation. In the ancient world – in both China and Greece – the workshop appeared as the most important institution anchoring civic life, and as a productive site practised the division of labour to a far greater degree than farming. The complications of craft labour were joined to the family value of continuity across generations; sons worked alongside their fathers as potters, daughters alongside mothers as weavers. The workshop spawned an idea of justice, that the things people make cannot be seized from them arbitrarily, and it enjoyed a kind of political autonomy, at least in Greece, since artisans were allowed to make their own decisions about how best to practise their craft.

As a cultural site, workshops from ancient times onwards developed elaborate social rituals. These were honour-code rituals, but, rather than being practised behind the scenes as in political coalitions, these rituals publicly marked the mutual obligations between unequal partners – between masters, journeymen and apprentices within each workshop. The Chinese master, for instance, swore an elaborate oath to the parents of a new apprentice to protect the child *in loco parentis*. Annual ceremonial feasts in ancient Athens bound masters in the same trade to support one another during famines or in times of war.[21]

Given this ritual solidarity, both Confucius and Plato believed that craftsmen made good citizens.[22] The artisan's understanding of society was rooted in direct, concrete experience of other people rather than in rhetoric, or floating abstractions, or temporary passions. The idea of the craftsman-citizen flew in the face of ancient fact; many artisans in ancient Athens, and most artisans in ancient Rome, were slaves, or near-slaves, and did not enjoy full citizen rights. Nor has the history of European workshops been a story of perpetual stability; no productive activity is ever fixed. Still, the idea of the craftsman-citizen persisted, appearing in medieval guilds in Paris, Florence and London. In the mid-eighteenth century, Diderot's *Encyclopedia* celebrated the crafts-man's skills as equal to those of warriors and statesmen and more necessary for the health of society; Thomas Jefferson imagined crafts-men to make good solid citizens for the same reasons Plato did.[23]

Nearer to Washington's own time, the workshop became an icon of reform. As industrial capitalism began to bite, the artisanal workshop appeared as a rebuke to the factory, more humane in its operations. But it was also doomed, since the factory appeared inevitably destined to crush this better way of life. It is sometimes said that the craft com-munities founded by Robert Owen in Scotland and in America, and by John Ruskin and William Morris in England, were self-conscious exercises in nostalgia for the pre-industrial era. If so, Booker T. Wash-ington differed, because the ex-slave had little to regret about the past. Moreover, he did not treat Owen as a backward-looking critic.

One of the interesting things about the idealistic Robert Owen is that, indeed, he thought through ways to make the workshop modern. He championed a 'putting out system' in which a large distributor parcels out work to small workshops; in modern terms, this is networked production, flexible in its staffing with people moving from one workshop or another as required; Owen's idea differs from outsourcing in that profit-sharing rules the whole network. One successful modern version of such an employee-owned business is embodied in Britain today by the John Lewis Partnership, while one failure was illustrated by the period when United Airlines in America was employee-driven. I am sorry to say that the year-end bonus was also one of Owen's bright ideas; this was for him a means of equalizing wealth, unlike the modern banker's obscene perk. Owen's basic idea behind profit-sharing and bonuses was to increase loyalty to a firm and strengthen solidarity in the ranks.

It remains a compelling idea, though we no longer apply the label 'workshop' to it; Owen did so because he believed, like Émile Durkheim, that the factory was a more primitive form of social organization, a regress in human civilization. The workshop idea extends beyond the Marxist focus on ownership of the means of production; it's a question as well of how to behave sociably once you are in control. To Owen, loyalty and solidarity are necessary for institutions to become productive; modern industrial sociologists have documented the truth of Owen's proposition.[24] Organizations, whether profit-seeking, governmental or charitable, need to build commitment; Owen's idea of the workshop is of an institution which combines long-term mutual benefit and loyalty with short-term flexibility and openness.

In a way, Owen's idea of the workshop was also that of GoogleWave. This program shifted people from window to window, task to task, role to role; unlike the fetish-of-assertion blog, the program hoped that something of mutual and equal benefit would emerge, and that people would develop loyalty to one another online. Another modern variant of the workshop is the scientific laboratory, which Owen explicitly foresaw. 'Factory-style science' appeared to him as the mechanical testing of hypotheses; a more innovative laboratory engages in true experiment, open to surprise – which is to say, discovery. Good laboratory work should run like an experimental workshop.

Socially, Owen envisaged what could be called mobile solidarity, cutting the workshop free from roots in just one community. Just as the network of production meant that labour moved around, and that the content of labour evolved, transformed by experiment, so too cooperation in the workshop should be flexible, and portable. Cooperative skills were meant to be built up in the worker's self, transferable from place to place. This is an itinerant-musician sort of cooperation in which performers become able to work with a shifting cast of characters in different venues. It was Washington's idea too. The experience of learning to cooperate well as a free man or woman would take form in specialized Institutes far away, and then be brought home.

Washington's rigidity as the creator and the supreme boss of the Institutes – so at odds with how he hoped his protégés would behave with one another – came from another source. This was Charles Fourier's version of the workshop at the turn of the nineteenth century. Fourier dubbed his workshops 'phalansteries' or 'grand hotels', giant buildings which provided housing, labour and education according to an elaborate plan; they are the origins of the modern company town. He envisioned face-to-face cooperation occurring in 'phalanxes', the wings and floors of the hotel.

Fourier subscribed to the eighteenth-century Utilitarian belief in the greatest good for the greatest number; he aimed to erase poverty for the masses, but not erase it for every one of them. He crowded the 'deserving poor' in his hotel onto the top floors, and the Jews, whom he hated, were confined to the ground floor, doing the dirtiest labour. But Fourier wasn't a completely malicious nut-case. He sought to work out just how the division of labour in a factory could be made more thoroughly interactive (the suggestion-box was one of his bright ideas). And he tried to figure out how work itself could become more playful and inventive, as in huge toy-boxes full of tools provided by the phalanstery so that workers could experiment with different ways of doing a particular job. Still, this was top-down planning with a vengeance, the workshop designed *in toto* before it existed, ruled over by an 'omniarch' who chose the tools in the toy-box and decided which rooms the most deserving of the deserving poor should live in. Much of early Soviet industrial planning derived explicitly from Fourier, the omniarch in Moscow designing factories and setting out production targets, like Fourier, with little or no hands-on experience; state socialism omitted, however, the freedom Fourier wanted to give workers within the shop.[25]

Washington, too, functioned as something quite like an omniarch. And like the Germans in Paris, he had a complicit relation to the dominant powers; rich whites paid for the Institutes, Washington avidly soliciting their patronage. The sneering phrase 'an Uncle Tom', derived from Harriet Beecher Stowe's novel *Uncle Tom's Cabin*, seemed to fit him, at least in the eyes of W. E. B. Dubois, the great radical leader a generation younger than Washington. The phrase refers to an African-American who grovels before white masters, who takes their occasional favours gratefully, who bottles up rage when confronted by their condescension and who treats his own people with scant respect.

In his defence, it could be countered that Washington thought of the workshop as forging a dignified kind of sociability. He wanted to heal the African-American community; he hoped that eventually blacks who strengthened their internal bonds would integrate as respected members of the larger society and would move in status to the upper proletariat and petit-bourgeoisie. Washington aimed at inclusion rather than revolution, a fate too easy for the armchair revolutionary to scorn.

Washington's creation, like Owen's, remains resonant because of the ways the Institutes connected cooperation and mutual respect.

We see this connection in photographs made by Frances Johnston of the Hampton Institute. Put on display in 1900 in Paris at a gallery near the Seine, these images supplemented the few objects displayed in the corner of the American room at the *musée social*.[26] To drive home the economic promise of the Institutes, Frances Johnston mounted before-and-after photographs of ex-slave homes, contrasting the hovels people rented before attending Hampton with the solid houses they purchased after graduation. But whether by design or artistic instinct, she looks harder than Washington writes. Her photographs show, for instance, ex-slaves and dispossessed Indians working together in greenhouses and in carpentry shops; there is a photograph of an 'Indian orchestra', its musicians holding European string and wind instruments. Washington's writing rather plays down this mixture; the photographs make a point of it. The images show ethnic differences resolved by people doing demanding things together, rather than simply being together. Johnston's eye honours her subjects by showing them addressing hard tasks, which is quite different from the emphasis on casualness and informality by which the settlement-house workers sought to engage their denizens.

The photographs also make a point about the tools that enable workers to cooperate. Each tool within the workshop is depicted as sharply as the human beings using it; Johnston was one of the first photographers to experiment with different depth-of-field lenses. She took great care in photographing the new tools, like the cheese-making press, in the workshops. This matters, I think, more than might first seem. Nostalgic utopians of the workshop idea lumped together the 'mechanical' and 'technology' as a single enemy; John Ruskin was the most extreme in this, but for many others the social evils of factory labour slid into attacks on the machinery itself. Johnston does not present tools as alienating; she makes them as visually important as the people using and sharing them.

At one point in her career, Johnston went to the outskirts of Paris to photograph factories, places where the simple, brutal division of labour ruled.[27] She placed her camera just as one worker would see the people around him or her; in the photograph these surrounding bodies become unfocused, or only the fragment of another person's body appears in the frame. In mechanical collaboration within the factory, what other workers are doing appears indistinct, whereas in the Institute photographs, everything is in focus and other people are clearly in the frame.

Johnston's most famous photograph shows six men constructing a staircase, each of the six deploying a different skill yet locked together, mutually aware yet absorbed in their own work. Perhaps the most striking thing about this photograph is the expression on the workers' faces: there is none. Intent on what they are doing individually, their faces are serene. The image is haunting in part because it avoids any suggestion of agitprop, as in images of fists raised in the air as a gesture of solidarity. Nor does it show them especially happy, nor include any facial sign that they are excitedly aroused – just absorbed.

But Johnston has also staged this photograph, rather like a chore-ographer, to show how these workers relate to each other. Put on display are all the different stages of building a staircase; present at a glance is a clear narrative of the work they are doing. The workers do not look at one another but the choreography makes evident that they are intimately connected. Working on their own they appear relaxed, but not informal as in the casual encounters of a settlement house; relaxed, even though they are performing a demanding task together; and relaxed in being comfortable with their tools. We sense, in con-templating this photograph, that the people in the workshop are just what they seem; there's no hidden backstory; they are not a coalition. The structure of the image lies in its narrative of making a staircase, which shapes their shared purpose in time; the project furnishes their mutual respect.

In this chapter I've tried to draw out a contrast between political cooperation in itself and what might be called the politics of cooperation.

Political cooperation is a necessity in the game of power, when one party is too weak to dominate or just survive alone. Political cooper-ation has to be humanly fine-tuned, through rituals of mutual respect; shared interests alone will not make it prosper. But political cooper-ation at the apex of power runs into serious troubles with the base, the mass, of people below: the compromises entailed by cooperation at the top often seem betrayals to those below; the identity of a political group can be washed out through negotiation; as organizations become larger and stronger, bureaucracy erects barriers between top and base; the rituals which bind leaders together in power's back-rooms are not transparent to those outside. All these factors can lead people to feel *ressentiment*, that sentiment of betrayal in which the elite seem more bent on cooperating with one another than with those below.

The politics of cooperation in non-political organizations can face some of the same tensions between the apex and the base, but if their purpose is direct social contact the danger is less. Such organizations have instead to address how people should relate, face to face. The settlement house took up the issue of sociality, as Georg Simmel first framed it, that of living in a complex society full of difference;

Hull House and its ilk sought to convert inner and often passive awareness of others into active engagement. To make this happen, the strategy of the settlement house, like that of the community organizing espoused by Saul Alinsky, emphasized informal contact, a principle organizers applied to themselves in 'Toll's Rule': advise rather than direct. But encounters on these terms could remain fleeting and shapeless long-term.

The workshop sought to counter that wandering experience by giving more shape to cooperative activity. The Institutes did so by focusing on building up skills in a community, skills that could then be used in other places, other circumstances. In this, the Institutes drew on a set of guidelines about working together first formulated in Robert Owen's 'Rochdale Principles'. But in practice these principles could produce a paradox: mutuality among members in a workshop, but still subservience to someone at the top about how they should live. Nonetheless, mutuality within the workshop was genuine in the Institutes: it made technical competence into sociable experience.

Perhaps the person whose life and work most dramatized this contrast was Karl Kautsky (1854–1938). Viennese by birth, he made in Germany a career transition from the calling of journalist to that of politician, founding when young the monthly paper *Die neue Zeit*, in middle age becoming a defender of the doctrine of inevitable revolution, and late in life, when revolution actually came to Germany at the end of the First World War, becoming an official in its foreign ministry. In his long years as a militant, he knew full well that the moment his movement lost its organized political edge, the process of social reform in Germany would stop. But disillusion came to Kautsky as an elderly man, travelling in Georgia and in Russia in 1920, when he contrasted social democracy in Georgia to proletarian dictatorship in Russia. Lenin attacked him in turn as a 'renegade' and as 'lacking in revolutionary will'.

When my mother went to visit Kautsky in 1934 in Vienna, where he had retired, he was trying to work the social in socialism, an effort recorded in his book *The Labour Revolution*.[28] Like Freud, Kautsky would later flee Vienna in the Anschluss of 1938 and die shortly thereafter. In Vienna, guarded outside, since Stalin was bent on assassinating him, Kautsky's flat struck my mother as like a library in which no one had ever shelved the books, as though this man of immense erudition no longer knew where to put them, how to bring order and coherence to this his private museum dedicated to the 'Social Question'. Still, he was bent on finding out what makes cooperation tick. The workshops celebrated by Robert Owen seemed the key to unlocking mutuality, but Kautsky did not believe that this utopia could become sustainable in everyday life.

The disorder in Kautsky's library is one legacy of the Paris Exposition Universelle, confusion about how to practise cooperation. Kautsky's own late-life urge to make sense of active cooperation, rather than mere toleration, is an equal legacy. This is not a challenge only for the Left. Any individual or group wanting to build change from the ground up faces it; the challenge is great when working with people who are not carbon copies of ourselves.

A silence, though, has marked our discussion. Competition is missing. In political coalitions, within civic groups, among people bent on doing a job together, competition may seem to get in the way of cooperation. In fact, as we shall next see, cooperation and competition are intimately related.

2

The Fragile Balance

Competition and Cooperation in Nature and Culture

Anyone who has played a team sport, cut a business deal or raised a brood of children knows that mutual cooperation and competition can combine. The undertow of competition is aggression and anger, sentiments which are hard-wired into human beings. Rehearsals, conversations, coalitions, communities or workshops can countervail against this destructive pull, because the impulse of goodwill is also imprinted in our genes. As social animals, we have to work out through experience how to strike a balance.

This chapter explores the possibilities for doing so. The monotheistic religions have provided one guide. They picture the destruction of Eden as unleashing contending natural forces; righting the balance requires renewed obedience to a higher power. Science has taken another view of natural dissonance. Ethology, a particular branch of modern science combining genetics with the study of behaviour, looks at how animals in groups go about managing mutual need and mutual aggression. It's easy – too easy – to take religion and science as implacably contending forces. Their concerns meet in one realm of behaviour: ritual. In Chapter 1 we touched lightly on the power of face-saving rituals to mediate between competition and cooperation; ritual has a broader and deeper scope, both as a biological mediator and in the practice of faith.

EDEN

The Peaceable Kingdom, a painting by the American 'primitive' artist Edward Hicks, shows all kinds of beasts at the edge of a forest, bears, lions, ducks and sheep sleeping together. True art has gone into this painting, since its colour tones are beautifully balanced, reinforcing the theme of harmony. This canvas is the Garden of Eden before the Fall, with God absent. The idealized image banishes any suggestion of aggression – and of course real nature looks nothing like this; sleeping sheep would in fact make their neighbourly lions hungry.

We shouldn't be too quick to dismiss Edward Hicks's painting as mere fantasy. The image of natural peace in Eden pervades the three great monotheistic religions, each believing harmony to be shattered by human striving. St Augustine thought that after the exiled Adam and Eve left Eden, the forest soured, becoming strife-filled for those creatures who remained behind.[1] The monotheistic religions want to account, in the Fall, for how we became our own enemies, with consequences for all creation.

Until the seventeenth century, the serpent's seduction of Eve and her revolt were usually framed in sexual terms: Eve destroyed Eden because she was full of desire. This was a framing which John Milton contested. In *Paradise Lost*, first published in 1667, he portrays Adam and Eve in Book Four as husband and wife having natural sexual relations; their union, in the words of one modern interpreter, is one of 'mutual dependence, not a relation of domination or hierarchy'.[2] Eve destroys this domestic harmony, and all of Eden, by her reasoning, by thinking for herself; independent reason turns her into a competitor with God; she seeks to convince Adam of the value of her own understanding, and she succeeds; in Milton's famous words, 'The mind is its own place, and in itself / Can make a heaven of hell, a hell of heaven.'[3]

Milton's framing of disorder contrasts sharply to that of his near contemporary, Thomas Hobbes. For Hobbes, Eden never existed. In his *Leviathan*, published in 1651, the natural man appears as a beast, blood-red in tooth and claw. Against Milton we could set Hobbes's equally famous declaration that in nature there are 'no arts; no letters; no society; and which is worst of all, continual fear and danger of violent death; and the life of man, solitary, poor, nasty, brutish, and short'.[4] In the war of each against all, human reason is weak; since no equilibrium rules the life of the natural man, the human capacity for peaceful cooperation is scant.

This terrifying image of natural anarchy cuts a huge swath through many non-Christian cultures, the gods being like mankind in impulse but eternal in existence, bent on competition of the most violent sort with one another and against us mortals. In the world-view of the Aztecs, for instance, human cooperation was no more than a tool for appeasing angry, jealous gods, via rituals which offered the Plumed Serpent food, gold and human sacrifices. Ancient Sanskrit texts similarly ascribed natural instability to battles among contending gods.

Hobbes would have known more nearly those Greek myths in which the gods sow natural disorder. Hobbes's solution for the war of each against all was not, however, so far different from that of the writers of the Old Testament. In his view, to survive people must give up on their natural selves that acknowledged no higher power. The Leviathan will impose disciplined obedience and submission; society will enforce cooperation. Milton, too, believed that mankind can return to obedience; the destructive power of reason depicted in *Paradise Lost* was balanced by the poet's view, expressed in the *Areopagitica* (1644), that reasoning can lead mankind back to God.

In philosophy's long pondering on the state of nature, there are gentler versions of its defects, notably, in the seventeenth century, John Locke's. In the machinery of philosophical thinking, the state of nature often serves as a 'counter-factual'; what would life be like if there were no social restraints as we know them? In the century after Milton and Hobbes, this was no abstract question; the Enlightenment wanted to reverse the belief that mankind cannot dwell in a natural state. These writers hewed to naturalness, which meant for them simplicity in their clothing, taste in food and everyday language. The eighteenth century was an era, for instance, in which women began to wear thin muslin chemises which exposed the shape of their breasts; at the end of the century it became the fashion among some French and English women to wet down the muslin fabric, so that it clung to the shape of the body. They wanted to reveal nature rather than repress it.

In modern times, science has returned to the proposition, posed in separate ways by Milton and Hobbes, that mankind will not or cannot remain in Eden; through analysing cooperation, ethologists have contemplated this proposition in a particular way.

NATURAL UNSTABLE COOPERATION

Today the word 'natural' equates with 'genetic'. The equation can easily seem rigid and implacable, the genes determining how we behave. A kindred form of determinism is neurological, the brain's neural circuitry fixing our experience of ourselves and each other. Such determinism seems to Steven Pinker too narrow: 'the fact that you can look at meaning and purpose ... as a neuro-psychological phenomenon does not mean you can't look at it another way, in terms of how we live our lives.'[5] But determinism is also limited science, because nothing in nature is fixed in form.

Certainly cooperation is imprinted in our genes, occurring, as the ethologist Robert Axelrod puts it, 'without friendship or foresight'.[6] But cooperation cannot be stable either, and for the same reason: the natural environment is never fixed. A bee, for instance, returning to the hive, communicates to its mates by dancing where to find nectar, and may seem to epitomize the animal who has mastered cooperation. Bees are indeed extraordinarily communicative dancers; the entomologist Thomas Seeley describes the astonishing choreography of bees whose 'angle of dancing corresponds to the direct air line between hive and food source. This [dancing] involves the integration of solar angle and length of different flight segments.'[7] Yet honey bees do not know yet how to dance the dangers of air pollution.

The Peaceable Kingdom shows the natural world come to rest; in real nature, the lives of all creatures are unstable due to such environmental changes, as well as the internal churning of chance variations in the course of evolution. This is one reason why we want to avoid mythologizing natural cooperation as laying down the law about behaviour. It's true that cooperation is marked by one fixed constant. All social animals collaborate because the lone bee, wolf or human cannot ensure its own survival. They – we – need one another.

There's more to this cliché than first meets the eye. 'Nothing in the brain of a worker ant represents a blue-print of the social order,' the entomologists Bert Hölldobler and Edward Wilson report. The genetic social knowledge of these insects is quite incomplete, no single leader or top ant possesses it, 'there is no overseer or "brain caste" who carries such a master plan in its head', and no single bee carries an entire 'master plan' of bee society in its brain.[8] If individual incompleteness grounds the lives of social insects, still 'environmental domination by ants and other social insects is the result of cooperative group behavior'.[9] How can the incomplete brain and social control be reconciled?

Another cliché helps explain this. Individually insufficient creatures compensate through the division of labour, each executing small, separate tasks, the group becoming thereby potent. But here again there is an unexpected twist. Social insects, for instance, possess enough genetic code to take over, when sickness or misadventure requires, some of the specialized tasks performed by other members of the nest or hive; the division of labour is flexible, and social insects can switch roles temporarily. This is surprising, because we usually think of a hive as efficient the way a factory is, where the division of labour is locked into fixed tasks. In the nest or hive, though, efficiency and rigidity do not equate; cooperation is more supple.

Communication skill is also part of the answer to the riddle of incompleteness combined with potency. At the heart of these natural communication skills lies pattern behaviour. It consists of signs which the animal knows how to make, which other animals can instantly read and which can be repeated. The key word here is 'instantly'. The moment the bee lands it can start dancing, other bees crowded around understand what the movements mean, and so speed off to the nectar. The code for this instant communication lies in an animal's genes; in the same way, human beings are coded at birth. The code provides a base in us, but as higher primates; as described in the Introduction, the code provides ingredients upon which infants and younger children build up more complex, less instantly legible behaviours.

It might seem that genetically patterned behaviour is the source of balance between cooperation and competition. Though eighteenth-century ethologists had no notion of genetics, they certainly thought this. Julien Offay de la Mettrie (1709–51) imagined nature balanced like a machine; like Voltaire, he derived this conviction from a rather peculiar reading of Isaac Newton. The mechanistic idea was applied by the philosopher and salonnier Baron d'Holbach (1723–89) to the social lives of animals and men. How, other than by balancing competition and cooperation, d'Holbach asked, could animal species perpetuate themselves side by side in the environment generation after generation, feasting off one another but not so gluttonous as to destroy their source of food? Surely they cooperated after a fashion to ensure their mutual survival? The Swedish botanist Carolus Linnaeus (1707–78) took another tack in developing the concept of the ecological niche, each species with its special place and role in the divine machine. Linnaeus was a careful naturalist; he documented in detail ways in which species did not overstep their natural territories, a respect for mutual boundaries which he saw as mutually cooperative.

If not evoking Eden, all these views emphasized the fact of equilibrium in nature; many of those who believed in the Divine Machine called upon mankind, mired in the muck of mutual hatred, to return to this first principle. Nature reconciles drawing on others and getting along with them. The Enlightenment emphasis on balance is echoed somewhat today in Gaia theory, according to which the earth, like a self-regulating mechanism, responds to physical changes like rising temperatures by rebalancing its living parts; other environmentalists today believe balance has gone missing and needs to be restored.[10]

If our eighteenth-century forebears were, so to say, on the side of the angels, their first principle is not entirely reassuring. Shifting climatic conditions, for instance, will change plant locations and prompt migrations and intrusions of animals in the midst of other species; like performers, the actors in nature will inevitably appear on unfamiliar stages. One key fact about evolution, then, is that environmental change frequently runs ahead of pattern behaviour. This is particularly true of the repertoire for communication ingrained genetically in social animals; though there may be a well-established division of labour, environmental change still moves ahead of the genetic imprint. We are one of those animals.

Early naturalists like Jean-Baptiste Lamarck (1744–1829) believed that animals could address the challenge of unpreparedness by immediate adaptation; Lamarck himself imagined that a creature could change its programmed behaviour within one generation. In the nineteenth century, the Austrian monk-scientist Gregor Mendel (1822–84) showed why this could not be so; genetic variations occurring by chance take generations to have an environmental effect, and yet more generations of sifting to select for a better adaptation. No act of adaptation could abridge evolutionary time. We are today able to manipulate and so speed up the process of genetic change in a single organism, but even so environmental readjustment among clusters of species takes time. The geneticist Stephen Gould, for instance, developed the concept of 'punctuated equilibrium' to highlight the fact of collective disruption; in his analysis, environmental ruptures occur suddenly, disorganizing previously established patterns.[11] This is not to say that chaos rules, that there is no equilibrium in the environment, but simply that it is a stay against time.

These general precepts have helped biologists make sense of the flux of cooperative behaviour among our near cousins, the higher primates. The primatologist Michael Tomasello finds that chimpanzees, for instance, switch roles suddenly, from helping out to competing against one another, when faced with an uncertain environmental challenge.[12] Reciprocity in sharing food, as Frans de Waal and Sarah Brosnan found in studying capuchin monkeys, can also take different and unstable forms; these monkeys are unreliable investors in and respecters of one another.[13] The quiver of behaviours helps these primates deal with a shifting, complex environment. It used to be thought that efficient reproduction furnished a secure bedrock of cooperation in higher social animals, but reproduction now seems insufficient to explain their social bonds. Primates often bond more to individuals of a similar rank than to their kin (primate groups have a class structure), or bond along same-sex lines, as in grooming behaviour.[14] Cooperative hunting among chimpanzees is similarly hard to explain solely in terms of efficient reproduction.[15] The external challenges of survival which species face, the disruptions with which they have to deal, such as changing hunting and feeding grounds, are just too complex to be met by family structure alone.[16]

Natural cooperation, then, begins with the fact that we can't survive alone. The division of labour helps us multiply our insufficient powers, but this division works best when it is supple, because the environment itself is in a constant process of change. Changes in the environment run ahead of genetically patterned behaviour; among social animals, no single institution, like the family, can guarantee stability. Given all this, how then are balances between cooperation and competition struck? The answer lies in the spectrum of exchanges ants, apes and humans experience.

THE SPECTRUM OF EXCHANGE

'Exchange' simply names the experience of give and take among all animals. It arises thanks to life's basic rhythm of stimulus and response; it occurs in sex, feeding regimes or fights. Exchanges become self-conscious among higher primates, in the sense that all primates show evidence that they ponder what to give and take, and that they experiment with different kinds of exchange.

The exchanges in which all social animals engage run a spectrum of behaviours from the altruistic to the viciously competitive. I dislike arbitrary categories, but for the sake of clarity I've divided the spectrum of exchange into five segments: altruistic exchange, which entails self-sacrifice; win-win exchange, in which both parties benefit; differentiating exchange, in which the partners become aware of their differences; zero-sum exchange, in which one party prevails at the expense of another; and winner-takes-all exchange, in which one party wipes out the other. In animal terms, this spectrum runs from the worker ant which offers up its body as food for other ants, to the wolf whose exchanges with sheep are invariably lethal; in human terms, the spectrum runs from Joan of Arc to genocide.

The balance between cooperation and competition is best and most clearly struck in the middle of this spectrum. In win-win exchanges, competition can produce mutual benefits, as in the market exchanges imagined by Adam Smith, or in political coalitions which aim to balance mutual competition and cooperation. Differentiating exchanges, whether occuring simply through physical contact, or in primates like ourselves, via discussion and debate, can define borders and boundaries; as in animal territories, so in urban communities groups may contend and conflict in order to establish turf which they thereafter respect.

Some scientists are prone to reckon all these exchanges as matters of costs and benefits (the baleful influence of accountants is felt everywhere in modern life). This habit is exemplified by the behavioural psychologists Natalie and Joseph Henrich, who describe cooperation as occurring whenever 'an individual incurs a cost to provide a benefit for another person or people'.[17] Another version of accounting appears in Richard Dawkins's popular book *The Selfish Gene* when he declares that 'niceness and forgivingness pay', though humans cannot reckon this benefit in advance.[18] The habit of keeping a ledger of life is not so much wrong as simple-minded. Social animals often switch from one kind of exchange to another, and so prove inconstant record-keepers: bent on finding a sheep to eat, the male wolf is suddenly struck by how sexy are the yellow-grey eyes of his female hunting partner ... as the pair roll on the soft mattress of the pine-forest floor, the night and its scents enveloping them, they forget for a while that they had set out to kill. Higher primates, moreover, often think in ways too complicated to be rendered neatly as losses and gains; they probe reality rather than price it.

Altruism

This loaded word makes many ethologists today uncomfortable, since its human connotations are of a noble and freely willed gesture. The insect that surrenders its body to be eaten by others is practising a genetic programme in which no ethical choice is involved. So too, in higher primates, when a mother ape exposes herself to danger to protect her offspring, rather than acting nobly, she may simply be protecting the genes her progeny carry. The ethologist's worry makes sense; we shouldn't equate the cannibalized ant or the self-sacrificing ape with Joan of Arc, who chose to give her life to a cause rather than ensure the survival of her genes.

Altruism proper focuses on gift-giving. The French sociologist Marcel Mauss was a pioneer in the study of gift-giving, and he was a politically engaged pioneer. He contrasted the strong bonds created by gift-giving in aboriginal societies with the weak social tissues of competitive capitalism. This may seem a cartoon-like contrast, or just the difference between charity and selfishness. Gift-giving is certainly not charity in the abstract, as the historian of early modern Europe Natalie Zemon Davis has shown; the donation of time to projects in local communities had the practical benefit of tempering religious hostilities during the sixteenth and seventeenth centuries.[19] Still, no law obliged them to go this extra mile; it was their choice to give.

In modern times the British sociologist Richard Titmuss has charted an equally practical role for altruism in a study of blood donors. His study contrasts those who donate for nothing with those who are paid for their blood; the donor who gives freely feels great satisfaction in doing so, while the paid donor has little feeling at all about the act. Practical consequences follow: the free donor provides, on the whole, blood less likely to be tainted, since the donor attends to the healthy state of his or her body in making a gift of it, whereas the person who is paid registers simply the cash; whether his or her blood is healthy is of little concern to the paid donor.[20]

Altruism can be spontaneous, as in leaping to the defence of someone injured or threatened; such a gift can be totally selfless when nothing at all comes back to the giver. This is, I think, one sense of the Talmudic observation that 'a man who gives charity in secret is greater than Moses'.[21] The more usual sort of gift-giving occurs when the giver does get something back, though in forms more elevated than settling a business debt, as in the well-being experienced by the blood donor. An exchange has occurred, and its rewards are internalized; thus, though children want to be praised for being good, altruism proper begins when they want to act well without being praised for doing so. One echo of this in adult life appears among workers committed to doing good work or helping out other workers even though their bosses offer no praise or recognition in return.

The author of the First Letter to the Corinthians remarks that 'there are diversities of gifts, but the same Spirit'.[22] One secular version of this biblical observation is that altruism is performed for a 'shadow self', a shadow companion with whom one conducts a conversation about how to behave. The secular shadow self is more a witness than a divine judge. In studying authority in labour relations, I found, for instance, that workers motivated to help others freely over a period of months rather than just in the moment hold a sustained conversation with this inner companion; the result is that altruistic behaviour shaped their sense of personal agency.[23] Though cooperation with other people, in itself, is not the point of altruism, the altruist is motivated by this internalized dialogue.

Let's make the matter more physical. One centuries-old version of altruism has appeared in monastery gardening. In principle, monastery gardens are a return to the original Garden of Eden. In practice, monastery gardening followed two forms. Saint Gall in Switzerland (the earliest monastery for which good horticultural records exist) divided its herbs, fountains, shrubs and pathways into logical divisions, asking of monks that they specialize and so collaborate rationally; the monks on Mount Athos (from what fragmentary records reveal) let its monastery gardens run wild; the monks sought to discover what they could eat or make into medicine from nature's sheer untamed profusion. If you are a keen gardener, you probably know that these monastery gardens, in either form, contested the idea of farming portrayed in Virgil's *Georgics*: Virgil's farmer struggles alone against nature, while the monks of Saint Gall and Mount Athos worked in nature together.[24] Cooperative labour in the garden aimed to strip away aggression and striving, returning the labouring monks to a gentler self.

Though these religious gardens entailed withdrawal from the world, there's a parallel with the secular shop floor. Normally people need and enjoy praise for good deeds; altruism proper begins when they would do the deed even if they didn't receive recognition from others, exposing their behaviour instead to that shadow self. In this, altruism retains the quality of a sheltered act – just the quality we recognize in the everyday observation that altruistic people seem strongly motivated from within.

Win-win

By contrast, win-win exchanges are much more overtly reciprocal. Nest-building is a prime natural example; every member of the nest shares in the effort and benefits from the result. Pattern behaviour is crucial in such win-win exchanges; it is the genetic prompt which guides animals in knowing what part others in a group can and should do to benefit all members. 'Behaviour sinks' consist of those occasions when animals cannot or refuse to play their part; when in a scientist's laboratory rats are prevented from building shared nests, for example, the rat pack disintegrates into aggressive, violent ferocity, and a war of each-against-all ensues. One natural version of us-against-them promotes win-win exchanges within groups of social animals; the perception of a shared menace welds rats – not usually the sweetest of animals in dealings with one another – into a phalanx.

There's a temptation among some ethologists to think that we humans are just the same.[25] We are and we aren't. Pattern behaviour is in our genes, but culture holds a powerful sway over the practice of win-win exchange.

The prime human example of win-win is the business deal where all parties gain. They may have competed to arrive at this happy result, but in the share-out there emerges something for everyone. At least this was Adam Smith's view of what happens in markets. He was not a naturalist working out in the field, but he subscribed to the belief of Linnaeus and others that nature balances competition and a live-and-let-live sort of companionable order. More famously, he accepted a social version of the eighteenth century's celestial machine; this appeared in his famous evocation of the invisible hand which makes sure in market competition that everyone gets something in the end. The same happy result has been what modern coalitions hope for, competing against one another during elections, then sharing slices of the political pie once in power.

The balance between competition and cooperation does not happen naturally, in the sense of inevitably, without will and effort, in business dealings or in other walks of life. Negotiating skills have to fine-tune the balance, and these skills constitute a craft of their own. The good negotiator, for example, learns how to deflect confrontation when things are getting so hot that one of the participants threatens to drop out; he or she puts unpalatable home truths indirectly so that an antagonist more readily can face up to them. Both are hard-nosed versions of 'sensitivity' to others, which means that a master of win-win negotiating skills has usually become adept at dealing with ambiguity.

In later chapters of this study, we shall explore in more depth the practice of this demanding craft among professional diplomats, job counsellors and community activists. At this point, we need to dwell on the sheer importance of ambiguity itself.

Win-win exchanges are more often an open-ended process than a neat list of gains and losses which people can reckon when they begin negotiating. Smith's invisible hand, for example, relies on markets that are expanding in unpredictable ways. By his time, three centuries of colonial conquest had produced an ever-greater number and variety of raw materials and finished goods to trade; competitors dealt in both what they already owned and what they might come to own in the future. Fantasy ruled much of this trade; in the 1730s, for example, some wholesale importers of tomatoes from Mexico genuinely believed the tomato would replace milk as a primary food source; from the 1720s onwards, sudden rushes of desire for tulips and mica convulsed European markets. People didn't quite understand what exactly made them valuable but for the moment believed they were big. At the bargaining table, negotiators shared these fantasies as a starting point; they then competed hard for a share of the market in them.

Even when not in the grip of tulip- or mica-mania, traders dealt in the cornucopia of strange goods flooding into Europe from abroad, goods whose inherent value was uncertain. Smith would have understood well modern commodities-trading in futures, or current deals about Internet companies in which the parties don't quite see what products will eventually be worth. It was, and still is, the ambiguous character of the market which enables people to believe that there can be something for everyone, whereas in a market governed by a scarce supply of goods whose utility or worth is established it is more likely that exchanges will sort into winners and losers.[26] As Smith puts the matter succinctly, the Wealth of Nations comes from expanding rather than static trade.[27]

A big social issue lurks in the flux of win-win exchanges. It may seem strange that many computer geeks, who spend most their lives in front of screens, are avid convention-goers, prone to spending a lot of time eating or drinking together; the reason, I think, is that unscripted face-time yields its own, win-win benefits. This is the role played by informal exchange, which is the very opposite of forging formal agreement. Formal cooperation sets down the rules of engaging with other people: the precise information you will act on, what you will expect of your partners, how a contract will be enforced. This is pattern behaviour, created through negotiation, to be sure, rather than implanted genetically. All these defined contours of action are left unresolved in informal exchange; in bars after working hours, in the office around the water cooler, as in encounters in the hallways of convention centres, people instead derive unexpected, valuable information through gossip; a chance remark may suddenly open up a new vein of endeavour for people spending time together. More generally, the dialogic conversation flourishes through informality; the odd twists and turns of these conversations can result in win-win exchanges.

We all know the sort of salesman who has learned not to push; he or she can foist almost anything on customers like me. He seems so relaxed and nice, so unassuming. Skill in dealing with people informally skirts close to the edge of manipulating them; people who relate with skill to others on easy terms, whether genuinely well-meaning or not, thus raise a cautionary flag: they signal that informality is not necessarily naive.

All of which is to say that win-win exchanges may well be mutually affirming, but this affirmation has to be hedged with caveats. In Smith's version of the win-win exchange, there has to be more than enough to go around; scarcity of goods does not promote the win-win exchange. Abundance in Smith's colonialist times was allied with goods of ambiguous or unknown value; fantasy about their worth served as the companion to wealth. Ambiguity marks the informal win-win encounter as well as the contractual deal; ambiguity can play a positive role in the odd bit of gossip which becomes information of value, or the stray remark during a conversation which sparks a new collective project. But people adept at informal exchange are not simple souls. They may countervail against aggressive, competitive displays of self; they may indeed promote the welfare of others, or, like the modest salesman, just make others feel good – in which cases the win-win exchange proves an illusion.

Differentiating exchange

In the very middle of our spectrum lies the differentiating exchange. In animal environments, these exchanges establish territories and define the borders between them. In her studies of chimpanzees, Jane Goodall has described the exchanges – meetings, if you like – of chimpanzees at these edges which result in each group laying down scent markers; the markers are then readjusted through further encounters; having agreed which group will occupy which space of the forest, the chimps then withdraw.[28] The idea of the exchanges is to minimize aggressive competition for territory.

Edges are fraught zones in natural geographies because they shift constantly. Inanimate forces like climate change can force communities of living things to readjust their internal edges; as water temperatures rise in the Antarctic, for instance, penguins and gulls are altering the ways they share space. Edges come in two sorts: boundaries and borders. A boundary is a relatively inert edge; population thins out at this sort of edge and there's little exchange among creatures. A border is a more active edge, as at the shoreline dividing ocean and land; this is a zone of intense biological activity, a feeding ground for animals, a nutrient zone for plants. In human ecology, the eight-lane highway isolating parts of the city from each other is a boundary, whereas a mixed-use street at the edge between two communities can be more of a border.

A more personal kind of border-condition arises when, for instance, in a city two strangers meet in a bar, talk casually and come away from the encounter with a sharper personal understanding of their own interests, their own desires or their own values; the same thing can happen when a dinner party draws together people who know one another only casually. Differences are exposed in the course of the talk; contact may stimulate self-understanding; something valuable will then have transpired through the exchange, though the people in the bar or at the table may never see one another again. This experience might appear as yet another sort of win-win exchange, but its point is reflexive, focused more on what people learn about themselves than on what sustains a relationship. Most of us have profited from such sociability.

The differentiating exchange is the province of dialogics. Our eighteenth-century ancestors sought to organize this exchange through the ways their cafés, coffee houses and pubs were set up to encourage strangers to talk. Money motivated the proprietors; customers spent more if they lingered. The customers sat at long tables of twelve to sixteen people; the small round table meant for just one person or a couple appeared only during the nineteenth century, and first in Parisian cafés. The theatre was an addiction for all classes in London, Paris and other large cities; facing one another across these tables, people used forms of address, turns of phrase and gestures modelled on what they heard and saw on stage.[29] Yet the pattern-behaviour of speech people imbibed from the theatre, providing strangers with a shared verbal code, was enriched in the coffee house by another Enlightenment value, that of speaking openly and directly to others without embarrassment; 'coffee-house speech', Addison and Steele observed early on, enabled people to speak 'freely and without reserve upon general topics of conversation'.[30] Were they modern philosophers, Addison and Steele might have called coffee houses scenes in which dialogic exchanges were at once formal and free.

Practical reasons prompted strangers to talk at once dramatically and forthrightly. The eighteenth century was the dawn of Europe's big expansion in urban growth. London and Paris, especially from the 1760s onwards, filled up with strangers who needed not only to share information but to interpret and judge its value – which is why insurance companies like Lloyd's began as coffee houses. To do so they needed to communicate expressively; the café, Diderot remarked, 'is a theatre in which being believed is the prize'.[31] It sufficed to be believed for the moment; in that era, few people sought to make intimate friends from encounters with strangers in cafés or coffee houses; they were perhaps more comfortable with meetings in these social borderlands than we are today, with our insistent demand for intimacy.

In the nineteenth century, public life shifted from verbal to visual encounter. By 1848, it was taken for granted in Paris that strangers would not speak to one another freely in the street or the café, unless expressly invited to do so. Leaving others alone and being left alone forged a new kind of protection, and strangers who remained silent in each other's presence formed a kind of compact not to violate the other's privacy. The eye took the place of the voice; a *flâneur* in the city looked around him (*flâneurs* were mostly men), was stimulated by what he saw, and took these impressions, as it were, home with him. The same shift occurred as the eighteenth-century traveller became the nineteenth-century tourist. The traveller felt free to knock at doors and then to chat with the owner of a house or farm; the tourist looked around, often quite carefully, Baedeker or other tourist guide in hand, but felt more reserve in engaging the natives in talk. The great guide to this shift, in my mind, was the poet Charles Baudelaire as *flâneur*; Baudelaire liked to venture out at dusk, wandering the streets of Paris, returning home at night to write; these stimulating journeys he took silently, observing closely without trying to speak to the strangers who aroused his muse. Photographing the city in his mind, he experienced differentiating exchanges visually.[32] As did Georg Simmel, who, as we have seen, made these moments of visual stimulation into a social theory of subjectivity.

This small excursion into the history of public life suggests two conundrums about cooperation. A conversation with strangers at once dramatic and forthright embodies obvious, active cooperation with others – but what of encounters of Baudelaire's and Simmel's sort? Does cooperation go entirely missing in silent visual encounter? The programmers of GoogleWave certainly hoped not; the screen was meant to make cooperation more vivid, more compelling, than a telephone call – but the program failed socially. Is the eye inherently less sociable than the voice?

The other conundrum concerns shortness. Sensing how different you are from someone else wears off in time; if you drink or dine with him or her twenty times the provocation is likely to disappear. It's certainly true that a brief encounter might change your life – the short love affair, the unexpected hour of personal straight talk from a colleague at work – but what of the lasting effects on how you cooperate? The short love affair might ripple out, altering your responsiveness to people more generally, but then again, it might not. What's contained in this conundrum is the uncertain relation between subjective illumination and everyday social practice. If you are a certain sort of romantic – and I think the Adam Smith who wrote so passionately about sympathy was tinged with that sort of romanticism – you will believe that inner illumination will transform your everyday behaviour. But then there's Baudelaire, whose subjective life consisted of inner, sudden, short, illuminations and whose social self was rigid, contained and unresponsive.

Apart from the conundrums about which sense is stimulated and how consequent inner illumination may prove, there's a whole other dimension to the differentiating, dialogic exchange: the experience can moderate competition. 'Different' need not mean better or inferior; the sense of being different need not invite invidious comparison. Affirming this principle animated the Hampton and Tuskegee Institutes and, I think, represented their great glory. The Institutes ended each day with prayers, during which the achievements of individuals were named; every individual was named as having achieved something, even if what they had accomplished would seem trivial to the sophisticated outsider, as in the formula, 'let us celebrate our sister Mary, who has this day shelved ten pounds of cheese.' In the history of workshops, kindred rituals have long addressed differences of ability; something similar to this prayer ended the working day of every craft in every medieval guild. The rites offered up at the end of each day singled out a distinctive contribution each person had made to the community for the common good.

By emphasizing that each person had something different to offer, Booker T. Washington hoped to overcome the 'acid saying of better or worse', that acid of personalized competition which is invidious comparison. Cooperation strengthened as a result; the rituals of recognizing that each and every one of the people in the Institutes had something special to offer contributed to the sheer productivity and quality of what the Institutes made; outsiders noted and took these results seriously, as they did the kindred work in Robert Owen's New Harmony, because emphasizing distinctiveness had a practical value.

These, then, are the complex facets of the differentiating encounter. In animal nature, it marks off territories; the edges of these territories can be inert boundaries or active borders; so too in the human habitat, a contrast we can make between highways and streets. Border encounters can happen inside as well as outside, as in eighteenth-century coffee houses and cafés. These patterned but open occasions for speech contrasted to the visual encounters the nineteenth-century *flâneur* had with the city; silent, episodic and inward, these experiences were more stimulations than exchanges; they frame puzzles about how much looking at others engages us with them, and about how important subjective arousal proves for everyday behaviour. But the differentiating, dialogic exchange has a practical value in the form in which Washington and Owen organized it; ritualized moments which celebrate the differences between members of a community, which affirm the distinctive value of each person, can diminish the acid of invidious comparison and promote cooperation.

Zero-sum

We all are familiar with zero-sum games, which occur in exchange when one individual's or group's gain becomes another's loss. We've played this sort of game since childhood, in school as well as on the sports field; almost every test of individual talent and achievement is framed by zero-sum reckoning. So in adult life at work are hirings and promotions; nations play zero-sum games with one another whether at war or not; so do religions, unfortunately, especially when they search for converts from other religions.

In adulthood two little lies frequently cover up the zero-sum exchange. The first is, 'I didn't want to hurt you, I'm sorry you are losing out, but in life that's the way the cards fall out,' and so on. The lie here denies that the winner often takes pleasure in the loser's fate. I think of a musical colleague who once described the concert of a mutual friend that received bad reviews; my colleague betrayed a slight smile while quoting from the reviews, even as he spoke of how stupid were the reviewers. The second lie, on the loser's part, is 'I really don't care'. Let's brush aside these lies and consider something more consequent. The win-lose, zero-sum exchange emphasizes competition but does not completely erase cooperation.

It's evident that zero-sum exchanges require cooperation among individuals on the same side, and in higher mammals, as for human beings, that coordination can depend on complex strategic thinking. Grey wolves, for instance, are subtle hunters. An elaborately orchestrated set of moves allows them to coordinate effectively as they spread out to surround prey, then tighten the noose in close formation as they come in for the kill. The military strategist Antoine-Henri Jomini (1779–1869) picked up on this ballet, basing his own military campaigns during the Napoleonic wars on observation of wolves, copying their coordinated circling behaviour.[33]

Between opponents, the zero-sum exchange also entails a certain kind of cooperation. This consists of setting the ground rules for a contest; these rules are set before individuals or groups compete. In lower social animals, rules of engagement seem to be set by genetic imprinting; even before genetic knowledge appeared, naturalists like Lamarck noted that contending animals 'instinctively agreed' on the shape and size of a field for battle. In higher mammals, negotiation comes into play. As described in the Introduction, children around the age of five become skilled in setting ground rules for games. More than sheer agreement is involved; kids learn that rules can be made up, and that rules can be changed.

Another sort of connection between opponents appears in human zero-sum exchanges. Win-lose is seldom total and absolute; instead, the winner will leave something for the loser. This remainder figures in Adam Smith's views on those market exchanges that are based on scarce resources whose worth is well established. Such competition must leave losers something so that they can try again, and are willing to continue competing. Such strict markets resemble sports; you don't want the losers to disband as a result of defeat. This is a ground rule for the end of the competitive exchange, paralleling the shared ground rules which set play in motion.

An element of fantasy also can bond winners and losers. Something like Aristotle's idea about the 'willing suspension of disbelief' in the theatre appears in economic contests: often, the willingness to take risks depends on players believing that they will somehow be exempt from losing, no matter how great the odds that are stacked against them. Shared fantasy also plays a part, as we've seen, in win-win exchanges, in defining the value of the prizes, eighteenth-century investors agreeing that tulips and mica were, somehow, immensely valuable goods. Competition may in itself inflate the value of the prize: if you are struggling so hard to get it, you think the prize must be important. This theme looms large in American literature, since the country worships success; the novels of James Fenimore Cooper in the nineteenth century, F. Scott Fitzgerald in the twentieth and Jonathan Franzen today portray people who have sacrificed their lives to winning, to success, only to find that the prizes once gained are less important than they had imagined. The sociologist Herbert Blumer (1900–1987) lumped these fantasies together as 'fictions of play'. This did not mean they were insubstantial; after all, people devote their lives to winning, or to nursing the consequences of losing. A young man during the Great Depression, Blumer knew all about economic necessity, but he saw something more at work in zero-sum games. He spent a lot of time early in his career studying the movies, and showed in his first writings ways in which people model their own behaviour on Hollywood screen fantasies. This capacity for fantasizing modulates into 'the fictions of play'. Conventions for behaviour are negotiated, both between players and in the heads of individuals; they become, he said, 'symbolic interactions'.[34]

Blumer's insights are important in dispelling the tough-guy idea that win-lose exchanges are the meat of social life, more generous forms of exchange being just a cultural or ethical garnish. Tough-guy realism, indeed, entails a kind of blindness: blind to the demoralizing consequences in classrooms where zero-sum tests rule, or to the erosion of productivity in offices when competition for promotion becomes an obsession. No less than cooperation, competition is symbolic in character and in gestation. More, it is framed by cooperation: the participants need to cooperate at the beginning of competition in agreeing its rules. Winners have to accept that they leave the losers something, if competition is to continue; total selfishness will abort new games.

If no Eden, zero-sum exchange is thus not quite Hobbes's state of nature, red in tooth and claw, a war of each against all. That honour is reserved for the winner-takes-all exchange.

Winner-takes-all

We meet, we compete, I take everything, you are destroyed. Pure Hobbes. In natural ecologies the apex predator is master of this encounter, in which there is no reciprocity. Wolves are apex predators, as are alligators; at the top of the food chain, they have no equal competitors; they can take whatever they like whenever they like – so long as human beings do not enter the picture. In human societies, winner-takes-all exchange is the logic of total war and genocide. In business, winner-takes-all is the logic of monopoly; the idea is to eliminate all competitors. About this state of affairs, let's be as succinct as Hobbes: it should be put an end to as soon as possible.

These, then, are five forms of exchange. Cooperation and competition are most balanced in the middle of the spectrum of exchange. The win-win exchange occurs in both nature and culture, but in both the balance is fragile. Dialogic exchanges which differentiate individuals and groups can also balance cooperation and competition. Establishing territory through marking out borders and boundaries is pervasive in natural communities, but becomes more specialized and subtle in human culture. At the extremes of exchange, altruism is an involuntary force in natural societies and an internalized experience among humans; reciprocity of a tangible sort need not figure in it. At the other end of the spectrum, competition prevails over cooperation in zero-sum exchanges, though it requires cooperation to begin; as much as cooperation, human competition is organized symbolically. In winner-takes-all exchanges all connections between the two are cut; the apex predator rules.

Since symbols, symbol-making and symbolic exchanges are so important in the middle zones, we need to know more about how they are structured. Rituals are one way of structuring symbolic exchanges; rituals establish powerful social bonds, and have proved tools which most human societies use to balance cooperation and competition.

THE POWER OF RITUAL

Many social scientists think an unbroken thread connects communication among animals to human rituals. The historian William McNeill has tried to show this thread in a study of dance rituals. In *Keeping Together in Time* he explored the relation of dance and drill, that is, bodily rituals which lead to discipline of a military sort.[35] McNeill roots these rituals in the coordination of activities which occurs in all social animals; indeed, he has found evidence that the chimpanzees Jane Goodall studied can learn to dance.

When insect ethologists use the word 'ritual' they mean genetically imprinted, communicative behaviour. Unlike bee-dancing, Goodall found that the chimps can learn to treat coordinated dance movement as a game; they experiment with how to do it, just as young children do; an element of creation is involved. In human beings, McNeill found, the game of keeping time together evolves further into a performance, into 'festival occasions, when almost everyone in the community joins in and keeps going for hours on end ... [marching] binds the community more firmly together and makes cooperative efforts of every kind easier to carry through'.[36] Such feel-good activity is an elaboration of primate behaviour, he argues, rather than uniquely human.

The argument has proved a step too far for many of his readers. The Joy of Ritual! Instead, we might want to consider the Beckhams.

The football star David Beckham and his spouse, Victoria 'Posh Spice' Beckham, faced a problem in 2004 when they decided to christen their sons Romeo and Brooklyn. Mr Beckham had told the press after Brooklyn's birth, 'I definitely want Brooklyn to be christened, but I don't know into what religion yet.'[37] They decided to invent a ritual. The tots, it has to be said, were somewhat overshadowed by the black-tie event. A six-course meal was served, rumoured to cost £2,500 per person; the singer Elton John arrived at the Beckham estate in his trademark silver Rolls-Royce; other celebrities had carefully briefed the press on when they would appear and what they would be wearing. Mrs Beckham organized the service as well as the food and flowers; two Buddhist shrines were set up outside the estate's chapel.

Though the event sounds like fun, and though the parents just wanted to make a gesture of speeding Romeo and Brooklyn into the world, the Anglican establishment howled with outrage; to date, no minister has admitted to performing whatever ceremony took place. The prelates of course loathed the luxury of it all; pouring expensive bottled water over a baby (or worse, according to rumour, vintage champagne) they found obscene. But more, the priests scorned the Beckhams' attempt to create ritual for themselves; the sanctity of true ritual arises from tradition, its origins buried in the mists of time. In their view, a ritual cannot be made up, cannot be created.

Made or found?

The priests have a certain psychological truth on their side. Ritual behaviour feels as though the celebrant has stepped out of time in performing a rite, the rite given to him or her by tradition or the gods. Rituals need not be giant in scale; some, like etiquette at table or who buys whom drinks in a bar, are quite banal. But whether cosmic or small, ritual seems to be behaviour coming from outside ourselves, which relieves us of self-consciousness; we focus on just doing the ritual right. But if ritual only dictated behaviour, if it were a shrine not of our own making, the rite would be a static force – and rituals are not frozen behaviour.

Consider another ritual: the teachers at my grandson's school are Leftists of the organic-food sort, appalled that my son and I smoke and that we take the little tyke with us to pubs. But these teachers are not simpletons. They know that gang life starts early in East London, and that something needs to be done to counter it. They have there-fore adapted an old English custom, insisting that their students shake hands after they played competitive sports; the teachers extended this custom to the classroom itself, particularly on those days when stu-dents are subjected to the relentless testing which marks British education; at the end of the day, the testees shake hands.

This ritual may seem to the worldly sophisticate just more of that politically correct thinking which enjoins an organic diet, but the kids love it, crunching one another's fingers in the shake, bowing with exaggeration, but, still, performing the ritual enthusiastically. By adapting an old custom, putting it into a new setting, the teachers' rite aims to ring-fence competition and the aggression it entails: the hand-shake signifies the kids' return to their bond just as kids.

Anthropologists now emphasize this adaptive process; rather than static, ritual is continually evolving from within. Clifford Geertz gave just this inner history to certain Balinese ceremonies that anthropolo-gists before him had frozen in amber.[38] The European historians Eric Hobsbawm and Benedict Anderson have described in the same vein the 'invention of tradition' in national or local values, inventions of the past which mutate as conditions in the present shift.[39] It's true that, as in natural evolution, the pace of change is slow; most ritual patterns evolve in small steps over years or generations, people mak-ing changes without being aware of doing so. In time the act comes to seem immemorial. But there's more to the invention of tradition.

When we shake hands, I'd wager, none of us recall that this greeting was invented by the Greeks to show that the hands hold no weapons. The handshake itself is now usually a low-intensity exchange. But for the children in my grandson's school the handshake is charged; a new context has made it so. We commonly speak of 'living rituals', and may mean that the past continues alive in the present – but a living ritual also implies the value of gestures and words in the present, for reasons different from those which spawned it in the past: we need to deal with an immediate problem or address an absence. The Beckhams wanted a ritual, of some sort, because they had new children; they had an absence to fill.

Three building blocks of ritual help balance cooperation and competition.

Three building blocks of ritual

In its early years, anthropology viewed ritual as an acting out of myth. The anthropologist's circumstances made this view seem reasonable. In the early twentieth century, anthropologists tended to be explorers seeking out cultures which had not yet been touched by Western civilization; they wanted to understand the world-view of these cultures, and myths appeared as the key to gaining that insight. Bronisław Malinowski (1884–1942) was a model for such exploration; he spent most of the First World War in the Trobriand Islands in the western Pacific, trying to deduce, for instance, what the rituals of giving and receiving Kula necklaces (beautiful objects made of shells and threads) revealed of the Trobrianders' beliefs about the cosmos.[40] He of course considered the setting, objects and participants in these rituals, but the point of these concrete facts was, to him, the cosmic myths they represented.

A great shift occurred later in the twentieth century as anthropologists began to explore rituals more as self-standing, apart from representing the cosmos. Clifford Geertz helped bring about this shift, as did Victor Turner, who believed that rituals inevitably morphed into theatrical performances in which the props, costumes, skills of the performer and relation to the audience took on a meaning of their own.[41] This shift went hand in hand with anthropological unease about the idea of engaging with pristine civilizations untouched by the West; by the late twentieth century there were few of these – and the idea itself seemed to smack of celebrating the noble savage. The anthropologist today is more likely to study the local use of cellphones in the Trobriand Islands, or focus on the West itself, as does Caitlin Zaloom in a study of the rituals practised by commodities-traders in Chicago and London, without worrying about metaphysics.[42] Myth and ritual have separated.

I understand why this shift happened, though am not entirely happy with it, perhaps because of poetry's power to connect the small and the great – as in Eliot's line in *The Waste Land*, 'I will show you fear in a handful of dust.' So, too, myth-making; it is a powerful, small-to-great use of language in which all people, not just poets, engage. Still, I can see three ways in which rituals can be built as self-standing practices.

The first is a bit of a paradox. Rituals depend on repetition for their intensity. We usually equate repetition with routine, going over something again and again seeming to dull our senses. As the rehearsal process discussed in the Introduction shows, however, repetition can take another course. Playing a passage again and again can make us concentrate ever more on its specifics, and the value of the sounds, words or bodily movements becomes deeply ingrained. In rituals the same ingraining occurs. This is what religious rituals intend, as in a rite like the Eucharist; perform it a thousand times and you will have ingrained it in your life. Its power will be a thousandfold greater than doing it just once. This is also true of secular rituals; the ritual of shaking hands after a test means more if it happens again and again; it establishes a pattern of experience.

Of course, repetition can go stale. As the rehearsal process makes clear, repetitions have to follow a certain course in order to stay fresh. Refreshment occurs by ingraining a habit, then examining and enlarging it consciously, then ingraining it again as unconscious behaviour. In my grandson's school the teachers first told the children to shake hands, then the kids discussed why they were doing it, then they practised it again and again without further discussion. The end-of-the-day ritual at the Hampton Institute began as a command issued by Booker T. Washington in 1870; there came a moment – hard to date exactly, though it appears to have arrived after about a year – when the artisans began to discuss why they had been issued this command and the form of words they might use to acknowledge the value of each person's contribution; thereafter they practised this daily work ritual without more mutual soul-searching. Rituals go stale if they remain stuck in the first stage of learning, that of a habit; if they go through the full rhythm of practice, they self-renew.

Rituals, secondly, transform objects, bodily movements or bland words into symbols. The point of a handshake is more than feeling another person's skin; the bread and wine of the Eucharist or the food at a Seder mean more than having something nourishing to eat and drink.

A symbol like a stop-sign warns of danger and tells us directly what to do. The symbol Eliot makes out of 'a handful of dust' engages us in a more problematic way; it tells us there is a large meaning to dust, but not exactly what that meaning is. Since Plato, philosophy has struggled with the relation between symbols as representations and as evocations. The semiotician Roland Barthes (1915–80) believed that if we think hard enough, every stop-sign becomes a handful of dust; that is, the seeming forthrightness of representation dissolves into a miasma of evocations.[43]

Ritual draws on both kinds of symbols, but sorts them out through the rhythm of practice. Directions are first given us, which we ingrain as habit; these directions dissolve into evocations we try to pursue more consciously; the pursuit is not endless; we recover our sense of direction in an enriched habit, re-ingrained as tacit behaviour. In rituals, objects and bodily gestures, no less than language, pass through this transforming process, becoming dense in meaning. But we know how to use the Kula necklace or the Seder goblet; the saturated symbols guide us.

The third building block of ritual concerns expression, specifically dramatic expression. Walking down the aisle if you get married is nothing like walking slowly down a street; even if your gait is similar physically, in the marriage ceremony you are on display and each step you take down the aisle seems immense. Just the expressive element was missing in GoogleWave, whose exchanges attended to the sharing of information rather than to emotional arousal; the dramatic content of the computer program was thin.

In a ceremony, you may be full of feeling, but that fullness represents a danger. In *The Paradox of Acting*, when discussing the work of professional actors, Denis Diderot puts the danger as follows: 'If the actor were full, really full, of feeling how could he play the same part twice running with the same spirit and success? Full of fire at the first performance, he would be worn out and cold as marble at the third.'[44] The same danger attends rituals: too full of feeling, you might start crying, forget what you are supposed to do, break down; other people might feel sympathetic if this happens in a marriage ceremony, but the ceremony itself will become a mess.

Professional actors focus on the content of their lines; professional musicians focus on the notes, are expressing something outside themselves; in performing, they turn outward. Some of the same outward-turn occurs in ceremonies, whose expressive power stands at the opposite pole from a person lost in the labyrinth of his or her own private feelings. This is one reason why, in performing a ritual, people become so exercised about getting it exactly right, whether it's a question of social etiquette or what version of the Bible to use in church; no matter what you feel, the power of the occasion depends on what you are performing.

There's a sociological nicety involved in focusing on content rather than on yourself. The sociologist Erving Goffman (1922–1982) launched the study of the role of drama in everyday life, coining the phrase 'the presentation of self' to evoke the roles people play in behaving like the characters in a play, understandable and credible to others as the sort of person a mental patient, his or her doctor, a prisoner, his or her guard, is supposed to be; in theatrical terms, Goffman explored 'typecasting'. Invaluable as Goffman's work was, there is something missing from it. In a ceremony, people are relieved of portraying the kind of person they are, of speaking on behalf of themselves; the participants enter a larger, shared, expressive domain. This is why the historian Keith Thomas (and I) deploy the term 'enactments', rather than 'presentations of self', to describe the outward turn in rituals.[45]

Unlike the performing practices of professional musicians or actors, everyday rituals have to be accessible and easy to learn, so that everyone can participate. In the world of work, these rituals are usually small events, like the rituals of the tea break, which are hardly soul-shaking dramas. Still, the participant gossiping during a tea break wants to hold the attention of others, rather than rambling and so boring them. He or she has to learn to gossip well, dramatizing what may be in itself undramatic, and in that sense becomes a performer.

The word 'performance' may suggest an illusion which suspends everyday reality. Tulip-mania was certainly dramatic; the conviction that you, personally, can somehow beat the odds in a zero-sum game may invoke theatre's willing suspension of disbelief. Yet there's another side to this story.

There's a wonderful moment in Machiavelli's letters when the disgraced servant of the state, exiled to a small farm outside Florence, describes a daily ritual. 'When evening comes, I return home and go into my study. On the threshold I strip off my muddy, sweaty, workday clothes, and put on the robes of court and palace, and in this graver dress I enter the courts of the ancients and am welcomed by them, and there I taste the food that alone is mine, and for which I was born.'[46] Is the ritual a flight from reality on the farm? Surely it is more than that. By donning the costume he no longer has a right to wear, Machiavelli suddenly springs to life; intense hours are ritual's gift to him. For a man in disgrace that's a real gift – as it is for others without power.

Ritual balance

These three aspects of ritual are tools for balancing the weights of competition and cooperation. The Book of Genesis describes no balancing rituals in Eden because there was no need for them; until Eve began reasoning, an undramatic, peaceful harmony pervaded that state of nature in which all creatures obeyed God's command. There was too much drama in the state of nature as Hobbes imagined it, but no balance; ritual was absent in the war of each against all.

The natural world as ethologists understand it has expressive rituals of a sort, as among dancing bees. It's a matter here of genetic pattern-behaviour whose content often lags behind environmental change. Cooperation and competition can be balanced in natural communities, within the same or between different species; establishing boundaries and borders is one way to effect this balance.

Balance depends on exchange. As we've seen, exchanges run the gamut from altruistic to winner-takes-all relations. In human exchanges, reciprocity diminishes at either end of the spectrum. Altruism in our species can be a pure gift in which nothing is expected in return, in kind, or the giver conducts a dialogue with his or her own shadow self. Competition with others doesn't figure in this process; there are rituals surrounding the gift of blood but these are gentle and civil in character. I haven't, I know, addressed the potlatch and similar contests in which people compete to see who can give the most; these contests, usually elaborate and dramatic in character (think of fund-raising drives), would indeed fall within ritual's balancing domain.

At the other end of the spectrum, among apex predators like wolves or soldiers bent on genocide, there can be intense cooperation within the predatory group, but no cooperation with those to be destroyed. Again there's a caveat to add, and an inflammatory one. Hannah Arendt argued, and in my view very badly, that, during the Shoah, Jewish leaders in the camps collaborated in the destruction of their own people; with the Nazi wolves they contrived rituals to routinize the process of killing more efficiently.[47]

Reciprocity comes to the fore in the middle zones of exchange. In win-win exchanges, there's enough to divide up equally for everyone among competitors on the same terrain; in certain zero-sum exchanges, there's enough left over for the losers that they are able to try again. In both, cooperation sets the ground rules and defines what's particularly valuable for people to compete for. Ritual can play a role in both. Ritual can give a shape to informal win-win exchanges; moreover, face-saving rituals make it possible for coalitions with strong and weak partners to work together for their common benefit. Ritual appears in zero-sum exchanges in the elaborate etiquette of meetings which set the ground rules for competition; such etiquette is founded on the adeptness with which children learn early on to negotiate the rules of a game.

Ritual occupies a special place in differentiating exchanges. As in encounters between strangers in a bar or casual acquaintances at dinner, rituals guide the process of compare-and-contrast. Eighteenth-century coffee-house talk modelled itself explicitly on the speech and gestures of the stage; we do so implicitly today when seeking to make gossip vivid rather than simply the imparting of facts.

There's a history to rituals which have sought to balance competition and cooperation, and in particular at a great turning point in the early modern era. This turning point particularly shaped the rituals people deployed to live with others who differed from themselves. The result of this historical turning point was, at the time, that the balance between competition and cooperation became fragile; we are still living with the consequences. The following chapter explores how it happened.

3

The 'Great Unsettling'

How the Reformation Transformed Cooperation

In 1533, Hans Holbein the Younger finished *The Ambassadors*, which now hangs in London's National Gallery. The painting shows two young men who face forward; between them is a two-tiered table stuffed with things, scientific instruments on the top shelf, a lute, a case of flutes, a hymnal, a mathematics book and a hand-held globe on the bottom. The two young men are arrayed in rich robes, especially the man on the left, his body outlined in white fur edging his robe; an intricate green cloth hangs behind them; an oriental carpet is draped behind the table. Amid this sensuous profusion a disturbing object lies in the foreground: a giant disk floating at an angle, with something obscure on its surface if the painting is looked at straight on; once the viewer moves to the side, this obscure image becomes clarified as a death's head: a skull.

Holbein painted *The Ambassadors* just as the secular consequences of the Reformation were coming to a head in Britain.[1] Henry VIII, in spearheading this change, was driven less by religious conviction than sexual desire; he wanted a divorce from Catherine of Aragon in order to marry Anne Boleyn, and the Church then as now forbade divorce. Henry was willing to overthrow the old faith, and embrace new Protestant doctrine, at least nominally, to get his way. The 'ambassadors' in the painting are two young men, Jean de Dinteville and Georges de Selve, envoys sent to England by Catholic France to deal with the havoc caused by Henry VIII's marital troubles, a complex mission since Anne Boleyn had links to the French court. Holbein's painting though, represents much larger changes in early modern society's understanding of cooperation.

The open hymnal on the lower shelf marks one social consequence of the religious schism: the effort in Protestantism to reform religious ritual, so that it is more cooperative. The hymnal is open to two songs written by Martin Luther (on the left 'Come sacred spirit', on the right 'Man, if thou would live a good life and remain with God'). Both hymns celebrate renunciation of the flesh; Henry VIII would have been unlikely to sing them fervently. Luther meant these hymns also to serve new church rituals that would bind congregants together more strongly than the old. He used simple words written in the native language congregants spoke, rather than in refined Latin, the language of the clergy; the bibles he used were printed, making them widely accessible. In these ways, Luther sought to strengthen religious community, a community in which all could directly and equally share their faith.

The tools which appear on the top shelf of the table in Holbein's painting signal a change in the organization of workshops. These are the precision tools pilots used to convert information about the heavens into precise mathematical calculations. There is a compound solar viewer used to calculate sunlight and solar time; a sextant used to locate the sun's position in the sky; a nine-sided object resembling a spinning toy, each face etched with circles measuring angles in different ways, used to reckon space in different configurations. All are tools used by navigator-explorers to chart unknown regions of the world, tools with political value, since they would assist Europe's project of conquering new territories, but which the first explorers did not understand very well how to use.[2] These instruments on Holbein's table are products of a new kind of workshop, the technical laboratory, a workshop which would alter how artisans practised cooperation.

Then there are the two young men themselves. They were not in fact professional diplomats, which is odd, since diplomacy was in the process of becoming an organized profession.[3] The profession took form around resident ambassadors, served by a newly articulated bureaucracy of consuls, secretaries and double agents. These young men were envoys called in as auxiliaries during a crisis. Though specialized, the diplomatic profession had a wider resonance in European culture because of the ways diplomats conducted conversations. Up to about 1500, Latin was the language of European diplomacy as of the clergy; now French began to be spoken as well, a French which combined vernacular, everyday forms of expression with diplomacy's formal codes of address.[4] In the same way that theatrical speech served as a model for discussion in eighteenth-century coffee houses, so in the sixteenth century diplomatic French spread like an ink-blot into ordinary social conversation. Speech which combined the formal and the colloquial migrated from embassies to aristocratic salons; in time, the language of salons migrated further into sitting rooms of bourgeois life.

The spread of diplomatic speech into everyday life may seem a small footnote in the history of European civilization. But it was in fact one sign of a sea-change in sociable behaviour: the shift from chivalry to civility. Chivalric values were woven tight into the fabric of aristocratic life; civilized codes were rooted in professional conduct, a profession requiring skill, a skill that non-professionals could learn and practise. Civility, moreover, generated new ethics of sociability, of how people ought to behave; these ethical standards applied particularly to the practice of cooperation.

Historians are rightly suspicious of strict periods like Medieval, Renaissance and Reformation; these are arbitrary divisions of time. And yet history is not a continuous flow; as in natural time, human history has punctuating moments. Apart from its beauty, *The Ambassadors* is an iconic painting in that it marks three great changes in European society in the sixteenth century. These were the transformation of rituals in religion; changing practices of material production; and the appearance of a new ethics for sociability. Holbein's painting signals turning points in all three ways people cooperated at the dawn of the modern era.

The artist was not simply a recorder. At the bottom of the canvas, the death's head makes one comment. This skull can be seen only by stepping sideways, a painterly technique called anamorphosis. When looked at from the side all the other objects and the people in the painting become flat and distorted. Death's heads were a traditional symbol of the vanity of human wishes. The lute makes another comment on the times; it has a broken string, another traditional symbol of discord. More novel was the mathematics book, written by Peter Apian in 1527, *On Mercantile Calculations*, open to a page on 'division'. The effect of all three is unsettling, but Holbein was a painter, not a preacher. Looked at straight on, the people and the objects on the table are arresting and beautiful in themselves; in the same spirit, let's look directly at each element in this great icon.

RELIGIOUS RITUAL

Luther's hymnal in the Holbein painting marks a huge shift in the social organization of religious ritual. Luther sought to draw in the faithful through words and songs in native languages, in part because he was convinced that medieval rituals had come to exclude ordinary people from direct participation in religion. They risked becoming mere spectators to their faith, watching it performed by priestly officials rather than cooperating in its enactment.

Luther's fear embodies one response in Western culture to the process described by Victor Turner in central Africa and Micronesia: the metamorphosis of ritual into theatre. Luther feared this structural change both theologically and socially; religious theatre split the community into two unequal parts. His fear can be charted in the bread and wine used in Communion.

Bread and wine

The ritual of Communion was a long-term work in progress. Up to the sixth century, bread and wine were shared in the communal meal of the Eucharist, recalling the fellowship of the first Christians; so far as is known, these were easy, informal occasions, prayers and blessings being offered spontaneously during the course of the meal. In the sixth century the formal rite of the Latin Mass began to replace this sacred supper party.[5] Still, up to about AD 900, both bread and wine came from offerings brought to the church by the congregants themselves; by the eleventh century, these offerings were replaced by products from specialized, priestly hands in the monasteries. The rite grew farther away in space from congregants in the church through the evolution of Romanesque into Gothic church architecture, the Romanesque church conducting services close to the congregants, the

Gothic pushing them further away with the creation of the altar rail and rood screen.

The sensate experience of wine and bread also became removed from the realm of the everyday. The cup of wine had in early times passed from the lips of congregant to congregant; by the tenth century it was often imbibed through a straw; in the twelfth century, the priest frequently drank the wine alone, on behalf of the congregants. Up to the ninth century the actual bread used in the Mass was leavened and eaten in chunks; this daily bread, usually confected from rye and spelt, was gradually replaced by special unleavened, thin white wafers made purely of wheat; only this special bread, the 'oble', could be altered into Christ's body during the Mass.

Beyond church walls the dominion of spectacle also flourished. The revival of cities from about AD 900 is one to define as 'medieval'. This was not only a geographic and economic revival; the revived city spawned rituals like parades of the Host or other sacred relics through the streets before the celebration of Mass. Like gifts of bread, early religious parades in Paris had been simple affairs in which people made their own costumes, carried home-made crosses, wandered rather erratically through the streets towards parish churches. Regulation then imposed its heavy bureaucratic weight on these events. In 1311, under the aegis of Pope Clement V, the Corpus Christi parade became an officially sanctioned *ex cathedra* part of the ceremony. By the fifteenth century costumes had become the product of specialist weavers, the ceremonial crosses precious objects encrusted with costly stones, parade routes laid out carefully by ecclesiastical authority.[6]

Theatrical spectacle in the community thus marked an increasing separation between spectator and celebrant, mirroring the divide between everyday and sacred material.[7] Inside the church, the priest used special gestures and tones of voice to act out Christ's last days; the visual Elevation of the Host was dramatized so that the event would register with those who might not hear or understand the priest's words. But there's a hitch in what seems the implacable march from cooperative ritual to less interactive theatre. The hitch was the behaviour of ordinary parish priests as performers.

The historian Henry Kamen observes that 'in medieval times the pulpit had been the chief moderator of public opinion', yet medieval priests were poor at public speaking. In one parish in Cambridge, a local adage ran, 'when the vicar goeth into the pulpit, then the multitude of the parish goeth straight out of the church, home to drink.'[8] The education of the clergy in the dark arts of rhetoric, recovering the power of the spoken sermon, aimed to attract parishioners back to active engagement with their faith. The power-logic was that control derives from formality, and formality entails theatricality of the sort separating celebrant and spectator.

At Christianity's origins, the ritual sharing of food aimed to promote *agapé*, men and women's love for one another inspired by faith in God. Sacred meals in private homes, the earliest meeting places for persecuted Christians, were meant to echo the Last Supper. The food itself had no magical powers; the feast of *agapé* made it sacred. A millennium later, the ever-increasing value put on spectacle intensified the magical experience of the bread and wine in themselves – their sacred 'presence'. In this, we could make a contrast of Christian bread to Jewish matzo. The unleavened matzo eaten annually at Passover is meant to recall the story of Jews eating on the run as they fled persecution in Egypt, lacking the time and the ovens to bake raised bread. The matzo is a mnemonic symbol; it awakens the historic memory of the Diaspora but acquires during the Passover ceremony no magical properties in itself. The Christian wafer, on the other hand, is a 'real presence' in the Catholic Mass, the bread and wine of the Eucharist becoming the flesh and blood of Christ – a god's living body. This doctrine of 'transubstantiation' was codified by the Catholic Church in 1215; magical food strengthened the spell cast by religious theatre.*

The transformation of cooperative ritual into spectacular theatre, like all great historical events, prompted resistance. The simple Lutheran songbook on Holbein's table represented one form of resistance – or an alternative assisted by a change in technology. The advent of Gutenberg's printing press at the end of the fifteenth century meant that ordinary people could own bibles and songbooks – previously,

---

* Due to the doctrine of the 'real presence', some of the peoples conquered by Catholic Christianity drew a logical if false inference. Some Amazonian Indians initially imagined Christians to be like themselves, kindred cannibals, both groups eating their gods for strength.

these manuscript books were costly objects. The Reformation wanted printed bibles to be translated into the language of parishioners, so that there would be even more direct contact with the Word. The songs in Luther's hymnal are simplified musically, much less complex harmonically than Catholic church music of the early sixteenth century, so that any parishioner could easily learn and sing them.

But a more radical form of resistance would be to devalue ritual itself, if the believer were convinced that ritual inevitably leads to the vice of theatricality. A handful of 'Lutherans', writes the religious historian Benjamin Kaplan, 'consider[ed] many rituals neither required nor forbidden. In theology such optional practices were called "adiaphoral" or "indifferent" ... precisely because the performance of rituals did not contribute to salvation.'[9] Quakers like William Penn pushed this rejection further; in the words of a modern commentator, they believed that 'only the inward is necessary ... ritual [in this case baptism] ... can be entirely dispensed with'.[10] But views of this severity were held by a small minority only; doing away with ritual completely proved too austere for most Protestants – including John Calvin – and too isolating. Faith had to be socially framed in some other way, and the ritual of baptism showed one way to do so.

Baptism

In the early Church, baptism was for adults rather than for infants; it could have no meaning for babies because it entailed making the most serious decision of one's life. The transformed Christian body reflected Christ's own death and Resurrection: Paul writes in his Letter to the Romans that we are 'baptized into his death'.[11] In time, though, baptism was practised ever earlier in Christian lives until it took place shortly after physical birth.

Baptism certainly had, and still has, magical elements of spectacle, and in its long history these elements proved troubling to many Christians. Like his Catholic predecessors, Martin Luther believed that during the rite water itself became 'no longer simple water like other water, but a holy, divine, blessed water'.[12] Unlike his forebears, Luther winnowed from Catholic baptism other elements of spectacle – the incense and lighted candles, the scented oils coating a baby's body – to focus on immersion in clear, clean water as a gesture of seeking salvation. He stressed the wet subject, not the priest doing the wetting, and refreshed the early Christian practice of adult immersion; what matters is the decision to be reborn.

After Luther, many Protestant sects emphasized baptism as a covenant with God. The religious covenant is a contract of sorts, an idea not entirely foreign to an age beginning to embrace political and economic contracts and celebrating the virtues of choice. More, the decision about whether to enter into a covenant falls on the individual. In the colonized regions of the world, Christians forced heathens to convert en masse; Jews in Europe again and again faced a 'choice' between conversion or exile (or death). Christians born into the faith instead were meant to choose of their own accord. For Luther, though, that choice became more contradictory in practice. In *The Babylonian Captivity* (1520), he argued that local communities should be free to choose their own ministers from among everyday parishioners, yet the peasant revolts of 1524–5 came to horrify him.[13] Rebelling against Catholic religious authority, he still believed in the right of princes to rule, and personally courted their favour, all too often over-impressed by their titles.

It might seem that the biblical adage 'Render unto Caesar the things which are Caesar's ...' would have eased this tension between an individual's free covenant with God and his or her subservience to a prince. But in Luther's case, it was not so easy. He had unshakeable faith in the virtue of direct engagement and personal choice in coming to God; despite himself, that faith meant the most to him, as it did to his ever-growing legion of followers. The new Christianity with its simple hymns, its bibles translated into languages the people spoke every day, its recovery of simplicity and purity in rituals like baptism, its willingness to reject rituals which impeded direct connection between Man and God, or at the extreme to do away with ritual altogether: all this contrasted with the elaborate spectacles of worship which seemed to have passed beyond their medieval ripeness and become rotten fruit.

As an intellectual exercise, I've sometimes speculated about which of the categories of exchange described in Chapter 2 might best fit this religious shift. Neither altruism nor win-win exchange fits very well, because of a heightened, personalized experience of sin that lay at the heart of the new Christianity. Luther declared, 'Where God built a church, there the devil would also build a chapel'; suffering is therefore inescapable.[14] This emphasis on sin and suffering cast altruism in a particular light.

From Quakers to Calvinists, the Reformation certainly celebrated selfless service to the community, particularly when it occurred face to face in local communities. But no good work can erase sin. Luther affirmed justification *sola fide*, 'by faith alone', whereas the Catholic Council of Trent in the 1540s proclaimed that mankind could redeem itself equally by good works – altruism – and by inner faith.

Similarly the experience of mutual solace, as in funerals or other consoling rites; solace is limited in power and scope, since suffering is mankind's lot. We don't want to draw a cartoon: the community pastor, like the rabbi, priest or imam, does not use funerals as platforms to remind people that the dear departed may be headed for Hell. But Luther, and even more Calvin, emphasized in their writings that this would most likely be the dead person's destination. For the same theological reason that Protestantism attacked the selling of indulgences, a profitable Church activity which veiled human sinfulness, so Luther's version of Christianity eschewed any form of ritual which diminished awareness of mankind's imperfection.

Luther's cast of mind best fitted, I think, the differentiating exchange: in choosing to come closer to God, without impediment, the Protestant believer was meant to become ever more aware of how different is the human condition from the divine. Remove the filters of ritual, particularly the glitz of theatrical ritual: then coming closer to God makes the believer ever more aware of mankind's sinful state.

The word 'Reformation' may make us think of reform's enemies fighting a rearguard action in the name of tradition, contesting Protestant versions of cooperation. Within the Catholic Church that is exactly what happened. But the formulas of theatrical ritual built up in medieval religion pushed forward in time into new domains. During the Reformation, some political performers picked up the torch of medieval Catholic theatricality. Let's look at one way this happened in the seventeenth century, with consequences that have continued into our own time.

Secular echoes

In the late winter of 1653, the First Minister of France, Cardinal Jules Mazarin, assembled for the court a thirteen-hour ballet.[15] The First Minister was not in search of amusement. The *Ballet de la Nuit*, which started at dusk and ended at dawn, and whose star performer was the fifteen-year-old King Louis XIV, was a piece of political theatre. The King was meant to display his authority, by dancing, an 'iconic representation', Georgia Cowart says, 'of the king's power'.[16] The story-line of this dance resembled an off-on switch: during most of the night the dances dramatized chaos, nightmares and disorder; then, at the break of dawn, Louis suddenly appeared, arrayed in rubies, pearls and diamonds, a glittering young king banishing darkness and misrule.

The reasons for this performance lay in the residue of the Reformation. Religious conflict had produced, within France, a secular crisis. During the internal convulsion known as the Fronde, Protestants had rebelled against the Catholic, monarchical regime; the boy Louis, waiting to become king, had been driven from Paris when aristocrats, seizing on this clash of religion, rebelled against the increasingly iron grip of the centralized state. The ballet sent a message to its rebellious aristocratic audience. These same noble rebels in 1653 watched hour after hour in a vast, smoky chamber dimly lit by candles as demons and furies represented their own brief era of revolt; when sunlight broke the room's windows, order returned in the King's dancing person. Almost all ballets of this period reverted to ancient mythology for character-labels; Louis was cast quite logically as Apollo, the guardian of light. Mazarin had summoned the old god for a new purpose; in this dance Louis adopted the persona which served him throughout his long reign, that of the Sun King around whom the planets of the aristocracy should necessarily revolve.

The point Mazarin was ramming home depended, to be convincing, on how well Louis danced. To the dance historian Julia Prest, he could seem either 'superlative and godlike on the one hand and all too human on the other'; if the boy stumbled or tired the dramatic message would implode; the young king had to dominate the stage as soloist for more than an hour.[17] The symbol of power depended on bodily self-control. Mazarin could trust the young king to perform well: like his predecessor, Louis XIII, the young Louis XIV had spent more hours of each day learning to dance than reading books, and was an exceptionally gifted dancer in his own right – the greatest dancer, by all accounts, of his time.

A precursor to the *Ballet de la Nuit* was offered in 1581 during a marriage celebration at the French court; this was the *Ballet comique de la Reine*, choreographed by Beaujoyeulx, one of the first native-born, professional dance masters; in the sixteenth century, Italy was the epicentre of European dance. Lasting nearly as long as Louis XIV's debut, Beaujoyeulx's ballet mixed noble dancing with ordinary dancing, with acrobatic displays and with buffoonery. The French-man also invited the audience to dance; many of those who took part in the *Ballet comique* were not adept dancers, and were best at infor-mal, local dances.

At Louis's debut, the clowns were expunged, social (that is, 'base') dancing became the province of mythological devils who were in turn swept away as the King entered. In Beaujoyeulx's choreography, imaginary triangles inscribed within a circle on the stage floor repre-sented a trajectory of 'supreme power', which different dancers were permitted to follow. In the *Ballet de la Nuit*, this route became reserved as the King's path; choreographic geometries concentrated single-mindedly on the placement of the King's body. Spectators got the political message. During Louis's reign, writes the modern historian Philippe Beaussant, the evenings of dance shifted 'from the sovereign mingling with his subjects, among and with them, to the sovereign as director of a choreography centred on himself alone'.[18] In something of a similar vein, the great nineteenth-century musician Franz Liszt once remarked, 'the concert is . . . myself.'

Like all performing arts involving more than one person, mounting a dance must be a cooperative venture back-stage; the spirit of win-win exchange has to prevail for the event to hold together. Dancing of the sort practised by Louis XIV and his troupe was such a coopera-tive, win-win venture based on strict hierarchy; it marked one origin, as Jennifer Homans says, for the star-system in dance we know today, with its elaborate ladder ascending from corps de ballet to principal dancer.[19] Out front, though, the star-system emphasizes the distance between performer and audience: no one in a disco moves like Nureyev. In the theatre, this distance can be thrilling; put to political use, as Louis XIV did, it is subduing.

This is just the divide we have traced, in an earlier time, as communal ritual morphed into a more spectacular religious theatre, producing the same gulf between high priest and congregation. It would be pushing matters to claim that archbishops and bishops schemed to produce subservience in their parishioners through their own theatricality, but Mazarin and Louis XIV were certainly conscious of, and aimed at, that result. As theatricality passed across the divide between sacred and worldly performance, it became more of a manipulative tool of power. 'The performance is ... myself' applies today perhaps even more to politicians; facing television cameras, they are carefully groomed and spin-doctored and have become very artful in speaking from the heart. To be sure, when Louis spoke to the mass of his subjects, he spoke as a king; he enacted that role rather than expressed himself. But there is a connection between Louis on stage and the ever-so-sincere politician before the cameras. Both performances embody charisma, and it's worth pausing on that word.

The Greek word *charisma* originally meant a favour granted by the gods, a favour which gave physical things transcendent potency. Catholic Christianity reflected this physical magic, as bread and wine were transubstantiated into Christ's flesh and blood; some monarchs in Christian countries are still, at their coronations, anointed with chrism, which is the same substance used in baptisms.[20] The objects become charismatic. In politics, charisma names an inexplicable halo of personal legitimacy – the 'sanctity' of a king – and, applied to secular political actors, charisma names their quality of seeming larger than ordinary life, even when each dramatizes him- or herself as an emblematic Everyman.

The magic of personal charisma requires acting skill to work. Just before the Reformation, Machiavelli had laid out some of the rules for performing charisma. His Prince hides reasons of state behind a mask, acting so as to inspire love and fear of the Prince's own person. Machiavelli had to hand the example of the monk Savonarola, who at the end of the fifteenth century had at first aroused, by the power of sheer oratory, Catholic Florentines to renounce sensuality, to make a 'bonfire of the vanities'. (Artists like Botticelli consigned some of their most beautiful paintings to the flames; Savonarola had also driven Machiavelli temporarily out of Florence.) But Savonarola did not control his stage well; called on to walk through fire, he trimmed and hedged, and his charisma 'deserted' him.[21] Louis was more skilled in practising charisma, at least in his early years, putting himself on display like a polished jewel, dramatizing the sheer fact of his self-control.

As a sociological force, charisma has a complex relation to cooperation. The charismatic leader can inspire his subjects to cooperate more fully with one another – Luther did just this. But critical judgement tends to disappear in the cooperation inspired by a charismatic figure. In this, a long, strong rope connects Louis XIV as a performer to modern, charismatic tyrants. The most notable instance is of course Hitler, who called himself 'the greatest actor in Europe', and who declared that 'the chief concerns of the politician were matters of staging'.[22] The theatre of belief was no metaphor to the Nazis; theatrical illusion was an essential ingredient of their power, one which they cultivated from the very beginning, producing a terrifying, mindless submission. One participant at Nazi rallies told Theodore Abel in 1938, 'I felt as though [Hitler] were addressing me personally. My heart grew light, something in my breast arose. I felt as if bit by bit something within me were being rebuilt.'[23]

No one four centuries ago, obviously, could foresee such events. But it was evident then that when ritual turns into spectacle something happens to communities and to individuals. Spectacle turns community into a hierarchy in which those at the bottom observe and serve, but do not participate as individuals with self-standing worth. In this, Luther's contradictions resonate even if we lack his religious convictions. Luther himself was charismatic, a powerful speaker and writer, a giant Everyman. Though he felt awe in the presence of other, worldly princes, he feared their effect on the community of believers; the Everyman and Everywoman of normal size must directly enter into a covenant – themselves alone or, better, in concert with others – but they must choose themselves to do it. 'My heart grew light' is not at all what this covenant is about; spectacle can offer no relief from struggling with oneself over sin and the prospect of Hell. That struggle may have diminished in our age of feel-good religion, but the Reformation did make clear the enduring inner cost of theatre, the seductive threat that 'leadership' poses to conscience.

THE WORKSHOP

The navigation equipment on Holbein's table represented a great change in productive life. This was the expansion of workshops organized as guilds to include workshops more like laboratories. This change gathered force during the three generations before Luther nailed his 95 Theses to a church door in 1517, and has endured ever since. Cooperation in the making of new sorts of technologies and things was also an unsettling transition to modernity; it posed the question of how people should cooperate in discovery and experiment – GoogleWave's question.

The workshop, as noted in Chapter 1, is one of the oldest institutions of human society. One reason it is so old has to do with where artisinal labour gets done. The traces of workshops from six thousand years ago in Mesopotamia show that shared labour had become rooted to one place. Like farming, the artisanal workshop terminated the wandering way of life; while nomadic tribes scavenged, workshops produced their own sustenance.[24] Chinese written records from the second millennium BC predicted that such settled labour would become ever more skilful than the work of nomads, the urban potter a better craftsman than his wandering counterpart. Part of the reason for this belief lay in the artisan's tools, which became ever bigger, heavier and more complicated, and so more difficult to transport. An example is the city potter's wheel, which replaced the itinerant potter's upturned gourd.

If we make a big jump in time up to the medieval period, the articulated skills of the urban craftsman had found a bureaucratic base in guilds. As cities renewed in Europe from the eleventh century on, they transformed the monastic workshop. The economic life of the city depended on producing more than the producers themselves needed. Each city sold the surplus on to people in other cities, inter-city trade becoming ever more important than intra-city commerce. Individual workshops produced the surplus; guilds orchestrated how these goods were fed into the system of trade.

The workshops had to practise efficient internal coordination if they were to provide for more than local needs. That was in large part a matter of organizing men's time. The monastery day had mixed labour, whether in the garden or in sheltered workshops, with long periods of shared prayer and solitary contemplation, but producing a surplus of things for the trading economy required more sheer hours at the bench. Moreover, innovation of a sort was required in the work itself. The urban workshop developed greater skill in the practice of old crafts. Goldsmithing in the twelfth century and glass-making in the fourteenth evolved new skills, thanks to the appearance of compli-cated tools. Pottery-making, the most ancient of all crafts, required the same sorts of implements in 1300 as the great potters of antiquity had wielded, but potters now experimented with different sorts of clay. Urban workshops emphasized efficiency, necessary to produce surplus, a subject for which the Old Testament provided no guidance. Still, the spiritual equation did not disappear in the medieval market economy. Labour remained God-sanctioned in principle, the Church remained an authority presiding over economic power. But the monas-tic refuge ceased to provide an adequate everyday model for social relations in the urban workshop.

Guilds managed conflict between competing workshops, and issued guarantees that goods were genuinely what the makers claimed them to be. Most important, they enforced labour rights protecting work-ers, especially young workers, from some of the physical abuse and exploitation which occurred in slave or serf communities. Each work-shop contained three levels of worker, who all lived on the premises: apprentices whose contracts ran usually for seven years, journeymen whose contracts ran for three, and masters who permanently owned the operation.[25]

These dry elements of structure came to life through the rituals which guilds evolved. In the city's parades and feasts, apprentices carried the guild's flags; all guild members were entitled to wear distinctive, often elaborate clothes. Within each workshop, ritual paid a special kind of tribute to skill. The apprentice presented at the end of his training a piece of work called the *chef d'œuvre* which showed to the workshop what he could achieve so far. The *chef d'œuvre* was sometimes then exhibited in the guild hall, to be commented upon by anyone in the city; up the workshop ladder, the journeyman presented a more advanced *chef d'œuvre* to a community composed only of masters.

The young apprentice or journeyman was not allowed to speak or explain; the maker's personality didn't enter the picture; the rituals aimed at judgement of a man-made object on its own merits, and the object had to speak for itself. Our medieval forebears went about establishing the objective fact of quality through discussions aiming at consensus, though in a peculiar form of speech-act. The standard form of address used for objects was 'you' rather than 'it'. Medieval craft-speech took this verbal locution one step further; the objects were treated as if alive, as though they had been magically transformed into beings with whom one discussed and disputed.

The ritual of the *chef d'œuvre* may thus seem a kind of spectacle akin to theatrical spectacles in the religious sphere. But there was a big difference. At parades or inside churches, congregants fell silent in the presence of the religious performers; here, the audience spoke up; they were judges rather than spectators. Religion imbued every aspect of medieval life, so that there was no deep schism between how people prayed and how they worked; the workshop emphasized shared critical thinking in these rituals judging the worth of things, however, while religious spectacle did not.

We might imagine, that rituals would prove socially divisive because the judges could decide the work wasn't good enough. But in fact these were win-win exchanges. Most objects made by apprentices and journeymen usually passed the test – in the metal-working trades c. AD 1200 nearly 90 per cent did, in Italian leather trades at the same time about 80 per cent did (these can be only very rough numbers). The makers of things judged not sufficiently 'lively' had a second, and more rarely a third, chance to try again the year following. The pass rate may seem to render test-day a fraud. Not at all. The event exemplifies the classic rite-of-passage ritual: a young person is taken outside himself, exposed to danger, then reconfirmed as a valued member of the community. In medieval craftsmanship, the maker's things took this journey for him.

This system changed between the fourteenth and the sixteenth and early seventeenth centuries. Individuation evolved into innovation; that is, making a particular chalice or cup, distinctive in character, full of life, began to suggest the making of whole new classes of objects; in tableware, for instance, the fork appeared in workshops which had first confected a few miniature, two-pronged knives as a novelty item. From about the middle of the sixteenth century the suggestive process accelerated, but not in any predictable fashion. A signal fact about all the navigation equipment on Holbein's table is that people didn't know at first what to make of the new classes of things. In one way, this is a general law in the history of technology: tools are invented before people understand fully how to use them. In the seventeenth century this general law had a special and social application.

This was an age in which scientific experiment lodged itself in workshops, making some of them places of research, research with no practical end immediately in view. The workshops that produced the first sextants were an example; their creators were not sure what they were making, and not too concerned about the sextant's practical value, though they knew it had one; application was for others – navigators – to work out.

The idea that laboratories have distinctive rituals all their own has become by now a commonplace, and an entire branch of sociology is devoted to studying codes of deference and assertion, cooperation and competition, in the lab.[26] At the time it came into being, the experimental workshop seemed to disrupt the sorts of rituals with which workers were familiar. Technical discoveries could disrupt established hierarchical relations between masters and assistants, if the apprentice made a discovery which dethroned the master's expertise. This occurred, for instance, in the invention of improved polishing cloths used for the glass in instruments like the double-sextant on Holbein's table; these polishing cloths were created by adolescent assistants, as the result of an accident occurring in a lens workshop in Antwerp in 1496. Their masters tried to suppress the innovation, the adolescents then 'betrayed' the workshop by striking off on their own.[27]

Even if the shop held together, innovation changed the meaning of cooperation within it. Cooperation had now to make sense of the accidents of work, the accidental discovery of something new or different. The laboratory-workshop thus brought dialogic communication to the fore, the sort of discussion in which someone in a lab says, 'look at that, that's strange', and shares it with someone else at his or her bench. Experimental process made one kind of win-win exchange particularly important: the mutual benefit which comes from lateral thinking. Cloth-making provides a graphic example. In medieval London there were separate workshops and guilds for cloth-weavers and cloth-dyers. By 1600, new dyeing techniques vouchsafed changes in the way cloth might be woven; the work of dyeing and weaving now had to be amalgamated, each trade exploring what the other knew.

This process, emphasizing what we would call interdisciplinary thinking, made the workshop itself a place for dialogical communication and informal association. The historian Steven Shapin thinks there was a binding ritual for the amateur experimenters who drifted into early laboratory-workshops; theirs was a gentlemen's pursuit, they observed the gentlemen's code of disinterested enquiry rather than sought personal advantage for themselves.[28] The word 'amateur' was indeed applied in the seventeenth century to people who were curious about many things, rather than to indicate their level of skill; amateurs of the arts collected paintings, made music and studied history, just as amateurs of science moved from astronomy to medicine to botany; given independent means, the amateur could become a *flâneur* of knowledge. The craftsman without a private income, though, could hardly afford to behave in this disinterested way.

Economic historians of the early modern period have argued that invention prompted entrepreneurial individualism – and thereby make a direct connection between past and present. The analogue today in Silicon Valley would be that someone way down the pecking order stumbles on a new technique or formula, then, like the lens polishers, leaves the organization carrying away the innovation in his or her head. The process of converting a discovery into cash, then as now, was not easy. The two boys in Antwerp, having made their discovery, struck out on their own but didn't know, as we would say, how to bring technology to market; another firm put their discovery to profitable use; the two apprentices ended up in poverty.

The multiplication of skill was embodied in printing. The printing process was originally Chinese, then reinvented in Europe in the

1450s. Before its appearance, scribes worked alone, but printing was a collaborative activity, requiring different skills among diverse workers. Paper had been manufactured in Europe since the thirteenth century; to print on it, craftsmen like Aldus Manutius and Johannes Gutenberg applied three innovations: movable metal type, oil-based ink and the fixed-frame wooden hand-press. Printing begat editing. Whereas the scribe's job was to make a faithful copy of words, the printer began to format texts visually with different typefaces, with title pages, tables of contents and various bindings; the handwritten words of an author were changed by the printer. The reason for this is that the printer had become a direct retail seller as well; his work was oriented to attracting a public. 'The advent of printing', the historian Elizabeth Eisenstein says, 'led to the creation of a new kind of shop structure ... which entailed closer contacts among diversely skilled workers and encouraged new forms of cross-cultural exchange.'[29] Guild hierarchy was replaced by a flatter shop structure of separate but equal skills.

For workers, one important consequence of printing was that technical knowledge became delocalized. Ways of making things began to be written down in how-to books, for application anywhere; the novice no longer depended solely on face-to-face instruction; communication about something new or strange ceased to be solely by word of mouth. An early, printed 'international letter' circulating among glass-blowers (in 1593), for instance, communicates exciting news about how to heat sand. The excitement is that sand can be heated to higher temperatures than people ever expected before; the international letter explains how to do this. As a result, the technical worker could more easily think of himself as belonging to a general trade than confined to a local workshop.

All of which brings us back to the instruments on Holbein's table. The navigation equipment was handmade, but the tools used to make the sextant involved precision metal-cutters and mechanical wood-etchers. New technical crafts made both possible, and the ateliers in which metal-cutting and wood-etching were practised resembled print shops more than carpenters' shops; lots of people were involved, innovating forms and not quite knowing how the products would be used. Information, distributed by international letters, came into local shops from all over Europe. In the allied trade of lens-grinding, crafts-men were engaged in a similar open-ended, dialogic process, in Holbein's time toying with the idea of how the telescope lens might be inverted to become a microscope.[30] No hierarchical ritual instructed them how to proceed.

In these ways, technical innovation changed cooperation in the work-shop. Technical change unsettled its social relations. Rituals based on shop hierarchy were subverted. Dialogical exchange was at the heart of the experimental method, and remains so, but in the seventeenth cen-tury it was unclear how these exchanges could bond artisans together in the struggle for survival. Gentlemen might cooperate as disinterested amateurs, but ordinary craftsmen could not afford to do so.

The changes occurring within workshops open a window on the great theme of Holbein's era: the divide between religion and science. Stated baldly, the Catholic Church hewed to the mysteries of divine spec-tacle, the Reformation plunged into the labyrinth of the individual's direct connection to God, while experimental science sought to under-stand and to exploit the material world on its own terms. Stated even more crudely, the difference was backward- or inward-looking versus outward-looking. Any black-and-white contrast of this sort is bound to be misleading; within the sixteenth-century experimental work-shop, for instance, the physical mysteries people explored seemed to be God's secrets.

Yet to understand what is modern about cooperation we do not want to let go this contrast entirely. Experiment invites the dialogic conversation, the open-ended discussion with others about hypothe-ses, procedures and results. The science emerging in the sixteenth and seventeenth centuries viewed positively the dialogic, open-ended con-versation, while Christianity feared it; Catholicism feared that it would undermine Church authority, Protestants feared that free-thinking discussion could lead to the sin of self-confidence – just the fear Milton expressed in his version of Eve's discussions with the Ser-pent and with Adam in the Garden. The dialogic conversation, Mikhail Bakhtin writes, 'affirms Man's faith in his own experience. For creative understanding ... it is immensely important for the per-son to be located outside the object of his or her understanding'.[31]

There was thus an ethics to the open conversation and to disinterestedness. Even if the participants were driven by the need to convert discoveries into cash, scientific cooperation could flourish only if conducted in a 'civilized' way. What did this mean?

CIVILITY

The sixteenth century saw a shift in emphasis from chivalry to civility as codes for conduct among the upper classes. Eventually this shift would shape the modern understanding of cooperation. But people slid into the new values rather than abruptly cast off the standards of the past, a slide made evident by changes in castles.

Chivalry's home was the castle, which like the monastery was a place of refuge in early medieval times. As a military fortress, the castle housed huge piles of *matériel* – bows, armour, battering rams – as well as horses. The castle yard served mostly for military drill, and in the castle's overcrowded space soldiers slept, shat, ate and drank on the stairs, in all the rooms save the chapel, or out in the open. In the later Middle Ages and early Renaissance the architecture of the castle was transformed. Its military functions diminished; soldiers were pushed to the nether regions or removed entirely, to the ever-larger barracks which appeared in French and Italian towns during the course of the fifteenth century. Changes in warfare made this shift possible; armies spent much more time permanently in the field, with the result that the castle became more and more a ceremonial and social space.

Ironically, the less the castle served for practical purposes of war, the stronger became its ceremonial codes of chivalry. Unlike the knight errant of fable, chivalry focused in fact and in large part on taming violent sexual behaviour, particularly rape. It sought to dignify Eros, as in the medieval chivalric epic the *Roman de la Rose*, an epic full of subtlety and tact in the knight's expression of desire. Medieval civilization regarded physical fighting and violent oaths as a normal part of everyday life on the streets, in workshops, even inside churches. The sexual restraints of chivalry sought to put up one barrier against such violence among the elite.

The other side of chivalry, though, was that knights were, in Peter

Burke's words, 'hyper-sensitive to reflections on their reputation', that is, quick to take offence.[32] Good Christian that he was, if insulted the knight did not turn the other cheek; he burned with revenge to restore his honour. Revenge fell on him as a moral obligation, since, as in most honour-cultures, it was an insult felt to his family as well as himself; blood feuds marked chivalry as much as sexual self-restraint.

Codes of courtesy marked a break from chivalry by expanding restraint into other realms of experience. An early evocation of courtesy appeared in Baldassare Castiglione's *Book of the Courtier* (1528), which focused on how to behave less aggressively in conversation and so give more pleasure. Successors like Giovanni della Casa's *Galateo* (1558) sought to codify the rules for performing courtesy among people, at court, whom one knows well; later, seventeenth-century courtesy books stressed behaving well towards people one does not know, and towards people from other courts or from foreign places; more, they explained to people who were below the elite social stratum how to practise the same behaviour, such as how to listen attentively or how to speak clearly, without referring to persons or places a stranger may not know.

Castligione dealt with insult in a way foreign to the code of chivalry. His book invents conversations at a real court, that of Mantua, during the year 1507, all of which explore the ideal attributes of a courtier. When in the course of one of these conversations the Lady Emilia feels insulted and comes close to losing her temper, Signor Bembo, her provoker, deflects her anger by laughing the whole matter off, conveying that it's too easy to take offence; no chivalric knight would believe that, especially if a lady felt insulted.[33]

This little passage exemplifies the most famous idea of conduct in *The Book of the Courtier*: *sprezzatura*. Count Lodovico defines it early on: '*sprezzatura* (to use perhaps a novel word for it) to practise in all things a certain nonchalance which conceals all artistry and makes whatever one says or does seem uncontrived and effortless.'[34] Lighten up. To do so, the courtier has to avoid taking him- or herself too seriously. It's hard to think of a value more foreign to Martin Luther than *sprezzatura*; for Luther, the self was a deadly serious business. In Castligione's view, lightness made people more 'companionable', that is, more cooperative in conversation. Less self, more sociable.

Restraint of a particular kind is required to practise *sprezzatura*. Throughout his text, Castiglione takes aim again and again at bragging. Bragging was a common practice among male aristocrats of his time, men singing their own praises without embarrassment. He wanted his courtiers to veil the good opinion they may have had of themselves; boasting can make other people feel small. His successor della Casa elaborated a set of rules, applicable to social life outside courts, about how to avoid pomposity.[35] The 'gentleman' is one such Anglo-Saxon application: the gentleman is modestly polite to his servants or tenants as well as to his own kind. Certainly no thought of equality is implied by such behaviour; the historian Jorge Arditi believes it only made social privilege and control more subtle. But transactions between gentlemen and their supposed inferiors became less confrontational.[36]

It's not too big a leap of imagination to connect these codes of civility to the face-saving rituals of political coalitions, touched on in Chapter 1. The coalition currently ruling Britain had initially an eerie resemblance to the court of Mantua evoked in Castiglione's pages: the same careful, gentlemanly politeness among the partners, and same self-restraint when appearing together in public.*

A grander connection between civility past and present appears in the writings of the sociologist Norbert Elias. His great book, *The Civilizing Process*, argues that courtesy marked a great sea-change in European civilization.[37] Elias was convinced that social behaviour in the courts of the sixteenth and seventeenth centuries laid the foundations for what we today call 'courtesy', behaviour which is non-aggressive and respectful in character, courtly behaviour which became the model in the eighteenth and nineteenth centuries for the bourgeoisie. The key to this change lay in bodily self-control; in the early modern period courtiers ceased farting in public whenever they felt the urge; they became more restrained in their eating habits, using forks rather than stabbing food with hunting knives or grabbing morsels with their hands; courtiers ceased to spit in public; the bedroom became a private space in which only spouses, lovers or servants saw the courtier

---

* If I may address a comment to British readers: don't you feel that the current coalition also practises *sprezzatura* in the way it presents grave issues to our nation? Our masters have a nonchalant faith in their own market remedies.

naked. So too in speech, people became more restrained; the new courtly code eschewed swearing in public, or the operatic venting of anger. Civilities of these sorts came at a great psychic price.

Self-restraint, in Elias's account, requires feelings of shame when a person loses verbal and bodily control, whether in farting or in blurting out whatever he or she thinks. Civility contested spontaneity. Elias took up a distinction, first drawn by Freud, between shame and guilt: we feel shame when we aren't behaving well enough, and so feel inadequate, whereas we feel guilt over a crime or transgression. People who lack social manners may feel inadequate because they are not masters of their circumstances and of themselves. Elias showed similarly why embarrassment and shame become cousins; embarrassment reflects the fear of exposing oneself, and so being found wanting. The fear of behaving naturally and spontaneously, the shame over lack of self-control and the embarrassment of being exposed all combine. People exile themselves from Eden and call that exile 'civilized behaviour'.

These were ideas, based on research into arcane documents of court life in the early modern period, that as an academic student in the 1920s Elias didn't quite know what to do with. The advent of the Nazi regime drove him out of Germany and eventually to Britain, where he remained for many decades. The Nazi earthquake made clearer to him the consequences of his student work: when shame breaks down as a self-governor, so does civilized behaviour; the Nazis knew no personal shame which might restrain their inner beast. The historical story the young Elias charted now seemed to illuminate the horrors of the present.

Without diminishing the scope of his great work, I would like to point out its special character. Though Elias was Jewish, his text presents a very Protestant account of civility. Shame about oneself serves to restrain animal aggression. Freud wasn't too far from the same belief in *Civilization and its Discontents*, another book written in the Nazi shadow: man has to feel guilt, to know himself as a sinner, in order to be less aggressive. Elias's historical materials prompted in part this point of view, though within a less cataclysmic framework. The courtesy books of the sixteenth century spawned many more manuals on proper child behaviour, including a great one written by Erasmus, and innumerable books of etiquette – many of which are indeed quite prim in tone to modern ears – all emphasizing how to avoid gaffes or improprieties. Elias argues that this tone shows the mass of society becoming ever more self-controlled, the motor of shame driving people to worry about doing the right thing, to fear behaving spontaneously.

But is shame the single driver of this effort? Is fear of losing control really what makes us civilized? Elias underplays the pleasurable aspects of civility, and he turns a blind eye to its cooperative character, at least as Castiglione himself understood it. Civility, more than a personality trait, is an exchange in which both parties make one another feel good about the encounter; for Castiglione, it is the very opposite of an encounter from which one person comes away feeling demeaned or shamed. It is a win-win exchange. To understand the more sociable consequences of civility, we would do well to pick up on a clue Castiglione offers: he likens its practice to that of a 'profession'.[38] Diplomacy was the profession which put the emerging codes of civility – its *sprezzatura* – to practical use.

Professional civility

The most important elements in Holbein's *The Ambassadors* are the ambassadors – which, as we've seen, these young men were not quite. In medieval times diplomacy was not a profession in itself, nor did most diplomats abroad command a physical place, an ambassadorial residence, devoted to their work. Sixteenth-century Venice, an international trading power, a city dealing constantly with foreigners, led the way in stimulating professional diplomacy, a model which was imitated as other European powers expanded their dealings to the limits of the Continent and beyond.

Renaissance diplomats came in two colours. The first were special envoys who travelled to a foreign court or city to do a specific task and then came home; the second were resident ambassadors who remained away for some years.[39] Most Renaissance envoys differed little from their ancient ancestors. Envoys travelled to celebrate the marriage or birth of an important personage, to negotiate a treaty of war or peace, to give an official speech or to deal with a dynastic mess. Holbein's young diplomats were such envoys, coming to London to broker a marriage.

Resident ambassadors served more like a sponge, absorbing information to then be conveyed home. In the first decades of the sixteenth century, Sir Henry Wotton was resident ambassador from England to Venice, Francesco Guicciardini served as the papal ambassador to Aragon, Eustace Chapuys was the Holy Roman Empire's ambassador to England. Bureaucracy followed in the wake of these top men abroad: the consul, who handled commercial affairs abroad, the secretary charged with the special task of encrypting information to be sent home. We feel the essential difference between envoy and resident diplomat in the novel of Henry James, *The Ambassadors*. Strether, its plain-speaking protagonist, arrives in Europe as an envoy to bring home a young man who has strayed, but once in Paris Strether becomes more like a resident ambassador; he smoothes and soothes in order to remain *en poste*.

The constantly shifting alliances of Europe's courts and states meant that today's friend was tomorrow's enemy; the Renaissance ambassador had to keep such stormy relations going. The historian of Renaissance diplomacy Garrett Mattingly describes successful diplomacy in the sixteenth century as divided between agreements among courts or rulers which could be written down, and spoken understandings that officials could not agree upon or that were too explosive to make explicit. Reformation diplomats split these roles; by the time of Louis XIV highly trained envoys occupied themselves with the first kind of diplomacy, their skills coming mostly from the law; resident ambassadors dealt with the second, their skills based on local knowledge combined with an almost forensic attention to verbal hints.

The ambassadorial building, in its architecture and furnishing, aimed to create a receptive atmosphere where foreigners felt welcome – otherwise the ambassador would learn nothing. From their origins, ambassadorial residences splashed out on comfort and indeed luxury. In most Renaissance buildings, people slept, dressed, dined and received in the same space, the different furniture required for these different activities being trundled in and out by servants. The resident ambassador of the sixteenth century pioneered the dining room as a special space; even when himself dining out, the foreign ambassador kept an 'open table' going in his residence, hoping to get unbuttoned information at the price of a meal.

Hospitality and comfort might prove a cause for regret among the ambassador's masters; more, if truly successful in making himself at home abroad, the resident ambassador faced the temptation of going native. Francesco Guicciardini found himself suspected of this and so excluded from much of the real negotiation between the papacy and his foreign hosts, the diplomat admitting that 'ambassadors often take the side of the prince at whose court they are. That makes them suspected either of corruption or of seeking rewards, or at least of having been bedazzled by the . . . kindnesses shown them.'[40] The risk of local seduction increased when, towards the middle of the sixteenth century, resident ambassadors came to be attached for many years or in some cases decades to a foreign place and power. The risk of a man going native prompted by the 1530s the development of the institution of the back-channel. Foreign courts began to regard the ambassadors' secretaries as agents who could work around the ambassador. The secretaries were encrypting and decrypting information, and so were at the fulcrum of communication; they could select or erase what the ambassador learned from his minister. Sir Henry Wotton famously defined a diplomat as an honest man sent to lie abroad for the good of his country – but this bon mot rebounded when secretaries began to lie to their own resident masters.

How could civility be of use in navigating these dangerous shoals? Guicciardini's cardinal rule for fellow diplomats was: avoid any display of triumphalism when your mission prevails, since today's loser may be tomorrow's friend. Self-restraint was indeed critical for the practice of diplomacy, but informal sociability proved more useful in knowing the local score than the ceremonial events which so often imprisoned diplomats; an unwise ambassador, Eustace Chapuys observed, was one who spends his entire day in meetings. *Sprezzatura* oiled the flow of informal, open talk – though the professional diplomat had also carefully to calculate each and every word he used; his *sprezzatura* had to avoid genuine spontaneity.

Latin served for formal occasions, French for more informal ones. The diplomat tended to deploy in both the subjunctive mood which we explored in the opening pages of this study. It is the mood which gives voice to 'I would have thought . . .' rather than 'I think', indirection making verbal space, inviting response from others. Early on, diplomats became masters of listening carefully when others spoke in this mood; whether at the foreign court or their own table, the professional listener attended to minute hints, clues and suggestions. Because they were professionals, the diplomats knew the game each was playing.

In diplomatic encounters, an ambassador's skill in managing silence became an essential element in deploying the subjunctive mood. Of course, he had to know what he couldn't say to others, but he had also to learn how to make silence speak. By the mid-seventeenth century silence punctuating the flow of talk had taken on its own ritual character. If you wanted to know how far along a certain path you could take a colleague, you led him just to the point where he fell silent; if you wanted to help him out in a difficult situation in a group, you papered over his silence with your own speech. These may be 'diplomatic' behaviours all of us practise, but few of us get the coaching in silence a junior diplomat received in the embassy's back-rooms.

The sixteenth-century diplomat Ottaviano Maggi, in one of the first treatises on how to be an ambassador, counselled that 'he should never seem to be struck by wonder or to stand in awe', even if he learned something dumbfounding.[41] The ambassador had to show himself equal to all occasions, wear the mask of self-control and competence – in a word, be a good actor. This counsel traces back to Machiavelli's view of how princes ought to act; in The Prince, Machiavelli spoke admiringly of the despot Cesare Borgia, who 'knew so well how to dissimulate his own mind', and Borgia, a great actor, knew, in Machiavelli's famous words, how to inspire 'love and fear' in his subjects.[42] But Machiavelli's Prince is a secretive actor, playing his cards close to his chest; The Prince, Douglas Blow observes, 'discloses a resolutely antibureaucratic writer'.[43] The Prince's sudden and surprising personal behaviour will keep his subjects on their toes. An ambassador might be as good an actor, but as the sixteenth century unfolded the professional diplomat became ever more enmeshed in bureaucracy, and in social rituals, within his own embassy's walls.

The upheavals caused by the religious Reformation put diplomatic civility to a huge test. The Victorian diplomat Ernest Satow observed that in 'the wars of religion in the sixteenth and seventeenth centuries [which] so embittered relations between Catholic and Protestant

States ... ambassadors reported that it was impossible to find out anything, because nobody wanted to talk to them'.[44] Yet the embassies stayed open. Holbein's young diplomats were housed by a French ambassador who survived the religious upheaval *en poste* for two decades; he and his minions went day after day to Britain's then equivalent of the Foreign Office, even though there was little or nothing to talk about. While religion fought, diplomacy met.

The legacy of professional civility may seem narrow, appearing perhaps most interesting to diplomats today who want to know how professional courtesy was first organized. But this is a story that has cut a wider swath, as Castiglione himself foresaw. At the end of *The Book of the Courtier*, he asks what the serious point of courtesy is; he answers himself by saying it is to prevent conflict spiralling into violence.[45] The usages of skilful courtesy in the early modern era deflected the chivalric knight's quickness to take offence; *sprezzatura* lightened the aggressive undertow of conflict. Diminishing hostility toward others was the point of civility also to Norbert Elias. But Castiglione – like the professional diplomats who saw themselves mirrored in his pages – emphasized the social skills of civility, rather than personal restraint bred by bodily shame. These social skills relied on rituals, the ambassador's rituals of the table or of seemingly casual talk drawing people together; unlike the early medieval rites of Communion, these were cunning rituals. The skilled ambassador became expert in striking a balance between competition and cooperation. It's a model, as haunting now as four centuries ago, but how can it apply outside the halls of an embassy?

One way to approach this possibility lies in looking a little more carefully at the psychology of civility, about which Norbert Elias gave so powerful if so Protestant an account. In order to do this, we might explore the first spread of diplomatic civility into civil society, in the salons appearing in private houses.

Civility and the self

By 1618 Cathérine de Rambouillet, a Mistress of the Queen's Robes, had had enough of court life and withdrew to her own house in Paris, in the rue Saint-Thomas-du-Louvre.[46] She learned the ways of courtesy at court, but she intended to leave behind court intrigue; she sought to create instead a space in the rue Saint-Thomas-du-Louvre which was intimate and friendly – and shielded from the prying eyes of power. Civility inside, she hoped, would become *spirituel*. In French usage of the time, this was a personal rather than a religious quality; the *spirituel* self practised self-deprecating modesty, played with irony and paradox, not for any practical end but just because these were qualities which nourished mutual pleasure.

She made the civility of friends come alive in her Blue Room, a chamber historians think to be the model for the later salon as a social institution. Mme de Rambouillet knew that she needed a new sort of house architecture to create a space of friendship. She built a dwelling with stairs at the side, making as much room as possible for tall, airy rooms with light flooding in from opposite ends; she did not want to live in a courtly cavern. The most important room in the house should be its most intimate, the Blue Room, in which, stretched out on a daybed, she received guests. They also perched on the bed or stood in the narrow strip between bed and wall, the *ruelle*, a sort of internal alley, crowded with visitors. The blue – walls, bedspread and curtains – broke with the dull tans and red of court interiors, a blue watered by abundant window light.

A daybed but no sex. People, perched on the bed, near to Mme de Rambouillet's toes, could speak of disappointments in love so long as they did not go into physical details, or of their disappointing children, or they could gossip wickedly, so long as they did this well – which meant amusing rather than agitating others. Her pet writer, Vincent Voiture, mastered the light, regretful tone of Blue Room love to perfection: 'the long regrets, friends to solitude, the sweet hopes and strange thoughts, the short vexations and the soft sighs . . .'[47] If this seems unbearably precious, we should remember that the purpose of such language was relief from a court infested with intrigue, relief also from the wars of religion, Catholic versus Protestant, that were beginning to convulse France.

As the protected space of the salon evolved, talk in it became more complex than gossip; the rituals contrived for talk enabled indirection and irony as social commentary. These changes started at the end of Mme de Rambouillet's life in the salon of her social heir, Madeleine de Sablé. In 1659 the writer François de La Rochefoucauld began to use this salon as a staging ground for his 'sayings' or 'sentences' which have come down to us as the *Maxims*. These take the distilled, polished form of paradox, such as 'austerity is a sort of adornment these women add to their beauty', or 'the mind is always deceived by the heart'.[48] Each alone seems self-contained, but spoken in the salon these civilities had a social effect: a person capable of creating verbal irony which he or she applies to him- or herself is the sort of person who earns trust. La Rochefoucauld sought to arouse just this trusting effect in a self-portrait appended to his *Maxims*, surely one of the greatest if briefest of autobiographies.[49] His physical appearance, his behaviour in society, his vices and virtues are all formulated in terms of paradox: a well-made man but not good-looking; happy in society but lacking curiosity; melancholy but also easily seduced by jokes: he mocks but does not demean himself. He has made a social connection to the reader by striking this balance; in the salon, he left others a space for themselves, above all not shaming them by his wit. His is a deep, sophisticated version of friendliness, to be sure, but also quite solid: the differences, difficulties and contradictions I sense in myself (as I sense them in you) permit us to be together. We are different from each other, as we are divided within ourselves: let's talk.

The salon was a protected space for aristocrats, as were the courts Norbert Elias studied for clues about the origins of modern civility. The large legacy of court civility, in Elias's view, was a certain sense of self, involving a quest for self-control and a fear of embarrassment. An alternative civility, focused on giving pleasure, the legacy of Mme de Sablé's salon, and of La Rochefoucauld's way of talking to friends in it, is perhaps best embodied by the German word *Bildung*. More than formal education, *Bildung* can be defined as learning one's place in the world, as placing oneself in relation to others. The historian Jerrold Seigel believes that the complexities of modern society helped spawn the idea of a 'multi-dimensional self', a self full of contradictions, paradoxes and ironies that could not be resolved easily – if at all.[50] This was La Rochefoucauld's belief as well. The phrase 'multi-dimensional self' sounds grand and abstract. Seigel believes it touched the ground of everyday life in the 'reading circles' which became widespread in eighteenth-century bourgeois German homes. These were the forerunners of the modern book club; people met in a living room to discuss the latest literature; these serious monthly meetings were devoted to contemplating life's complexities. They were intimate versions of civility. The coffee house and café were bigger public versions, mixing social classes and including strangers. If more casual in tone than the reading circle, these public, urban institutions were socially more 'multi-dimensional'.[51]

In sum, the diplomats, hymnal and sextant in Holbein's *The Ambassadors* might seem to be jumbled together arbitrarily, but there's more coherence to be found in the painting. Civility largely understood provides the thread between these icons. The professional civilities taking form in early Reformation diplomacy opened up possibilities for everyday sociability. These civilities contrast to the shut-down of mutuality that occurred when religious ritual became transformed into theatre; they contrast, also, with the anguished struggle Luther imagined for his followers, whether together or alone. Civility made sense of how people in experimental, innovative workshops could best learn from one another, civility as an open, inquisitive discussion about problems, procedures and results rather than as the mark of the gentleman-amateur. Civility implied a certain sense of self: subjunctive or indirect, ironic or restrained in expression but not self-ashamed. Civility was the social frame our Reformation ancestors put around lively communication. It remains a good frame.

As befits the richness of our subject, the cooperative experiences explored in Part One have varied and complex shapes. The Introduction opened with a caution: cooperation is not innately benign; it can bind people together who then do harm to others. In exploring rehearsals and in conversations, we sought some principle that would make cooperation more open. That principle is dialogic cooperation. This kind of cooperation is our goal, our Holy Grail. Dialogic cooperation entails a special kind of openness, one which enlists empathy rather than sympathy in its service. As the experiment with Google-Wave revealed, dialogic cooperation is not easy to practise; the programmers who created this technology did not understand it.

In Part One, we have looked at three facets of cooperation: its relation to solidarity, to competition and to ritual. Solidarity has been an obsession in modern politics. In Chapter 1, we explored in depth one moment a century ago when the Left grappled with it; solidarity then, as now, was divided between those who sought to forge it top-down and those who sought to create it from the ground up. Top-down politics faces special problems in practising cooperation, revealed in the forming and maintenance of coalitions; these often prove socially fragile. Solidarity built from the ground up strives for cohesion among people who differ. This is another side of the dialogic principle: how can people be open to and engaged with those who differ from them racially or ethnically? Community organizers, like the organizers of settlement houses a century ago, have had to address this question. Organizers of workshops had to deal with another sort of difference, that of the division of labour; their question has been how cohesion can be kindled among people doing different kinds of tasks. The social bonds forged from the ground up can be strong, but their political force is often weak or fragmented.

In Chapter 2 we explored the relation between cooperation and competition. Striking a balance between the two means considering our nature as social animals. The great monotheistic religions have treated man in the state of nature as a flawed creature, destroying the peaceable kingdom of Eden; for tough-minded philosophers like Thomas Hobbes, Eden never existed; natural man engages in lethal competition, and is not at all minded to cooperate with others. Modern ethological science takes a more hopeful view: social animals do strike a fragile balance between cooperation and competition in dealing with one another. The balance is fragile because the natural environment is constantly shifting, but it can still be struck through exchange. We saw the forms of exchange run the gamut from altruistic to winner-takes-all encounters; in the middle of the spectrum, balance between cooperation and competition can most easily occur. Ritual is a particular way that the human social animal organizes balancing exchanges, rituals of our own making, rituals endowed with passion when they become skilled performances. The journey Chapter 2 charts is a passage from nature to culture.

In the present chapter we've explored a more particular journey in European culture, the changes in cooperative culture which appeared at the dawn of the early modern era, within religious practice, the organization of labour in workshops, and in the emergence of civility among professional diplomats and in the conduct of everyday life.

We might want to pause over the label 'Reformation', usually applied to the religious shifts we've explored. As an idea, it has a further reach. 'Reformation' contains the appeal, indeed the demand, for reform. The next part of this book will take up that demand, applied to our own time. Our social arrangements for cooperation need a Reformation. Modern capitalism has unbalanced competition and cooperation, and so made cooperation itself less open, less dialogic.

PART TWO

Cooperation Weakened

4

Inequality

Imposed and Absorbed in Childhood

Part Two assesses the state of cooperation in modern society. What has society made of its early modern inheritance? How well do our institutions develop the natural endowments and everyday capacities people possess to cooperate? Exhibitors in the 'Social Question' rooms of the Paris Universal Exposition of 1900 were in no doubt about capitalism. It was an article of faith that the economic system demeaned and demoralized workers; when a rash of suicides broke out among American workers in the mid-1890s, no one in the radical press was surprised. Whatever the promises of high culture in the past, indeed whatever the promise of cooperation in our own early biological development, the capitalist beast has crushed these promises in everyday adult life.

Capitalism today is in some ways a different, in some ways the same animal as a century ago. Different, because services play a bigger role in the economy than a century ago. Industrial production once lay at the heart of the advanced economies; today manufacturing has been moved offshore and exported, its place filled by technical and human services. A century ago, three countries furnished the bulk of the world's investment capital: America, Britain and Germany; today, global capital comes from everywhere. A century ago, mass consumption, fuelled by advertising, was in its infancy; consumers preferred to pay for what they could physically touch or weigh in the hand. Today, on the Internet, the imagery of objects dominates consumption.

Some old ills have become deeper. Most notably, inequality has extended its reach, as the gap between the rich and the middle classes grows ever wider. In the United States, the wealth share of the middle quintile has increased 18 per cent in real dollars during the last fifty years while the wealth share of the top 5 per cent has increased by 293 per cent; today the odds of a student in the middle classes making as much income as his or her parents are 2 to 5; the odds of the top 5 per cent becoming as wealthy as their parents are over 90 per cent.[1] These numbers are signs of zero-sum competition veering toward the winner-takes-all extreme; the capitalist is becoming an apex predator.

As much as the economy has changed in the last century, many analysts believe the social question still remains as it was. In capitalism, social cohesion is inherently weak. The new reach of inequality seems only to confirm the gravity of an old evil. Even if you are unshakeably on the Left (as I am), you should want to worry about this judgement, for the old conviction has become by now too familiar, too instant. It risks assuming that getting rid of an economic vice will by itself produce positive social results.

Alternatively, the promotion of cohesion and cooperation can appear in discussions of 'social capital', an approach popularly associated with the work of Robert Putnam. His is not primarily an economic analysis; rather, Putnam and his team survey attitudes, such as trust in leaders or fear of foreigners, and they chart behaviour like participation in churches or unions. In his view, American and European society has less social cohesion than it had even thirty years ago, less trust in institutions, less trust in leaders. As appeared in the Introduction, Putnam invokes the image of people now 'hibernating' from those who are different; in another famous image, he characterizes people as now 'bowling alone' in society.[2] The latter image he links to cooperation by saying that passive participation now marks civil society; people may belong to many organizations but few ordinary members become active. This passivity he finds true in European and American trade unions and charities, and in European churches, though the great exception in his scheme to declining participation is church-going in America. The sociologist Jeffrey Goldfarb takes Putnam a step further, saying that we are seeing today the emergence of a 'cynical society' whose denizens are ill-disposed to cooperate.[3]

This stinging judgement has its critics. Some say that the picture of participation is not as grim as Putnam paints, because people are participating in new ways, for instance on Internet sites.[4] Other critics dislike the very phrase 'social capital', since it suggests that social relations can be reckoned like money in the bank, a quantity people own or lose in precise measure.[5]

Sometimes it helps to see ourselves by stepping into another person's shoes, looking at how cultures quite foreign to our own assess social capital and cooperation. Modern China offers one way to do so. The country is now aggressively capitalist, yet it has a strong code for social cohesion. This code the Chinese call *guanxi*. The systems analyst Yuan Luo describes *guanxi* as 'an intricate and pervasive relational network which Chinese cultivate energetically, subtly, and imaginatively'.[6] The network means a Chinese immigrant feels free to call on a third cousin in a foreign city for a loan; at home, it is the shared experiences and memories among friends, rather than written contracts or laws, that lay the foundations for trust in business dealings; in families, *guanxi* has a further reach in the practice common to many non-Western societies of young people sending home whatever they can spare of their usually meagre wages, rather than spending all they earn on themselves. 'Duty' better names these social relations than 'social capital'.

So is honour a better name? *Guanxi* invokes honour as a key ingredient of social relations. Douglas Guthrie, an American student of Chinese *guanxi*, explains that it is akin to the old Western business code, 'My word is my bond.'[7] You can count on other people in the network, especially when the going gets tough; they are honour-bound to support you rather than take advantage of your weakness. *Guanxi* entails something other than sympathy; people in the network criticize one another and they nag; they may not be nice but they feel obliged to prove helpful.

Guanxi is an example of how a social bond can shape economic life. In essence, this bond is informal in character, establishing a network of support outside a rigid circle of established rules and regulations. The bond is a necessity in the fast-changing, often chaotic conditions of China today, since many of its official rules are dysfunctional; the informal, personal network helps people go around these in order to survive and prosper. The value of informal cohesion has already appeared to us, in dialogic exchanges, whether in a conversation or in the community organizing of Saul Alinsky. We want to establish the scope of these exchanges in our own society: do they have an equal practical value as they do for the Chinese? There are two reasons why we might want to think like the Chinese about cooperation.

First, if informal, the *guanxi* network is also meant to be sustainable. Sometime in the future the one who gets help will give it back in a form neither party may now foresee, but knows will occur. *Guanxi* is a relationship meant to endure from generation to generation. By the standards of a Western contract, there's no reality in such an ill-defined expectation; for the Chinese student, government worker or businessman, the expectation itself is solid, because people in the network punish or shun those who later prove unresponsive. It's a question for us of holding people accountable in the future for their actions in the present.

Secondly, people in a *guanxi* network are not ashamed of dependency. You can establish *guanxi* with someone who needs you or whom you need, beneath or above you in the pecking order. The Chinese family, as traditionally in other societies, has been a site of dependency without shame. As described in Chapter 3, in the writings of Norbert Elias shame has become deeply associated in Western culture with self-control; losing control over your body or your words has become a source of shame. Modern family life and, even more, modern business practice, has extended the idea of self-containment: dependency on others is taken to be a sign of weakness, a failure of character; in raising children or at work, our institutions seek to promote autonomy and self-sufficiency; the autonomous individual appears free. But looked at from the perspective of a different culture, a person who prides him- or herself on not asking for help appears a deeply damaged human being; fear of social embeddedness dominates his or her life.

Had he known of it, I think Robert Owen would have found *guanxi* congenial in spirit; so too, I suspect, would settlement-house workers and community activists a century ago. The common thread is an emphasis on the qualities of a social relationship, on the power of duty and honour. Yet China is ferociously capitalist. By our lights, that fact seems difficult to reconcile with cultural practices. Some

Chinese believe that *guanxi* is beginning to break down as the country more and more comes to resemble the West in its ways of parenting, working and consuming. If so, we want to know why Western culture has this corrosive effect. The three chapters in Part Two seek to explain this effect, upon ourselves.

This chapter explores the issue of dependency and inequality. It focuses on the lives of children, exploring how they can become more dependent on the things they consume than on one another. Chapter 5 takes up the issue of honour, in adult work. One strength of Robert Putnam's research lies in connecting attitudes about authority and trust to cooperative behaviour. By drawing on ethnographic field-work, I show how these connections translate into experiences of honour in the workplace. Chapter 6 explorces a new character type appearing in modern society, that of the uncooperative self. *Guanxi* sets the positive standard against which to contrast this character type, which resists the very idea of duty to others.

INEQUALITY IMPOSED

The Introduction presented some findings explaining why infants and very young children have such a vital and rich experience of cooperation. Once children enter school, these capabilities can suffer a kind of cardiac arrest. One large reason why this happens concerns inequality: inequality makes a profound difference in the lives of children, inhibiting their capacity to connect to and cooperate with one another. To make good on this large claim, I'll look at two dimensions of social inequality: first, inequalities that are imposed on children, not of their own making or desiring; secondly, inequalities which are absorbed and naturalized, so seeming to become part of the child's self. One way in which children naturalize inequality does something quite special to their psyche: they can become more dependent on the things they consume than on other people.

Inequality in childhood is often imposed by how children are slotted into different tracks or different classrooms or different schools. By now a mountain of contradictory evidence has accumulated on whether selection is good or bad for children, but sorting them out by ability is, in the long sweep of time, relatively new. Up to the early eighteenth century the schoolroom jumbled together youngsters of quite unequal talents; in France and Germany, mixing lasted to adolescence, while in Britain and America, into the mid-nineteenth century, it continued through adolescence in many schools. Evidence on the effects of sorting in our own time is contradictory because so many different factors have come into play: family background, society's hunger to identify ability at an early age, the specialization of knowledge that destines some youngsters for vocational training while others are afforded broader scope. Some of these reasons for streaming in the classroom alienate children from one another, others seem to have little effect on their solidarity, and they bond, just as kids.

A massive report by Unicef, the international agency for children, looks at inequality in larger terms, evaluating the well-being of children and adolescents in twenty-one countries in North America and Europe.[8] The study uses numbers, surveys attitudes and probes behaviour; it charts, for instance, the percentages of children in single-parent homes, the numbers of children living in poverty and the state of infant health. Equally factual evidence comes from questionnaires which ask whether or not children eat their main meal of the day with their parents, and how often they study with other children. More qualitative are questions which ask children how much they like school, and about the experience of being bullied.

All the countries in this study have competitive economies but as societies they are not cut from the same cloth; some induct children into a realm where mutual support is weak, while other societies manage to promote cooperation even as they teach children how to compete. The Unicef report, however, starts with the fact of wealth itself.

The authors caution against equating a society's raw wealth with the well-being of its children: 'there is no obvious relationship between levels of child well-being and GDP per capita.'[9] The Czech Republic is, for instance, a better place for children to grow up, according to Unicef's measures, than its richer neighbour Austria. This finding reflects a familiar truth, that riches do not make for happiness, but that old truth is easy to romanticize; malnutrition is certainly no recipe for well-being. Exhibitors in the Paris Exposition like Charles Booth grappled with societies in which many children were starving; in Britain, southern Italy and much of the United States, childhood poverty still looms large. So the old adage should be reframed; once social conditions rise above basic deprivation, increasing affluence does not translate into social benefit. Under these conditions, inequality of a particular sort enters the picture.

This is internal inequality, that is, the spread between richer and poorer sections within a society. The 'Gini co-efficient', a globally standardized measure of wealth inequality, shows wide differences between countries within the prosperity-zone of Western Europe and North America; a century ago, Britain, the Scandinavian countries, Italy and the United States were more of a piece in terms of the Gini co-efficient. On the whole, Unicef's benchmarks for a good-quality childhood now are set by countries along the northern rim of Europe, countries that have relatively low levels of inequality internally. Norway's standard of living equals that of the United States, but its wealth is far more equalized.

The Unicef report engages schooling in a particular way. It's long been known that societies with high Gini co-efficients erode educational achievement among the great mass of ordinary students. For instance, Richard Wilkinson and Kate Pickett make clear how inequality can lower the motivation of adolescents, when few believe they can get ahead.[10] This is partly a matter of unequal class sizes or access to computer and book resources, but also has a social side. The Unicef report probes the consequences of inequality in terms of behaviour outside the formalities which rule the classroom. At one pole lies bullying by other children, at the opposite pole, studying with them outside school. In its sample countries, the Unicef data show that internally unequal societies evince more bullying behaviour among children, while relatively equalized societies show a greater disposition among children to studying with others. Another study, done by the Demos Institute in Britain, homes in on the tie between physical bullying and social class: poor children are twice as exposed to it as rich.[11]

Unicef's report on the quality of life among children makes uncomfortable reading for Americans and Britons. 'The United Kingdom and United States find themselves in the bottom third of the rankings for five of the six dimensions reviewed.' The results apply to such physical measures as child health (eating breakfast or being overweight), and risk measures like drunkenness and drug use. Socially, British and American teenagers are very frequently bullied; they score low on believing peers supportive; children in the Anglo-Saxon world are less likely than children elsewhere to help one another learn.[12] The Unicef study correlates weak cooperative ties at school to less 'quality time' spent with parents and siblings over meals at home.

Of course kids everywhere are rough with each other; even if angels in the classroom, monsters on the playground. It's a matter of countervailing forces which might bring them also together. Moreover, the Unicef report does not portray childhood in the English-speaking world as unrelieved misery; to the same degree as children elsewhere, children here are personally hopeful about the future. However, in Britain and America, with their high levels of internal inequality, countervailing social forces are weak.

Because this report is unabashedly Eurocentric, it's important to set the contrasts it draws in a wider context. A kindred though small study of middle-class children's quality of life in urban Japan and China likens these Asian societies to Unicef's Scandinavian benchmarks in balancing competition and cooperation: Japanese mothers spend much more time than British mothers in helping their children study; children in China spend much of their time studying in groups.[13] For the Chinese, *guanxi* is strengthened, among peers, in these study groups.

School bullies may be no more than anti-social kids, yet the sociologist Paul Willis believes that they have an awareness of what their fate will be later in life; his research has shown a consistent attitude of working-class British children to peers who are doing well in school; Willis argues that the violently aggressive children already sense that they are the ones who will be left behind later. Studies of bullying among poor African-American youngsters show a similar foreshadowing.[14]

The infants Alison Gopnik studied, as we saw in the Introduction, seem full of wonder and curiosity, their 'capabilities', to use the keyword of Amartya Sen and Martha Nussbaum, are an open book. By the time a child gets to the age of ten, these capabilities can become impaired. The unequal internal distribution of wealth has played a key role, correlated to family patterns and the organization of schooling; in capitalist societies with strong family cohesion, in schools which emphasize the value of studying seriously together, the social consequences of economic inequality can be countervailed. The Unicef study shows this occurring in countries with less wealth than Britain and the United States, societies where childhood appears to be socially impoverished.

A child of ten will pass a watershed in absorbing these external realities; economic facts and social institutions will in the course of a few short years shape the sense of self. I'll trace just one way this happens, in the behaviour of children as consumers. In particular, I want to show how children can become more dependent on the objects they consume than on one another.

INEQUALITY INTERNALIZED

As any parent knows to his or her cost, a giant market today aims at child consumers, a market of cool toys, to-die-for clothes, necessary electronic gadgets and games. In the United States, the purchasing power of children aged four to twelve rose from just over $6 billion dollars in 1989 to over $23 billion in 1997 and to $30 billion in 2002; teens spent $170 billion in 2002.[15] Like all consumption, this huge market aims to convince juvenile shoppers that they need what they lack, or, in the words of Juliet Schor, the marketing aims to convince kids to believe they are what they own.[16]

It isn't just a matter of shopping at the mall. Medical consumption also marks the lives of many children. Modern society is supposedly in the grip of an epidemic of depression; 6 per cent, or 3.5 million American children, are taking medication for it.[17] Attention Deficit Hyperactivity Disorder is a newly named disease of childhood; such distracted behaviour is treated by drugs like Ritalin, and, as of 2000, over 6 million American children were taking drugs of this sort.[18] Drugs for childhood depression and ADHD are marketed aggressively because these are low-investment, big-ticket items on companies' balance sheets.[19] For children, the message of the pills is that there's something really wrong with you, a message that can make kids feel deeply, personally pill-dependent.

Even in its teddy-bear form, the commercialization of childhood is a huge worry to adults, though the worry appeared as long ago as the seventeenth century in the Netherlands when children first had access to mass-produced toys. The worry relates to inequality in a particular way. This is the phenomenon of invidious comparison. As a general concept, invidious comparison is the personalizing of inequality. Consumption brings invidious comparison to life: the kid with cool shoes looks down on the kid without them, that is, you are yucky because you wear the wrong clothes. Invidious comparison, as the advertising guru Edward Bernays (nephew of Sigmund Freud) was the first to point out, exploits feelings of inferiority; in his tart phrase, the advertiser needs to convince 'someone who is nobody that he is someone special'.[20] The adman David Ogilvie has called this 'status' advertising, the adman's challenge being to provide consumers with a 'sense of recognition and worth' through buying mass-produced goods. 'I'm better than you' is an obvious sort of invidious comparison; more subtle is the reverse measure, 'You don't see me, I don't count in your eyes because I'm not good enough.' This is what *ressentiment*, discussed in Chapter 1, is all about, ordinary people feeling that they don't get any recognition, that they have no standing in the eyes of more educated or simply richer people. The status object is meant to salve that feeling.

The worry among people who study the commercialization of childhood is that children will not be able to detect what's going on in the marketing of status; they will take implied, unspoken, invidious comparisons just as a fact. This worry is grounded, in academic psychology, in a view of child development which traces to Jean Piaget. In Piaget's schema, children are particularly vulnerable consumers from the ages of six to eight, because of an inability to define the value of things apart from how they use games or toys; unlike Gopnik or Erik Erikson, Piaget thinks that children in this stage make only crudely functional comparisons of themselves with others, as in 'Matthew runs faster than Joey'.[21] Piaget's observations of children at this stage are compelling economically: he shows how almost infinitely suggestible they are, a susceptibility which translates practically into the lack of sales-resistance.

We want to dwell more on this behaviour, since feelings of status inferiority might erode cooperation with others. It's true that susceptibility to a sales-pitch does not inevitably lead to making invidious comparisons with other kids. In Juliet Schor's survey and ethnographic work among children in Boston, she found the young to be passionate consumers, yet drawing few invidious comparisons on the basis of that passion. Children were posed propositions like 'I feel like other kids have more stuff than I do', with which two-thirds disagreed. More tellingly, her study put the proposition 'when I decide who to be friends with, I don't care what toys or stuff the person has', with which 90 per cent agreed.[22] These juvenile American avid consumers – all just entering Piaget's vulnerable stage – would seem not to make invidious comparisons, but Schor cautions that matters are not so sunny.

The danger comes a little further along in development, among youngsters aged eleven to fourteen, and particularly among those who have become extremely materialist, compared with their peers. They are 'more likely to suffer from personality problems such as narcissism, separation anxiety disorder, paranoia, and attention deficit disorder' than young teens less attached to material goods.[23] In other studies of children, this connection is framed as a matter of self-esteem; in Britain, Agnes Nairn and her colleagues have shown that children with low self-esteem often try to compensate by accumulating toys and clothes.[24] In studies done by Tim Kasser and Richard Ryan of older teenagers and young adults, heightened materialism was associated with feelings of personal vulnerability.[25]

All this shouldn't surprise the reader of F. Scott Fitzgerald's *The Great Gatsby*. Material objects can compensate for feelings of inferiority; Bernays and Ogilvie understood that those feelings are something to exploit commercially. If relatively few children are budding Gatsbys, the more ordinary menace of consumption in children's social lives appears when they come to depend upon consuming things more than relying upon other people. If that happens, they may lose the capacity to cooperate. Social networking sites are an example of how this does in fact happen.

'Friending'

As face to face has become replaced by Facebook, friendship has become commercialized in a particular form.[26] Half a billion people use this site globally; Facebook seems entirely familiar. Its economic undertow, though, is less transparent. 'While only 28% believe what the adman says [in print],' one study reports, '68% trust their [on-line] friends'; advertising on social networking sites benefits from that association.[27] Social networking sites can be hugely profitable enter-prises also since embedding advertising into screen images is so easy technologically. Side-bars are now simple to create; a future possibil-ity in the technology lies in embedding hypertext links to products within the messages friends send to one another; the insertions would be unbidden, but in time, some admen hope, taken for granted, like product-placement moments in movies.

The term 'social networking' is in one way largely deceptive. Just as children distrust the print ads they read, some recent research suggests that they trust peers present in the flesh less than when they see peers on screen. The result is to render them machine-dependent for friend-ship.[28] Why this should be so is not as yet well understood. One explanation given concerns the technology itself. The images people take of themselves and their surroundings, especially on mobile-phone screens, may resemble old-fashioned candid-camera photographs; in being instant and seemingly artless, these images arouse trust. Another explanation focuses on sociability; in social networking sites, social transactions are less demanding, more superficial than face to face. You see where your friends are and what they are doing, you may send a comment but need not get deeply involved with what's happening – the logic of sending a short, coded text rather than spend-ing endless hours on the phone, as teens used to.[29]

As in GoogleWave, the issue is programming and use rather than the physical machine; with a different mindset, you'd make a tele-phone call whenever you see something arousing on screen. More, superficial sociability is not the inevitable consequence of online social networking. In China, the new technology has deepened *guanxi*; in the far-flung networks which characterize these relationships, with young people far from village homes, often far from peers in the same city, the nagging, advice-giving and practical support that characterize *guanxi* has strengthened thanks to the mobile phone.

Our own cultural history helps illuminate why superficial social bonds may form online. As described in Chapter 3, a great tension at the onset of the Reformation lay in the contrary claims of mutual ritual and religious spectacle, the first engaging people in a common rite, the second dividing them into passive spectators and active performers. Victor Turner argued that such a tension between ritual and spectacle exists, structurally, in all cultures; his claim may be too broad, but certainly makes some sense now in explaining the difference between telephoning and texting, between discussing things with other people and sending them mobile-phone images. I want to make more of this than is probably prudent. On modern social networking sites, as on blogs, something like the old Catholic theatre holds sway: people perform to a mass of spectators who watch.

I believe Phillipa, a teenager who tells my local newspaper 'we're not socially abnormal' about the fact she has 639 friends on Facebook, knows 'the vast majority' but has met few of them and knows little about them other than what appears on screen.[30] If all 639 equally texted and transmitted, say, just one text and one image each, this would yield 816,642 messages each day; impossible to digest. As the number of online friends increases, gradually just a few friends will stand out, the others becoming their passive observers. The same number-logic applies to blogs: a blog site with 2,000 members could produce 400,000 messages if each person contributes just one every week. What are the chances a hundredth of them would be read? Phillipa could be said to be a consumer of friendship, but it would be better to say that she has become a star performer, producing images and texts which the other 639 consume.

Unequal visibility also governs the circle of friends Phillipa forms online. In terms of social class, conventional wisdom invokes a 'digital divide' to describe inequality online and in ownership of online tools – computers, mobile phones or iPods and iPads. In general, the sociologist Paul DiMaggio and his colleagues say, inequality appears online in terms of access to the machines and fluency in their use.[31] This scarcity follows the biblical saying that to those who have, more is given.[32] Within affluent countries like Britain, though, the digital divide is turned upside down in terms of use. The researchers Ed Mayo and Agnes Nairn have found that 'children in the UK's most deprived households spend far more time in front of TV and internet screens than do their affluent counterparts'.[33] Their data are striking: children in poor households with computers are nine times more likely to eat their meal in front of the computer and five times more likely to be on the computer before they go to bed than more privileged children.[34] This finding accords with others about television use; poor children spend more time alone in front of the box when eating, before bed and before going to school. All of which is to say that poor kids are consuming screen-life more than their wealthier counterparts.

Here is a basic but often ignored fact about social networking: face-to-face connections, personal relationships and physical presence can be forms of privilege. This basic fact is known to anyone looking for a job who has emailed a résumé to an unknown prospective employer; the chances of its being read are very slim. Privilege and propinquity, presence and access go together – the principle of the old-boy network. In most poor communities, face-to-face connections are not empowering to children, the network of friends does not open doors.

Facebook's origins reveal something about the inequality of the friendships it puts online. Facebook and its ancestor Friendster were originally social networking sites used for dating. At Harvard, where Facebook took form, the network emphasized attractive self-display; as it expanded from dating to other social connections, competitive display became stronger; in the words of the historian of Facebook, David Kirkpatrick, '"friending" had an element of competitiveness from day one . . . if your roommate had 300 friends and you only had 100, you resolved to do better.'[35] The site initially prospered as an elite in-group; as it grew, it still carried that edge, defining how attractive a person is by the quantity of the people he or she is connected to.

It may be that among Phillipa's 639 Facebook friends there will be some from poor backgrounds who will be drawn into her sphere (I'm deducing from her diction that her family is well off), but sociological research argues against it. In his study of elite American secondary schools, for instance, Shamus Khan stresses the importance of living together in dormitories for forging the friendships that the American elite counts on in later life; at Harvard, significant relationships develop in extra-curricular activities and in clubs like the Porcellian or the Signet; Facebook, at its origins in that cushy milieu, was a tool of connection rather than the connection itself.[36]

We commonly associate the word 'inclusion' with cooperation. Social networking sites challenge that easy assumption. They can exclude rather than include; one way they do so occurs through the arithmetic of having hundreds of 'friends', an arithmetic which privileges display, particularly competitive display. 'Consumption' becomes a name for watching others live. In operation, class inequalities shape that sort of spectatorship. The machinery standing behind social networking sites was not built with class differences in mind. But 'friending' is no more neutral in use than GoogleWaving.

In sum, I've tried to show how in children's lives inequality relates to sociability, and more particularly to cooperation. The inequalities imposed on Anglo-American children make them less sociable than children in more equal European societies. Inequality is absorbed in children's lives when they make invidious comparisons. For children today, social relations are increasingly consumed online, and theatrically. Online sociability, so far, appears to be diminishing sustained social interaction with youngsters across class lines. Which is hardly any child's fault.

In a talk she gave at Columbia University, Martha Nussbaum set the matter of inequality in larger terms. She remarked that a capability sets a standard not just for what human beings can do but also for how society may fail to nourish them. Inequality constricts the capacities of children; they are endowed to relate more fully, to cooperate more deeply, than institutions allow. This is not always and everywhere so, and not attributable to capitalism in the raw, at least in the way people a century ago in Paris believed. Relative inequality within society makes for the failure. So too do social norms. *Guanxi*, that deep bond of the duty to cooperate, is not a bond children see brought to life online.

5

The Social Triangle

How Social Relations Become Embittered at Work

Fieldwork led me as a young sociologist to interviewing American, white, working-class families in Boston in the 1970s.[1] The boom after the Second World War had provided these workers with an immeasurably better life than the one they had known growing up in the Great Depression; they now owned houses and cars, they consumed. The research team I assembled with Jonathan Cobb forty years ago interviewed about a hundred families in Boston. Factories and shops in Boston were organized so that each person had a fixed niche and was meant to stay in it. This formal structure had deep roots in time, deriving from industrial organization in the nineteenth century. The social critique of this system was also deep-rooted; when reformers in Paris spoke of the 'soulless' system of production, they referred to niche-work, to the mechanical division of labour.

Our research team found in Boston, however, that manual labourers forged strong informal bonds at work which took people out of their niches. These informal relations consisted of three elements composing a social triangle. On one side, workers extended grudging respect to decent bosses, who returned equally grudging respect to reliable employees. On a second side, workers talked freely about significant mutual problems, and also covered in the shop for co-workers in trouble, whether the trouble was a hangover or a divorce. On the third side, people pitched in, doing extra hours or other people's jobs, when something went temporarily and drastically wrong in the shop. The three sides of the social triangle consisted of earned authority, mutual respect and cooperation during a crisis. In a factory or office, such a social triangle does not transform work into Eden, but does make work experience something more than soulless; it countervails against the niche, against formal isolation. Put more largely, the social triangle of this sort creates civility in a workplace, a civility between labourers and bosses which seems lodged in a different universe from the courtesies inside a diplomatic embassy but nonetheless shares some of the same structural features.

Forty years on, I am involved in interviewing quite a different group of workers: back-office, white-collar workers on Wall Street who lost their jobs in the crash of 2008. Many of my subjects are not victims; they have technical skills which have already seen or will soon see them back in work. Still, the sudden jolt that forced them into temporary unemployment made these bureaucrats, technicians and low-echelon managers more critical about the quality of their working life before the crash.

The financial industry is a high-stress business requiring people to work extremely long hours, and time for children, spouses and social pleasures is sacrificed to the job. Many of my subjects, passing across the trauma of 2008, are no longer willing to make those personal sacrifices; looking back, they feel a good deal of bitterness about playing the financial industry's game on its own terms. They've realized how little respect they had for the executives who once bossed them, how superficial was the trust they had with fellow workers, and most of all how weak cooperation proved within businesses in the wake of financial disaster. My subjects now feel that they were not much attached to the people and to the places where they once worked. In interviewing Wall Street back-office workers, I've posed to each person the question, 'Do you want your old job back?' The answer has usually been, 'I want to do the same sort of work somewhere else.' The bonds of the social triangle have proved internally weak.

So far, employers haven't had to worry much about the political consequences; the financial back-office is not out on the streets protesting. Even so, the weakness of the social triangle should be disturbing. Significant communication in bureaucracies occurs informally; when informal channels of communication wither, people keep to themselves ideas about how the organization is really doing, or guard their own territories. More, weak informal social ties erode loyalty, which businesses need in good as well as bad times. My subjects are too far down the corporate ladder for bonuses or huge salaries to make much difference to their behaviour; put another way, the social bonds at work are of more value to them. Many have come to feel embittered by the thin, superficial quality of these ties in places where they spend most of their waking hours. Though they wouldn't put the matter this way, they've suffered from the absence of a countervailing culture of civility which would render their social relations at work more significant to themselves.

This chapter explores the implications between the two realms of work, then and now.

THE SOCIAL TRIANGLE IN THE OLD ECONOMY

It would be quite wrong to imagine working-class cohesion made for happy citizens. Outside the workplace, the workers I interviewed in Boston felt slighted by the elite liberals who made policy for the city, and they transformed these slights, as in a distorting mirror, into negative attitudes about poor African-Americans below them; Boston workers were all too vehement in expressing *ressentiment*. The social bond occurred more narrowly inside the workplace.

Earned authority

In the 1970s, many older American workers on the factory floor had fought in the Second World War; many younger ones were fresh from Vietnam. Military life had instilled in them a two-sided measure of authority. They accepted that an officer provides the strategy for battle, indeed they wanted him to set the strategy, to lead, to direct; he is the superior, he should know what to do. Yet equally he ought to give troops freedom to fight once the orders are issued; indeed, he must do so. Micro-managing every soldier's flick of the trigger-finger would result in chaos on the field.

This military experience of officers and soldiers applied to domestic labour relations. In the Boston factories, when bosses behaved like petty tyrants, workers who had seen active military service tended to stand up to them. But bland, polite foremen were a greater goad; being relentlessly nice to people seemed a way of putting them off; foremen who shouted and swore and then let people get on with the job seemed better leaders. Though combat on the factory floor generated a lot of human heat, the workers still felt these hot, hands-on foremen earned the right to command, by being so passionately engaged; by then letting go, they showed a measure of respect, trusting that the workers were competent enough to get on with the job. Such outbursts became a monthly, occasionally a weekly, ritual which ended well for both sides. It might seem odd to think of this rough, regular ritual as expressing civility, but it did so, as a mutual acknowledgement. 'Yeah, he blows off steam,' a machinist remarked of his foreman, 'but he's not really bad, you know?'

Authority is often equated with raw power. This is a sociological mistake. Authority is, instead, power endowed with legitimacy. Since the time of Max Weber, sociologists have defined legitimacy in terms of voluntary obedience. Soldiers willing to follow the command 'Attack!' knowing it means they will die furnish an extreme instance; in civil society, legitimate power is framed in terms of laws people obey just because these seem right. The Weberian test for legitimacy is, will you obey even though you might get away with disobeying? Sensible as the Weber test is, still this sociological way of thinking is too narrow. It focuses on the subject rather than on the master. The master has also to earn his or her legitimacy, and usually does so through small behaviours and exchanges which have little to do with formal statements of the right or entitlement to rule.

Long after I left Boston, I came across a statement from an architect which seems to encapsulate how authority can be earned personally. The Swiss architect Peter Zumthor says of his studio, 'At the beginning I come with a sketch, and we talk. We talk about the idea, we talk about how to start.' Then, for a period, he lets his draughtsmen go their own way: 'Somebody starts with a model.' Zumthor then re-enters the picture: 'As I walk through the office, I pass all the work . . . I am good at giving structure to our talks . . . where we have several opinions, I cut off all academic, theoretical arguments.' He is not withdrawn while working: 'I get other people in, even the secretary, and ask "Would you like a hotel bedroom with a bed like this or like this?"' When he then does decide on the design, his decisions are final.[2]

Rather than just self-praise, the description makes an important point. In a pure exercise of power, the architect would never ask the secretary his or her opinion; he would already know where to put the bed, or believe he knows what the secretary really wants. Zumthor is obviously no pussycat in the studio, a mere mediator; he's in charge. But he engages others seriously, and by all accounts he elicits deep dedication from his staff.

Earned authority manages the everyday experience of inequality in a particular way. It moderates humiliation in the relation of command and obedience. In the Weberian way of thinking, humiliation occurs whenever a servant has no choice; in a fuller view, humiliation occurs when the master shows no recognition. A boss who does not humiliate can shout and swear, as in the Boston factories, then let the guys on the shop floor get on with it, or he can wander quietly from desk to desk, as in Zumthor's studio; either way, he is not closed in upon himself. We might think, as Norbert Elias does, that humiliation inevitably produces shame. As appeared in Chapter 3, Elias couched this process in terms of individual experience, the farting person humiliating him- or herself, but more, Elias imagines shame to have a long-lasting effect. In the rituals which earn authority, moments of anger pass; though they may temporarily humiliate, shame also passes. Containing emotion is one aspect of ritual's civilizing power.

Even if the relations between bosses and employers do not turn on such outbursts, informal discussions can become binding rituals; these talks just need to happen regularly. The discussions may seem quite trivial, as in when to grease a machine or where to put a bed. But if a workplace is organized so that exchanges of this sort are regular, the people involved know that they are being taken seriously. At least it did so in a Boston shoe factory where I spent time, in the days or weeks between storms, when during coffee breaks foremen and machinists discussed which brands of industrial lubricants, washers and shields were best for the machines. Here, too, the foremen who listened and took notes were earning their authority.

Leap-of-faith trust

The second side of the social triangle concerns trust. Georg Simmel once described mutual trust as requiring a leap of faith, trust being 'both less and more than knowledge'.[3] If we know exactly what's going to happen in dealing with someone else, trust doesn't arise as an issue. Simmel's contemporary, the pragmatist philosopher William James, didn't accept that trust is entirely blind. In his essay 'The Will to Believe', James likens trust to a hypothesis 'which appeals as a real possibility to him to whom it is proposed; trust is then tested, with the risk it may turn out to be misplaced'.[4] Still, like Simmel, James thinks trust requires a leap of faith; as he says in another essay, when we trust, we are ready 'to act in a cause the prosperous issue of which is not certified to us in advance'.[5]

Trust is like the instruments on Holbein's table: you are willing to use them even though you don't quite know how they work. Trading derivatives a banker doesn't quite understand requires the leap of faith; his will to believe in these financial instruments is stronger than what he knows are the dangers. In an architect's studio, people believe in projects that have yet to be, projects that in a corner of their minds they know will never get funded; Simmel's leap of faith keeps them at their desks. Similarly trust in others: it is faith in them, despite not knowing whether that faith can be justified.

In factory life in Boston, trust took on this complex coloration when people 'covered' for a fellow worker in trouble. Alcoholic workers, for instance, were quite clever, indeed manipulative, in hiding the signs of their drinking, but not clever enough; sluggishness on the assembly line usually betrayed them. When another worker sussed them out, he or she would slow down the line if possible, or simply whisk incomplete work out of the alcoholic's hands. In reformer mode – I was then quite the priggish young Harvard lecturer – I argued that people shouldn't be doing this; the alcoholic should be made to face up to the consequences of his drinking. But people on the assembly line weren't prim reformers; when they covered, they were responding to a fellow worker just as he was. When covering occurred, the alcoholics were at first puzzled, indeed suspicious; they couldn't quite believe that people would do this for them; there must be a hidden agenda. To accept the cover, they had to make their own leap of faith: they believed someone could genuinely be helping out. Just this bond of trust enabled the alcoholic to keep drinking.

Bonds of trust on an assembly line look a little different than they do in the abstract. The matter is more a two-way transaction: will people accept help and so trust in others? Trust can be built up on the shoals of weakness and self-damage. If covering seems unusual, it's worth noting that all these line workers were Catholics, devout if not theological. Year after year, decade after decade, they heard the Christian exhortation not to turn away from people who are frail, that frailty is also in them. Mutual trust can be built on such a conviction, and proves a stronger bond, I would say, than trust based on low levels of risk.

Cooperation and disruption

On the assembly line, cooperation was most tested when things went wrong, as at a large bakery in which I spent a good deal of time observing (and eating), when its ovens overheated and the risk of fire became acute. At these moments foremen suddenly yielded to orders from stokers who for the moment took charge. Unstable people were now shoved off the shop floor. Women who normally did packaging work outside appeared with buckets. People stepped out of their niches as the chain of command was suspended.

Moments of crisis like this reveal the fragility of formal organization and correspondingly the strength of informal collaboration. That's the great theme of novels like Joseph Heller's *Catch-22*, in which soldiers survive only by ignoring directives and working out together how to cope; the sociologist Tom Juravich has shown that the real world too often parallels catch-22 on the shop floor.[6] At the dawn of the industrial era, in *The Wealth of Nations*, Adam Smith depicted routine labour in factories as relentlessly desensitizing and mind-numbing, a view which in time has become nearly universal.[7] The industrial workplace can have this effect, though not implacably. Any break in routine can rouse people – and when roused, they shift to the informal zone; seemingly trivial things, rather than great crises, can rouse and shift them. Among a platoon of cleaners in one factory I came to know, people remarked on unusual scraps, food, even clothes, they found in the waste-paper baskets; in a post-office sorting room, which involves truly grinding routine, people's heads were into gossip as their hands sorted an unending stream of envelopes passing along a conveyor belt. These little incidents reflect a natural impulse: people want stimulation. The catch-22 crisis provides stimulation externally; people can also create it for themselves.

Gossip tends to stimulate people by dramatizing trivial information or events; it is most gripping when it becomes a mini-theatre full of shock-horrors – 'You won't believe this!' Moreover, the person gossiping assumes other people will 'get it', or will keep on explaining until they do; he or she doesn't want passive listeners. Most gossip tends to be malicious; we aren't usually gripped by an account of someone's generosity as we are by something outrageous that they've done. Still, during the time I spent in Boston's factories, I became increasingly aware that the engagements which animate gossip also stimulate people when actually working; like chit-chat which relieves boredom on the job, so can problem-solving, which entails dealing with another sort of break in routine.

The shoe factory, for instance, was once sent stained leather from Argentina; one leather-worker knew immediately what to do, but didn't proceed until he had explained to others what had caused the stain and the chemicals required to remove it; he made sure they understood. Though neither a crisis nor gossip, the problem-solving still required alerting others to something unusual, and effectively sharing knowledge: a non-routine, cooperative communication. As in any good conversation, in dealing well with a vexing problem people can't just fall back on procedures they have taken for granted; socially, and perhaps counter-intuitively, disruptions at work often prove bonding events.

Explosive bosses, lies told on behalf of alcoholic fellow workers and gossip are certainly not icons of what we think of as good-quality work. But they figure in social behaviour that can be positive: rituals of anger yielding to respect, the willingness to take a chance on others, the desire to get out of the prison of routine. And again, if we step behind each of these behaviours, we can detect the social relationships in which they are embedded: the rituals are part of the fabric of earned authority, the covering lie is enmeshed in leap-of-faith trust, and – putting gossip to the side – crisis-management and problem-solving link cooperation and disruption. Negative or positive, these rela-tions all involve sometimes quite subtle communication. The sides of the triangle are strengthened, moreover, by association; trust grows stronger when a disrupting event is dealt with, as does authority. This is in sum both a subtle and a coherent social structure.

The Boston Labor Bureau classed most of the jobs in the sites I studied as unskilled or semi-skilled labour, which is incorrect. To practise informal social relations of this sort, people needed a thor-ough knowledge of one another; they had, for instance, to know who to call on and who not to rely on in an emergency, or who is worth lying for. They had in equal measure to know their institutions well: the bakers knew where in Boston the supplies they needed could be found when a burn-out occurred, the cleaners scheduled their activ-ities, not by the union rule-book, but by adjusting to the shifting needs of different departments. Informal social relations required context-ual knowledge, a context to be queried and interpreted together.

The informal social triangle can appear in all sorts of organiza-tions, hospitals and schools, church and community groups, the military, offices as well as in factories. It might seem, indeed, that any organization would want to encourage internal, informal bonds of these sorts, in order to cohere socially. But the social triangle has one big requirement which an organization may not be able to meet. It requires institutions that are relatively stable in time, long-established. Only when this requirement is met can people learn in depth about how the organization works. In the last generation, however, capital-ism has moved away from the time-stable institutions that grounded workers like those in Boston. In part, this is because America and much of Europe have shed factory labour altogether, these advanced economies now seeking to become service economies. In part, time itself has become more short-term in most modern organizations, whether in the private or the public sector; people's experience of one another and knowledge of their institutions has shortened. The financial-services sector is in the vanguard of this change, its shaping of institutional time least resembling the experience people once had on the assembly line. Not surprisingly, then, in the financial-services sector the social triangle has fallen apart, and dramatically so.

THE SOLVENT OF TIME

At the onset of American prosperity after the Second World War, Wall Street, perhaps oddly, did resemble its industrial cousins; people spoke accurately when they invoked the image of the 'finance industry'. Most firms had existed for decades if not for a century or more: Lehman Brothers, JP Morgan and the like prided themselves on being venerable partnerships. In the banks and investment houses most employees made decades-long careers within a single firm. This aura of permanence and practice of long-term employment was not peculiar to New York. The historian David Kynaston has traced the way firms like Barings and Coutts in the City of London touted for business, quietly, by emphasizing their venerability; City of London firms took pride in the fact that most employees stayed for life.[8] Long-term employment equally marked my interviewees in Boston, who worked in perhaps two or three plants over the course of a lifetime, in factories that were permanent features of the community.

Apart from the contrast between wealth and poverty, there was of course one big difference between bankers and factory workers in their respective experiences of time: after the Second World War, the industrial proletariat suffered recurring bouts of traumatic unemployment, while redundancies in the financial services caused by the business cycle were more muted. Still, when work returned to industrial workers, it meant returning to their old plants. This is a striking fact about the three decades that followed the Second World War; within both America and Britain industrial workers tended to stay put, rather than move to look for better work elsewhere.[9] Throughout the nineteenth century and up to the Great Depression this was not so in either country; industrial communities were in flux.

It's important not to view post-war stability with nostalgia. In both industry and finance, long-rooted firms were often rigid, sluggish and complacent. Moreover, industrial bureaucracies made the experience of time within plants rigid and authoritarian. When in the 1950s the sociologist Daniel Bell studied General Motors' Willow Run factory in Michigan, he was struck by how the plant 'divides the hour into ten six-minute periods . . . the worker is paid by the numbers of tenths of an hour he works'.[10] Similar micro-calculations were made for low-level, white-collar workers in banks. This deregulation was, for workers, not entirely mindless. Punching the clock at least made labour legible to both sets of workers: in micro-time, they could calculate their wages and accrued benefits from those six-minute segments; in macro-time, the passage of years and the acquisition of seniority established where they stood in the plant or in the office.[11]

A host of studies began to chart, in the 1950s, the personal and social consequences of the industrialization of the white-collar classes, notably William Whyte's *The Organization Man*, C. Wright Mills's *White Collar* and Michel Crozier's *The Bureaucratic Phenomenon*.[12] For Whyte, long-term service tamped down sudden bursts of ambition and innovation; Mills believed stability led to an increase in conformity; Crozier, whose researches concerned France, where the state loomed larger in business, more emphasized the political consequences of white-collar workers becoming docile. None of these studies attended much to informal relations among workers or between workers and managers; formalized time seemed to possess an overwhelming, self-contained power.

That power began to loosen its grip in the mid-1970s, the financial-services industry on Wall Street especially feeling the effect. If one event could be said to spark that change, it was the breakdown of the Bretton Woods monetary agreements during the oil crisis of 1973, a collapse which unleashed huge amounts of global capital onto markets which before had been more national and fixed, the flood of cash flowing at first from the Middle East and Japan. Thirteen years later, the 'Big Bang' deregulation of financial services in London allowed more investors to enter the global market; cash appeared in capital flight from South America, from offshore China; in the 1990s markets drew in Russians spiriting away ill-gotten gains from their homeland; at the dawn of the present century, mainland Chinese became important investors in European industries as well as in American government bonds.

Suddenly, everyone was competing with everyone else. During the decades of stability, a gentleman's agreement partitioned the stock and bond territories that Wall Street and City firms controlled; moreover, hostile takeovers, like that engineered in 1957 by Siegmund Warburg of Britain's major aluminium company, were deeply frowned on. Collusion, of course, never disappeared; commodity markets and IPOs (initial public offerings of stock from young companies) were, to put the matter plainly, often rigged; were he alive now, Bernard Mandeville could have written a new *Fable of the Bees* based entirely on Wall Street. But those who now colluded also sought to subvert one another, to break up competitors' firms, especially to wipe out small players. The gentleman's agreement sought stability in the industry, while the new regime was more short-sighted, seeking momentary advantage.

Most of this new money has been, in the words of the economist Bennett Harrison, 'impatient capital', seeking short-term returns on share prices and financial instruments, rather than long-term ownership of the firms in which capital was invested.[13] Shareholder returns focus on the price of shares rather than the health of firms; you can make money by going 'short' on companies whose share price, you bet, will decline, even if the company continues to post profits. This in turn puts pressure on companies to 'make their numbers' quarterly or monthly rather than think long-term. Even pension funds, which should have been most minded to the long term, began in the last generation to play by different time-rules: in 1965, the length of time a stock was held by pension funds averaged 46 months, in 2000, it averaged 8.7 months, in 2008, 4.9 months.

Wall Street's particular role in the shift became the packaging of vehicles for impatient investment, while the City of London's role, drawing on old imperial connections, focused more on global execution and coordination.[14] Like the City of London, 'Wall Street' now denotes a generic space for finance – and in New York mid-town Manhattan has become as important to finance as Rector Place downtown, just as in London financial work occurs as much in Mayfair as in Moorgate.

The advent of the new timescale changed, in both cities, how firms are structured and how people work in them. As in other businesses today, set against the fixed 'core-business' model is the 'portfolio' concept, in which many different and often unrelated activities go on under the same corporate roof; the portfolio model is claimed to be a way to respond to fast-changing global markets, and to 'make the numbers' in one domain if not in another. The portfolio concept works against a coherent corporate image or identity; the corporation is conceived as a set of component parts which can be sold off, added to or reconfigured at will.

The financier-philosopher George Soros has conveyed the difference short-term time makes to organizations as a contrast between momentary 'transactions' versus sustained 'relationships'.[15] Unlike the sociologists of an earlier era, Soros recognizes that an organizational relationship is informal as well as formal; informal trust plays an important role in sustaining a relationship, especially when either the financial entrepreneur or his or her clients are under stress, needing their partners to cut some slack in the payment of bills or the furnishing of credit; the willingness to do so usually requires a long-term, personal tie.

More abstractly, the sociologist Manuel Castells has characterized today's political economy as 'a space of flows'.[16] He argues that thanks to new technology the global economy operates in synchronous real time; what happens to stock markets in London or New York instantly registers in Singapore or Johannesburg; computer code written in Bombay can be used for IBM as instantly as code written in the firm's home offices. Castells calls this condition 'timeless time'. The computer screen, which is the great symbol of our era, embodies it, window piled upon window without temporal relation; time is suspended. The social consequence is just as Soros puts it: a momentary transaction rather than a sustained relationship.

Short-term time has restructured the character of work. Today's labour market is a scene of short-term stints rather than of sustained careers. 'No long-term' is well conveyed by an executive for ATT, for instance, who a few years ago declared, 'At ATT we have to promote the whole concept of the work-force being contingent ... jobs are being replaced by projects.'[17] Temporary, often part-time labour is one reflection of this ethos; today, temporary work is the fastest-growing sector of the service economy. Even if employed full-time, the young middle-level university graduate can expect to change employers at least twelve times in the course of a working life, and to change his or her 'skills base' at least three times; the skills he or she must draw on aged forty are not the skills learned in school.[18]

These time-changes have a big impact on people's contextual knowledge. 'When I first came to work on the Street,' an auditor observed to me, when 'people made a career for life in a firm' they 'couldn't help but get to know the business, especially when the shit hit the fan; now you don't'.* Perhaps there is a new context: no one is irreplaceable; at least, a famous bit of showmanship by Jack Welch, one-time head of General Electric, sought to make this point. He kept an office empty in the executive suite, one he pointed out to any prospective recruit to dramatize that no one had a permanent place in GE. I asked the auditor what he thought of this. 'Sure, no one is irreplaceable but the point is, the office is empty,' there's no one inside that you've come to understand, rely on or not, know how to work with.

The rule of short-term led employers during the long boom, the years leading to the crash of 2008, to frame the ideal worker in the mould of the consultant, whose skills are portable, whose attachments to any particular place are temporary. In management, this consultant model evacuated the content of labour. For instance, a recent advertisement for a quite technical job, head of price-control regulation in Britain's Civil Aviation Authority, states: 'you will be a versatile manager . . . using your ability to convert ambiguous problems into clear solutions . . . a flexible and positive attitude and the ability to write and speak clearly . . . [your rewards include] the intellectual challenge and stimulus from working as part of a high calibre team.'[19] These attributes have little to do specifically with aviation.

Denial of the importance of context and contextual knowledge, like the focus on short-term or temporary work, reinforces among manual workers a grave sense of insecurity. Their knowledge of workplaces and the people in them counts for little in the job market; their social capital, to use again Robert Putnam's phrase, has little economic weight. Insecurity is a more tangible fact, as manufacturing jobs have disappeared, or people in work move from temporary job to temporary

---

* I ask the reader's forbearance: I'm quoting from research on modern Wall Street before explaining, as I will later in this chapter, how I gathered it.

job. Insecurity is configured differently in the finance industry. It's a daily experience for auditors, accountants, IT teams and human-relations officers on Wall Street, a normal fact of life in which upsets and crises occur every day. But the importance of long-term contextual knowledge does not therefore disappear.

It matters, for instance, in the ways rewards are doled out for good or hard work. How much do people know about you when they come to judge you? The answer to this question involves a peculiarity. Short-term time is faster among the financial elite than for those in Wall Street's back-offices; that is, upper-echelon executives began in the last generation to pass through a revolving door, moving from firm to firm after a few years or only a few months in one place, or from different departments in the same institution, whereas switching posts was less frequent in the middle echelons. The difference in speed has meant that within firms the managerial witnesses to and judges for hard work have often disappeared, moved on somewhere else, when it comes to evaluating a middle-ranking employee. 'My job got harder,' a human-relations officer remarked to me, 'because I had little personal information to go on' in handing out end-of-year bonuses to junior workers in a bank. Managerial short-time deprived him of that information.

Personnel departments sometimes judge back-office workers by the speed of change at the top. Another human-relations officer at a high-tech firm observed that 'in this business everything changes all the time. So if I see on a guy's résumé that he has been five, six years at the same place I have questions.' Which is to say, stability became a stigma during the long boom in finance.

The replacement for face-to-face judgement has become standardized evaluation forms, formal, box-ticking exercises which do not measure such intangibles as a willingness to work late, making up for the incompetence of a co-worker, or, more deeply, belief in the firm itself. One quite unusual accountant I interviewed had risen from factory labour to the back-office of a now-defunct investment bank, taking courses at night and putting off starting a family to do so; he compared monitoring in manual and white-collar labour as follows: 'Report forms are just normal in the glassworks. I imagined it would be different at the bank; you'd be seen more for yourself but it turned out not much different.'

The spate of mergers and acquisitions stimulating finance capitalism in recent years has reinforced the impersonality of judgement. A new set of managerial faces will come on the scene, people unfamiliar with those who already work there, and often unfamiliar with the business itself. These new bosses have little to go on but numbers in judging the employees they have bought. From experience, they cannot know who does good work. 'It was odd that this could happen to me,' a back-office employee at an investment bank remarked; his bit of the firm was lucky when it went bust in 2008 and was bought by another investment bank, but 'it was like we were a blank slate to them'.

All these aspects of short-term time converge in the informal social relations between people in finance firms. Project labour in chameleon institutions acts like an acid solvent, eating away at authority, trust and cooperation.

THE TRIANGLE COMES APART

The lives of back-office workers in finance began to interest me in the mid-1990s, when I was studying another kind of technical labour, the work of computer programmers in New York and in Silicon Valley. It was a time when computer programming was growing hugely and unpredictably, the possibilities of programs in use no clearer than were the uses of the navigation equipment on Holbein's table. I began to be aware that behind this buzz of creativity there was another kind of buzz; venture capitalists visited the pizza-littered, airless small offices where the programmers worked, the suited capitalists hoping to discover in this smelly chaos The Next New Thing. The visitors were in turn linked to Wall Street investment banks who doled out more capital when the 'venture vultures', as they were known, transformed small start-up ventures into businesses that offered shares for sale to investors suffering from that modern version of tulip-mania, the 'dot-com bubble'.

When I came back from Silicon Valley to New York in 1997, I tried to find out what was happening at this end of the food chain. Top investment bankers had little time to spare for me as a professor with no programs to sell, but they were polite – I'd taught two of my contacts the History of Early Social Thought at Harvard – and they diverted me to people in their back-offices. The screen was in that year decisively displacing the ticker tape and telefax as a means of financial communication; the back-office workers talked to me, distractedly, while staring, obsessed, at three or four computer screens across which moved, ceaselessly, row upon row of numbers. Despite the figures dancing before their eyes, I gleaned enough to understand that these people, who managed bills, cleared transactions, prepared documents for audit and processed purchases, were craftsmen of sorts. They were skilled and they took pride in their work; had Booker T. Washington launched the Hampton Institute in 1997, he might have trained his charges to learn these technical crafts rather than make cheese.

They seemed peripheral to my main interest at the time, an emerging new culture in capitalism.[20] I realized I should have paid more attention to the back-office when, a little more than a decade later, in September 2008, the crash occurred in the financial-services industry. I began interviewing people on Wall Street who had been personally affected – particularly people who had lost, or left their jobs – a project still in progress.[21] Those most affected were back-office workers, the first to lose their jobs in the collapse of firms like Lehman Brothers; the crash caused many other back-office workers to rethink their lives, some leaving Wall Street altogether.

You could find back-office men and women, in the winter of 2009, at a job centre near Wall Street, well-dressed people filling out forms, occasionally glancing around in bewilderment. Though not capitalism's big beasts, few of these skilled white-collar workers had seen the inside of an unemployment office before; now they sat on plastic chairs, bent over clipboards illuminated above by shadowless fluorescent light, surrounded by Latino teenagers, barrel-chested construction workers and elderly janitors also hunting for work.

As job centres go, this one in lower Manhattan is quite good.[22] The big intake room is clean and quiet, most of the computers are connected and the staff are mostly courteous and experienced. Clients of the more usual sort are led to cubicles or recesses; there, the staff fill in the paperwork for immigrants whose English is poor, or make the effort to draw out manual workers cowed by officialdom. With the unemployed white-collar employees from failed banks or brokerages the job counsellors face a different challenge. These clients need to think about personal strategy, short-term and longer-term.

In the short-term, they have to do whatever necessary to pay their bills; some are clerking in stores, others patching together temporary jobs on the fringes of the financial world. Long-term, employment in New York's financial sector is expected to decline from 9 to 7 per cent in the wake of the crash; a similar contraction is expected in the City of London. In the last three recessions, once unemployed, a person's chances of recovering middle-class status have been no better than 60 per cent. For this reason, middle-class workers are beset, the sociologist Katherine Newman writes, by a constant fear of downward mobility.[23] That fear isn't quite so pronounced among the people I talked to at the Wall Street job centre and at a larger centre uptown. Their skills are specialized and in demand among many businesses; while a few were having long-term trouble, most of the people interviewed so far are recovering.

This doesn't mean that losing a job isn't traumatic. There is a class structure among the unemployed as among the employed which affects how the loss is experienced. At the top, executives have termination agreements providing large cash payments; the elite unemployed also have company-paid access to specialist executive-search firms; above all, they have an extensive network of personal contacts, associates willing to go out to lunch or just to take a call. By contrast, the big problem facing workers lower down the ladder is their much weaker network of contacts. When in work these technicians mostly knew people like themselves, many of whom are now chasing after the same jobs. Mailing résumés 'cold' – that is, to unknown employers – has proved largely useless, since employers have neither the time nor inclination to read through the sheer volume of these applications.

That trauma, even if temporary, can serve as a wake-up call, if people ask themselves 'What do I really want to do?', or 'How do I want to live?' A senior filing-clerk remarked to me, 'Suddenly a Chinese did my job cheaper and they let me go, and the first thing I thought was, what a fool I was those days I stayed at the office extra time just to get the job done.' Looking back, many of the people I've come to know – whether the unemployed themselves or their colleagues who survived in their old jobs – are reflecting on the sacrifice of family life, or the limited scope of their jobs.

How reliable as informants are people who have come through a trauma like that of 2008? Anxiety and frustration, particularly among the unemployed, certainly can make for bias. In interview research, one's judgement of bias turns on how rounded a picture informants provide: can the person see another's point of view, does he or she talk dialogically rather than combatively about experience, is he or she curious? So far, with a few crude exceptions, the people I've encountered are balanced in assessing their recent past, but also focus in a particular way: rather than dwell on economics, these economic craftsmen have treated the crash as a rite of passage, causing them to think seriously about quality-of-life issues.

Three of those issues illuminate the weakness of the informal triangle of social relations at their workplaces. In retrospect, informants think that cooperation proved superficial in their relations with one another; the back-office was a more isolated work environment. Theirs is a rounded view; they blame themselves in part for poor cooperation and isolation. Trust in the office seemed minimal, and seemed to explain why they make invidious comparisons of a particular sort. They feel that their superiors did not earn authority in dealing with the crash, indeed that executives in many financial firms eschewed their roles as authority figures while holding onto power and perks. These views add up to an embittered sense of the workplace, a bitterness that back-office workers hoped to salve either by finding a better firm or by exiting from the financial-services industry altogether.

Weak cooperation

Isolation is the obvious enemy of cooperation, and analysts of the modern workplace know this enemy well. In management-jargon, it is called 'the silo effect', an image drawing on the immense tubular silos in which grain is stored. Workers in silos communicate poorly with one another. A study done in 2002 by the American Management

Association of executives showed, for instance, that 83 per cent thought silos existed in their businesses, and 97 per cent thought the effects of isolation were negative.[24] The structure of an organization can create silos. In a later study, the AMA researchers found that less than half of organizations collected organized feedback from their employees; communication was dominantly top-down. Other studies report, similarly, that management is not taking seriously the views coming to them from below.[25] The silo effect is modern management's version of what community organizers a century ago sought to combat, a structural effect built into top-down organizations on the political Left.

In the interviews, however, isolation appeared to be more self-imposed. 'I'm just so stressed out', an IT worker remarked, 'that I can't get involved with other people's problems.' Stress is a Janus-faced experience; an auditor told me, 'I didn't want other people interfering with me, I had too much to do.' Her use of the past tense is important; she wants to turn over a new leaf, she says, and is leaving Wall Street for a 'warmer work environment' in a university (I hadn't the heart to comment on this expectation). Beyond the isolating effects of stress, many old hands on Wall Street blame the advent of computerized screen-work: people stare at the screens rather than talk to one another. The old hands also think email diminishes cooperation. 'I'd send a message to the girl three work-stations away,' said an elderly lady doing account reconciliation, 'rather than walk over to her.' And then there is the matter of bonuses.

These are fabled year-end gifts at the top of the Wall Street pyramid. Lower down, in the bowels of the back-office, they are much smaller but still substantial. Six Lehman Brothers junior accountants my team interviewed averaged bonuses of $45,000 annually in the five years before the firm collapsed – a reason, perhaps, why though unemployed they could treat me and my students to quite an expensive lunch. But the awarding of bonuses is no win-win situation, a group of workers being rewarded collectively; it is instead a zero-sum game that sets individual employees against one another. 'Here's my friendliness calendar,' one accountant told me about the run-up to hours-time: 'March, very [friendly]; July, a bit in-your-face; September, aggressive; December, each-man-for-himself.' I can't judge how much this bothered people during the long boom, but the accountant, in retrospect, didn't think it was good for either communication or morale.

Today, the silo effect seems to most managers a recipe for low productivity; employees tend to hoard vital information they think is to their personal advantage, and people in silos resist feedback from others. One remedy is to encourage teamwork, indeed to impose it, but such enforced cooperation suffers from the solvent of short-term time.

Managerial wisdom about how to organize teams stresses, ideally, the team's small size, usually no more than fifteen or twenty people meeting face to face. Cooperation is thought most effective when the group dwells on a clearly defined immediate problem or project. Teams typically stay together from six months to a year, which reflects the reality of corporations whose business plans and very identities are shifting constantly in the global economy. Long enough to get a job done – but not so long that the members of the team become too attached to one another.[26]

Teamwork therefore entails portable social behaviour which team-members should be able to practise anywhere and with anyone. Some business schools and companies, for instance, now offer coaching in how to display cooperativeness as a team-player; new recruits learn how to shake hands, make eye contact and offer succinct contributions to a discussion: whomever you meet and wherever you meet them you can evince team-spirit.

The labour analyst Gideon Kunda has called this kind of cooperative behaviour 'deep acting'.[27] He means that underneath the surface of working cooperatively, team-members are showing off personally, usually to a manager or superior who is judging team performance; teamwork, he says, is 'feigned solidarity'. Short-term time makes a big difference to performances in this theatre of work. Because people are not really engaged with one another, their relationship being a matter of at most a few months, when things go wrong team-spirit suddenly collapses; people seek cover and deniability by shifting blame to other team-members. This weakness contrasts with teamwork in the bakery with the faulty oven; cooperation there did not fall apart, because people knew one another well and had formed long-term informal

relationships; they thus called on one another, and knew, more precisely, whom they could or couldn't count on.

The situation in the Wall Street back-offices was paradoxical in this
respect. As described above, back-office workers on Wall Street have
tended to be rooted for longer periods in firms than executives at the
top. Yet the firms themselves are in a constant state of internal flux,
departments being continually reorganized, their personnel reconfigured, as the finance industry expanded during the long boom. Teamwork
proved, to our informants, no strong social corrective to this febrile
structural change. 'Of course we work in teams,' a computer engineer
succinctly observed, 'but things keep coming up and we are constantly
losing focus.' This may seem a matter of the tasks at hand, rather than
the players involved. But Wall Street firms during the long boom constantly merged or bought up smaller businesses; they hoped to make
labour cost savings in doing so, those famous 'synergies' in which a
smaller, consolidated troop of workers provision an expanding organization. Team-spirit suffered as team-players were squeezed to 'do
more with less', as the executives hoped.

Short-term teamwork, with its feigned solidarity, its superficial
knowledge of others and its squeezing, contrasts dramatically to the
Chinese social bond of *guanxi*, the benchmark for a durable social
bond discussed at the beginning of Chapter 4. *Guanxi* is full of criticisms and sharp advice, rather than studied handshakes; people accept
the sharp advice because they know others mean to help, not display
themselves as exemplars. Most of all, *guanxi* is sustained; it's a relationship which is meant to transcend particular events. And the
network develops in time to include more partners, each depending
on others in particular ways. Unlike a sports team, the players are
involved in many games at once. There are no efficiency savings in a
guanxi relationship; instead, the network grows stronger through
becoming an ever bigger mosaic.

Trust eroded by invidious comparison

As described in the last chapter, invidious comparison – the personalized experience of inequality – can erode social bonds. Consumer
goods may provide the reference for making invidious comparisons;

youngsters are frequently persuaded to think about 'cool stuff' for drawing personalized comparisons without being conscious of what they are doing. In the adult world of work, invidious comparison can arise in a much more self-conscious manner; here, ability furnishes the reference point. Invidious comparison based on competence has a particularly corrosive effect on trust: it's hard to have faith in someone you think is incompetent.

The back-office in finance capitalism rightly views its labours as a craft. In banks and investment houses, the accountants and auditors do much more than mechanically register trading results; organizing numbers for institutional use is a complicated skill. The craftsman's ethos is both to want, and to do, good work. The sociologist Matthew Gill has found a pecking order among British accountants, based on the craft ethos; the most admired accountants he studied were those concerned about the soundness of numbers.[28] Good work of this sort is context-dependent. 'You need to learn your organization,' a Wall Street accountant remarked to me, 'you need to find out who to call when an entry looks funny, for the explanation; they don't teach that in business school.' An IT manager for the defunct Lehman Brothers said: 'Anybody can buy technology off the shelf; which shelf it goes on means understanding your user . . . that takes time.'

In technically skilled labour, trust in other people is founded on respect for their competence, on faith in them because they seem to know what they are talking about. The back-offices in Wall Street have harboured little respect, however, for the technical skills of executives in the front-offices. In the wake of the crash, the suffering public has learned how little many of the players in the finance industry understood what they were doing. The back-office, even during the boom which preceded it, regarded many of their superiors as incompetent. For example, many acted on perceptions of executive incompetence in terms of their own investing. They prepared for a business downturn by avoiding the high-risk gambles of their superiors, putting money away in safe places and cutting debts as much as possible. The vocabulary used by our prudent subjects to describe these products would warm the heart of any Marxist: 'fairy gold', 'crap certificates', 'junk bonds and I emphasize the "junk"' all used to describe the financial products sold by front-office executives. This is the rude vocabulary of financial craftsmen, contrasting their own labours to the activities of people higher up.

Executives would of course like to believe that excellence rises to the top. The inverse view appears, for instance, in a large survey done by the Chartered Management Institute of Great Britain: exactly half of its respondents believed they could do a better job than their current manager. This number does more than reflect employee self-esteem, since 47 per cent reported they had left a job because of poor management, and 49 per cent indicated they 'would be prepared to take a pay cut in order to work with a better manager'.[29]

In a way, the inverse view is a stereotypical complaint. The upper echelons appear installed by title – the Harvard MBA seen as a sure passport – or because they are good at office politics. But trust disappears if and when this stereotype is grounded in fact, just because the top don't know what's going on every day in the firm; they lack hands-on knowledge. My interviews elicited a small but telling refinement in this regard, one which does not appear in the Chartered Management Institute's survey. Informants do single out individual leaders in investment banks and hedge-fund management firms who seem competent and prudent; these executives are spoken about using their first names, while incompetent executives are referred to generically as 'he', 'she' or 'they'.

In the craft of finance, the inverse relationship has a technical foundation, as in understanding the algorithms used to generate financial instruments like credit default swaps. These mathematical generators are often as impenetrable to the top brass as to the general public; the executive eye seems to glaze over in discussions of technicalities with the back-office craftsman. 'I asked him to outline the algo [algorithm] to me,' a junior accountant remarked about her derivatives-trading, Porsche-driving superior, 'and he couldn't; he took it on faith.' The content of an operation is neglected. 'Most kids have computer skills in their genes,' noted one member of an IT support-team, 'but just up to a point . . . when you try to show them how to generate the numbers they see on-screen, they get impatient, they just want the numbers and leave where these came from to the main-frame.' This technician showed a certain admiration for Nick Leeson, the young man who destroyed Barings Bank by manipulating its financial numbers,

Leeson being curious about the construction of numbers and so alert to the possibilities for fraud.

Of course, you can't know everything, even if what you don't know is making you whopping-rich. Yet modesty is not involved when executives try to duck the matter, resorting to superficial chit-chat – lots of sports talk, for instance – in place of learning. Of an executive in an investment bank, one back-office crafter of algorithms said that 'he's perfectly nice, a good guy, but he [the head of the bank's gold trading] never asked my opinion about anything; perhaps he was afraid of being shown up, or that I'd trade on my own account . . .' Insouciance masking incompetence eventually begins to tell; the executive is, after all, calling the shots. Friendly or not, he tells you what to buy or sell; in time you come to distrust him but are still obliged to obey him.

Back-office technicians stressed, it should be said, inattention on their superiors' part during the run-up to the crash, rather than raw inability to interpret spreadsheets; the issue is more a matter of attitude than raw aptitude. And they faulted not so much the managers immediately above them (many of whom also lost their jobs) as people at the top of the organization, executives and boards of directors who seemed not to be paying attention. The result, however the ingredients are mixed, has been an inverse relationship between competence and hierarchy, a bitter reversal which dissolves trust in those above.

Invidious comparisons of this particular sort reinforce the 'silo effect'. The desire to communicate withers if there is no real interest in listening. Back-office workers who have experienced the inverse relationship for sustained periods appear to become relentless judges of their bosses, looking for confirming signs, in every detail of behaviour, that executives don't deserve their powers and perks. This doesn't make people drawing the invidious comparison feel good about themselves, since they are stuck in the relationship. At work, in these circumstances, invidious comparison is more likely to be embittering than a cause for secret satisfaction.

Power abdicates authority

The third element of the social triangle is earned authority. When it is strong, earned authority concerns more than formal or technical competence; it also involves that dreaded phrase 'leadership skills', and, more pointedly, an open dialogue with subordinates rather than rigid dictation to them. Further, the ethical frame of earned authority is the willingness to assume responsibility, for oneself and for the group. In the frame of *guanxi*, honour is a key ingredient of earned authority.

Among our informants, this ethical frame for earned authority translated into the practical matter of whether, and how, executives would defend their firms in the collapse of 2008. They distinguished sharply, in the banking sector, between executives like Jamie Dimon, head of JP Morgan Chase, who put great energy into holding his firm together, and other executives who sold off real assets, shut down departments or simply looked after themselves. The absence of leadership did not entirely surprise my informants, given the weakness of corporate loyalty during the boom years, with its revolving door in the executive suites. Some unemployed back-office employees even tacitly subscribed, against their own interests, to the argument made by the economist Ludwig von Mises, that downturns in the business cycle are opportune moments, when the sector purges itself of unsustainable businesses.[30] Still, they judged that most of their employers failed to lead, instead denying responsibility and abdicating their authority.

Signs of this abdication appeared when bankers argued, for instance, that regulatory bodies should have done a better job of restraining bankers. Or, in another vein, an AIG insurance executive declared, 'we are all victims' of hermetic, unfathomable credit default swaps, bundled mortgages and the like. Explaining a crash as a force beyond one's own control evinces a certain cunning; when things go well, those at the top can claim personal credit; when they don't, fault lies in the system.

Abdicating leadership does not mean renouncing power or advantage. This truism has unfortunately been vindicated in the years since the 2008 crash, as top executives quickly recovered their perks and bonuses while leaving behind a devastated society. Abdicating authority is more complicated, however, than simply walking away from a mess. Richard Fuld, head of Lehman Brothers, declared shortly after its failure that he felt bad about the way events had turned out; 'That's a cost-free apology,' one of his ex-employees remarked to me. A proud and combative executive, Fuld was surprised by this kind of response among former staff, since admitting regret had actually cost him a lot personally. But his regret lacked reference to any specific, concrete actions for which he took responsibility.

Whether plunged into long-term unemployment or suffering a short-term blip, informants were of one mind about the way they were treated when they lost their jobs. The sudden death of giant firms like Lehman Brothers meant that people in the back-office learned via email they had lost their posts, and were given only a day to clear out their desks. 'I had some specific issues about share-options but all I got was standard email boilerplate,' one accountant told me; 'no one would answer the phone.' Another remarked, 'It's like they've gone on vacation.' 'Why did they even bother?' one IT coordinator, who lost her job in the crash, remarked to me as she held out the statement of her firm's emailed appreciation for the service of its dedicated employees who, unfortunately in these hard times ... Visual metaphors informed the way people conveyed their upset: 'He was afraid to look me in the eye,' and, more pointedly, in the words of an auditor given a day to clear his desk, 'She [the head of human relations in his section] never really saw me; the only person who looked carefully at me that day was [the guard at the firm's door] who looked through my box of personal stuff to make sure I wasn't stealing any of the firm's data.'

Hurt feelings are inevitable whenever someone loses a job, and there may be no humane way to fire a person. But there is a larger reason, I believe, why my informants have emphasized indifference. This emphasis reflects the socially isolated position the financial-services industry occupies in society, particularly in New York City.

The city's traditional elite operated as what Germans call a *Bürgerlichgesellschaft* – the kind of civic society which appears in the pages of Thomas Mann's novel *Buddenbrooks*, a society led by a few long-rooted families. In American cities, this leading position has entailed taking responsibility for a city's voluntary organizations, the elite serving on the boards of hospitals, charities, schools, as well as arts organizations. When a man is promoted to vice-president, Vance Packard observed in the mid-twentieth century, he is expected to join a board. With the arrival of more globalized businesses, executives in large part eschewed such engagements; by one measure, less than 3 per cent of the city's hospitals now have board members from corporations headquartered abroad.[31] The disengagement is structural rather than personal. The top echelons move constantly from city to city, country to country; they are not locals.

In the long boom, it should be noted, there were two exceptions to such civic disengagement: members of the global elite who are Jewish have tended to remain in the *Bürger* mould, since the culture of Jewish life in New York, as elsewhere, emphasizes philanthropy and service to the community. The other exception has been board membership in museums, since these are prestige posts in an area of the arts which itself has become a global business. It's common to describe high finance as 'clubby', but all elites are. This particular club is different; few of its members apply to join the Century Association, for instance, the club for the great and the good in New York; if cosmopolitan, the Century is too local.

How big is this new elite? The best current estimates of its size are international in scale. By one reckoning, before the 2008 crash global finance was dominated by five accounting firms, twenty-six law firms, sixteen leading investment banks, six central banks and two credit rating agencies. The top staffing of this constellation in 2007 numbered about 6,000 individuals.[32] Satellites to top players are usually reckoned by who has regular face-to-face contact with the leader; the ratio comes out to about 10 to 1, so that the international 'front-office' consists of about 60,000 individuals. Generously assuming that New York houses a quarter of this elite, it constitutes at most 15,000 in a city of 8 million.

There are, to be sure, a good many native New Yorkers in the executive suites, but they aren't doing local business. High-flying, and constantly flying, executives seem, as one human-resources manager remarked, 'always somewhere else'. On the ground, in place of civic association, the new elite has carved out for itself little islands of sociability in Manhattan. These appear, for instance, in the city's late-night restaurants. During the long boom, late-night restaurants began to cater to people making big money on Wall Street; after 10 p.m., these places became scenes of self-conscious expense for people who had already spent dawn to dusk together. Places catering for this clientele have a well-defined character: a famous chef coupled with sleek-spare decor, a menu of internationally recognizable dishes, though made locally 'authentic' by naming the particular farms where the food is sourced; the restaurants stocked up on magnums, jeroboams and methuselahs of very expensive wine that could be ordered to celebrate deals. A lawyer from London or investor from Hong Kong can easily spot these places and feel at home – which is the point.

It's no wonder that, as a social island within the physical island of Manhattan, the elite of the new financial-services industry turned inward. This island mentality has affected conduct within the firm, reinforcing the 'silo effect' in dealings with more locally rooted subordinates. The perception of absent, island life, I think, stands behind the complaint of people who lost their jobs in the crash that they were treated with indifference. Being 'always somewhere else' or dwelling inside the cocoon of globalized luxury makes it easier to abdicate responsibility – at least it proved so with my two former Harvard students when I caught up with them again after a round of interviews with the unemployed.

'You're making too much of this,' one of them remarked; 'it's business; they have to expect they can't have it always their way.' Of course, but, perhaps because I am more tender-hearted than these relative youths who make ten times my salary, I asked if other executives felt the same way. They seemed surprised I would ask; 'the Street is such a mess, nobody can do hand-holding.' To their credit, my ex-student investment bankers were trying to hold together their 'boutique' investment firm rather than breaking it up and cashing in. Even so, they spoke in a way quite different from the owner of the shoe factory I'd interviewed forty years before; they were not much concerned about earning authority.

How then would employees in their back-offices reckon the changes described in this chapter? The informal social triangle might appear to belong to a world of work foreign to their own, in old-style banks just as much as in factories. They certainly knew all about short-time and its solvent effects on social relations. Silos and superficial teamwork were facts of daily life for them; they knew weak cooperation first-hand. So, too, they felt a diminished sense of trust, focused for them on losing faith in superiors who lacked their own technical competence. The crash appeared a litmus test of authority, one which many of their superiors also flunked. This occurred when the leaders failed to defend their own firms, eschewed personal responsibility by blaming other leaders or 'the system' and treated the newly unemployed with indifference.

Bitter as these experiences have been for many, however, these back-office workers do not speak the language of victimhood. There's an American explanation for why not. During the Great Depression of the 1930s, unemployed workers took personal responsibility for events beyond their control. In part they had to; the American safety net for the unemployed was weak then. Yet the American emphasis on personal responsibility continued even after the basics of state-guaranteed security were put in place; as an unemployed manual worker put it to me in the 1970s, 'At the end of the day I have to answer to myself.' This is one version of American individualism, and for this reason many informants are believers in the Tea Party movement, which advocates less government control and more 'answering to myself'.

Yet when people do invoke the virtues of self-reliance, it is like repeating a mantra by rote while thinking about something else. Economically, the unemployed may well be feeling superfluous – the sentiment would come to anyone emailing résumés he or she knows are likely to remain unread. But even for those who have recovered quickly from the crisis, the crash is not something they are likely to forget. The front-office may want to get back as quickly as possible to the old regime, to business as usual; lower down the institutional ladder, the various views people conveyed add up to a judgement that something was missing in their lives during the long boom, something connective and bonding at work; to use the Chinese standard, *guanxi* was missing.

The ethnography of the social triangle shows both a connection to and a difference from the early history of civility. The relation is that civility then, and now, has meant paying serious attention to other people. The difference is that politeness was then the crux of early forms of civility, whereas today good manners alone do not define civility; rather than calculated tentativeness at the diplomatic table or well-turned ironies in a salon, modern forms of civility can encompass rhythmic explosions of rage, can eschew easy friendliness and the superficial courtesies of teamwork. Above all, our ancestors sought to codify politeness almost the moment they began to practise it, whereas now civility is more informal in character; people tend not to be self-conscious of its codes. Whether codified or informal, ritual is what makes civility work; outward-looking behaviour is repeated so that it becomes ingrained as a habit. Short-term time is the solvent of civility. For this reason, finance capitalism has tended toward incivility; its elite has benefited from the short-term but more ordinary workers have not.

6

The Uncooperative Self

The Psychology of Withdrawal

We've looked so far at two forces weakening cooperation: structural inequality and new forms of labour. These social forces have psychological consequences. A distinctive character type is emerging in modern society, the person who can't manage demanding, complex forms of social engagement, and so withdraws. He or she loses the desire to cooperate with others. This person becomes an 'uncooperative self'.

The uncooperative self occupies a middle ground between psyche and society. One way to clarify the middle ground of social psychology lies in making a distinction between personality and character. Let's say you are full of anxiety and fear due to your overbearing parents, your early, repeated rejections in love, etc. etc.; you carry this inner weight inside you whatever you do and wherever you go in adult life; it's your personality. But full of anxiety and fear as you are, if pitched into a fight in the army or at a political demo, you surprise others, and yourself, by acting courageously; you've risen to the occasion, an occasion not of your own making or desiring. You've then displayed character, your psyche rising to difficult occasions. The 'uncooperative self' names a condition in which you withdraw from such challenges.

ANXIETY

The greatest of mid-twentieth-century sociologists, C. Wright Mills (1916–62), thought about character in this way. His study, written with Hans Gerth, *Character and Social Structure*, argues that anxiety is character-forming.[1] In his view, social actors try both to adapt to and to distance themselves from the roles allotted them by society. People develop inner strength by dealing with anxiety bred by circumstances not of their own making.

Mills's view was based on a great dilemma in his time. He pondered the behaviour of ordinary Germans during the Nazi era and ordinary Russians oppressed by Stalin's terror. Most of the denizens of totalitarian states did not resist, but nor did all succumb emotionally; a few became ambivalent about the behaviour imposed upon them. Like Winston Smith in George Orwell's novel *Nineteen Eighty-four*, they became increasingly disillusioned yet, unlike Winston Smith, did not take the further step of exposing themselves to danger. Not everyone can be a hero, but unease should still not be slighted; anxiety about their own behaviour at least keeps people alive to the prospect of change. Mills enlarged upon this condition to frame his own version of the sociologist's jargon-term 'role anxiety', a condition in which people both play their allotted roles and doubt them. Mills's idea of such anxiety contrasts sharply with that of Søren Kierkegaard, who believed that anxiety is bred out of the 'dizziness of freedom'.[2] Mills thought anxiety expressed alertness to, passed judgement on, the roles a person is obliged to perform; anxiety was in these ways character-forming.

C. Wright Mills is sometimes thought to celebrate the 'Age of Anxiety', as W. H. Auden called the mid-twentieth century. Today his views remain important in furnishing a yardstick for measuring, by contrast, the diminishment of character. This occurs when anxiety about playing a role disappears. That's the story of the uncooperative self; in this diminished condition, people feel little ambivalence, little inner unease, about behaving uncooperatively.

What signs do people give that they are feeling anxious? Heart palpitations, shortness of breath and nausea are bodily signs; a gene called PLXNA2 has been named a candidate for causing states of physical anxiety. Cognitive dissonance expresses mental anxiety; it occurs when people keep uneasily in their heads contrary views, or when, as in the religious cults studied by the psychologist Leon Festinger, people both believe the world will come to an end on a particular day, and somehow don't believe it; they anxiously hold on to their old beliefs, knowing them false.[3] Pigeons and mammals can suffer cognitive dissonance, fretting in their cages when they are trained in contradictory ways to get food.

In social life, anxiety can be managed through wearing a mask: you don't show what you feel. One way to do so was described in Chapter 1, in Georg Simmel's account of the social mask people wear in cities full of street life. The richness of what's happening and who is in the street prompts urbanites to appear cool and impassive outside, while seething with stimulation inside. This is an all-important tool of character.

Oppressive politics, too, requires masking. At the height of the Stalinist era, for instance, in 1948, the journal *Sem'ya i Shkola* (Family and School) proclaimed: 'The socialist regime liquidated the tragedy of loneliness from which men of the capitalist world suffer.'[4] 'Liquidated' is the key word here; the regime had murdered tens of millions of people who didn't fit into the collective scheme. How to defend against liquidation? The mask is one tool. A Soviet exile once remarked of his behaviour in meetings: 'You can express with your eyes a devoted attention which in reality you are not feeling . . . it is much more difficult to govern the expression of your mouth . . . that is why [I took up] smoking a heavy pipe . . . through the heaviness of the pipe the lips are deformed and cannot react spontaneously.'[5] This remark expresses exactly what Mills meant by doubleness.

The need for a protective mask is hardly confined to totalitarian societies. A half-century ago, in his studies of factory life, Reinhard Bendix probed in depth the old idea that the assembly line offers little stimulation; unlike the factories and shops in Boston, the West Coast industrial establishments he studied were huge, foremen ruled in cubicles removed from the assembly line, white-collar employees were further removed into separate buildings, operations were conducted strictly according to time-management principles first laid down by Frederick Taylor for the Ford Motor Company; under these conditions, it was hard for informal social triangles to take shape. Bendix found that workers caught in the vice compensated in their heads by imagining what more stimulating work should be, but kept these thoughts to themselves, for fear of being labelled or punished as 'troublemakers'. After work, they did share ideas over a beer, but at work they donned the mask; they dwelled in the double state.[6]

Mills hadn't much patience with academic psychology. He lived in a time when Freudian psychology, in particular, was hardening into an orthodoxy in America. He attributed these protective masks to social conditions in the city, in the state or in industry; so, too, social masks of another sort. The 'deep acting' Gideon Kunda remarks in teamwork would, I think, be sufficiently explained to Mills by the framing of short-term time in the modern office. But we want now to add more emotional depth to this sociological account. Psychology has something to reveal, in particular, about dealing with social anxiety in a different way than feeling and masking it. Psychology can illuminate the desire to withdraw, to isolate oneself, and so diminish anxieties about one's place in the world.

WITHDRAWAL

The word 'withdrawal' implies a decision a person takes, as in Robert Putnam's image of people hibernating from those who differ ethnically, racially or in sexual orientation. We need to clarify the various words for living in a withdrawn state: solitude, isolation, loneliness. The sociologist Eric Klinenberg has sought to give solitude a distinctive meaning of its own.[7] He finds that about a third of the adult population in big, dense cities such as Paris, London and New York live alone. Sometimes such solitude is chosen, other times not; yet it's hard, he argues, to characterize people's feelings about solitude; sometimes they suffer from living alone, something they embrace it. Divorce is a compelling example: the person who has chosen to abandon a mate may discover, in solitude, that he or she has made a big mistake, while the abandoned mate can discover, to his or her surprise, that an intolerable intimate burden has been lifted off the shoulders.

No more is solitude's kin, isolation, always a wound. While many prisoners who suffer involuntary solitary confinement think it worse than physical torture, Carthusian monks who choose isolation in their silent cells impose that suffering on themselves for the sake of enlarging their spiritual horizons. In secular life, the walks Jean-Jacques Rousseau took, as described in *Reveries of a Solitary Walker* (1778), provide something of the same illumination. Rousseau preferred to walk alone, and sought to avoid conversations with any friends he might meet; solitude, he says, made him whole. Loneliness itself hurts, but Jean-Paul Sartre believed that all humans need to experience its pain; loneliness of the sort Sartre, in *Being and Nothingness*, called 'epistemic loneliness' makes us aware of our limited place in the world.[8] This existential necessity is what Samuel Beckett conveys in plays like *Waiting for Godot*: absence is a basic ingredient of the human condition.

The withdrawals we are concerned with, voluntary withdrawals whose purpose is to reduce anxiety, don't have that existential or spiritual reach; they don't, indeed, arouse feelings of loneliness or lack. When the purpose is just to relieve anxiety in dealings with others, these withdrawals produce, instead of illumination, a kind of blindness. There are two psychological ingredients of this blindness: narcissism and complacency.

Narcissism

Narcissism may seem just a synonym for selfishness, but psychoanalysis long ago made it a more complex matter. When Freud published his foundational essay on narcissism in 1914, he imagined it to be an unbounded libidinal drive, seeking sexual satisfaction without restraint. Later, he reformulated his idea of narcissism, believing it to be a 'mirror state' in which the person sees only him- or herself reflected, as in a mirror, when dealing with others.[9] The psychoanalyst puts a bitter spin on identification, that key ingredient of sympathy discussed at the beginning of this book. The spin lies in whether we identify with others in their particular circumstances and sufferings, or with others as though everyone is like ourselves; the first is a window, the second a mirror. Freud detected the 'mirror state' internally in those patients who instantly associated new events in adulthood with familiar childhood traumas; for these patients, nothing truly new ever seemed to happen in their lives, the present always mirrored the past.

Freud's work on narcissism was further refined after the Second World War. To the mirror state, Heinz Kohut introduced in psychoanalysis the concept of the 'grandiose self'. 'Me' fills all the space of reality. One way such grandiosity is expressed lies in needing to feel constantly in control; in Kohut's words, the emphasis falls on 'the control which [a person] expects over his own body and feelings [rather] than the grown-up's experience of others ...' People subjected to this grandiosity indeed 'feel oppressed and enslaved' by the needs of others.[10] The result, in the view of another psychoanalyst of Kohut's era, Otto Kernberg, is that action itself is devalued; 'What am I doing?' is replaced by 'What am I feeling?'[11]

A person dwelling in this self-absorbed state is going to feel anxiety when reality intrudes, a threatened loss of self rather than an enrichment of self. Anxiety is reduced by restoring feelings of being in control and so reducing anxiety. When this inner psychological transaction occurs, social consequences follow, the most notable being that social cooperation diminishes.

Military life shows one way this happens. The sociologist Morris Janowitz has described as 'cowboy warriors' those soldiers who on the battlefield want to cover themselves in glory, in their own eyes, even at the expense of helping other soldiers, their feats of derring-do putting others at risk.[12] Janowitz says the cowboy warrior is performing for himself; the psychoanalyst would say he's made fighting into a mirror state. The narcissist is a dangerous figure on the battleground where, to survive, soldiers need to focus on helping out one another; in the nineteenth century, the German military strategist Karl von Clausewitz, all too familiar with self-serving heroics, advised commanders to punish such 'adventurers' as severely as deserters. Elevated in the chain of command, the cowboy warrior appears in Stanley Kubrick's film *Dr Strangelove* (1964) as General Jack D. Ripper, whose real-life counterpart in the Vietnam War was General William Westmoreland; in Joseph Heller's novel *Catch-22* a twist is added: the cowboy warriors in the Second World War are aware of their buddies when showing off, and want to make more prudent soldiers feel small – an invidious comparison. The difference between art and life is that the cowboy warriors in *Dr Strangelove* and *Catch-22* are very funny; on the real battlefield, they are just terrifying.

Heroic exploit is a universal feature of all cultures, and usually it has a morally demonstrative character: this is what courage looks like. So too is the raw competitive element that is nearly universal in heroism; on the Homeric field of battle, for instance, warriors on the same side competed to show their bravery. But heroism of a morally demonstrative sort has an unselfconscious character. Narcissism kicks in when the warrior looks in the mirror when fighting, seeing the fact of his or her own bravery.

But surely, it might be objected, warfare is the most anxiety-laden of all experiences? The psychiatrist Robert J. Lifton has pondered that issue in studies of soldiers since the time of the Vietnam War.[13] What he calls 'numbing' enables soldiers to deal with stress. The soldier in the midst of a fight goes numb, suppressing anything that distracts from the fight; it masks his inner feelings. When soldiers return home, the suppression lifts, fears or remorse kick in; post-traumatic stress ensues. In Lifton's research, one group seems relatively immune from this retrospective reckoning: the cowboy warrior. Narcissism provides, he says, so protective a carapace that the cowboy soldier in retrospect sees nothing to regret. This interpretation may seem one-dimensional, but it is borne out in those war-crimes trials where a certain kind of soldier can't understand why he is in the dock; he doesn't subscribe emotionally to the just-following-orders defence; what he remembers of war, Lifton says, is its excitement.

Socialist kitsch has often borrowed from the battlefield, for instance by mass-manufacturing posters of Eugène Delacroix's great painting *Liberty Leading the People,* made during the Revolution of 1830. This kind of kitsch, though, does not fall within the scope of narcissistic emotion. A nearer connection might be to the cowboy warriors of the stock market, indifferent to the larger consequences of their exploits, as became evident in the crash of 2008.

Chapter 2 was preoccupied with the issue of how a balance can be struck between cooperation and competition. In warfare, the balance depends on intimate cooperation within a squadron or a platoon; similarly, studies of military life consistently show that troops are more willing to sacrifice their own lives for the sake of their immediate comrades than for an ideology.[14] This intimate cooperative bond is the warrior's code of honour. On Wall Street, self-sacrifice of this sort certainly went missing during the crash; more, as we've seen, executives renounced their responsibility – 'we are all victims' – without compunction; nothing like an officer's code of honour applied. Lift-on's version of narcissism as a protective carapace numbing the actor may provide the psychological depth necessary to explain their behaviour.

Warfare has one thing further to reveal about narcissism. At the dawn of the Great Unsettling, the social code of the early modern era began to shift by emphasizing civility in place of chivalry. This emphasis fell particularly on replacing the warrior code of chivalry with more peaceable social bonds. To make this shift, a certain kind of character had to come to the fore, self-ironic rather than aggressive, indirect rather than aggressive, preferring the subjective, a character type formed around self-restraint. Civility of this sort was a counter to nar-cissism. But a kindred value resides in military honour itself; indeed, survival of the group depends on restraint of the grandiose self.

Narcissism, then, is one ingredient prompting withdrawal from other people. But it is usually mixed with another: complacency about one's position in the world.

Complacency

Complacency seems a straightforward matter: everything seems fine just as it is. Complacency motivates Dr Pangloss in Voltaire's *Candide*, who famously believes that 'all is for the best in the best of all possible worlds'. There's an important difference, though, between feeling secure and feeling complacent. When we feel inwardly secure, we can become willing to experiment, to unleash curiosity; such a feeling of inner security in oneself appeared among the gentlemen-amateurs of the early modern era described by Steven Shapin. The sociologist Anthony Giddens speaks of 'ontological security' as the expectation a person has that there will be continuity in his or her life whatever its ups and downs, that experiences will be threaded together.[15] Compla-cency is not outward-looking, nor is it ontological in Giddens's sense. Rather, it is a cousin to narcissism in expecting experience to conform to a pattern already familiar to oneself; experience seems to repeat routinely rather than evolve. That difference between security and complacency has been drawn out philosophically by Martin Heidegger; he contrasts being in the world, engaged with its shifts and ruptures, to a disengaged state of being frozen in time.[16]

Complacency had no place in the world-view of the Great Unsettling. Religion of Martin Luther's sort, technology of the sextant-maker's sort, diplomacy of Chapuys's sort, all sought to make people less complacent about themselves and their surroundings. Today, however, new forces are rooting complacency in everyday life, forces our ancestors could not foresee. This new formation of complacency turns on individualism. When complacency is married to individualism, cooperation withers.

Our guide to all this must be Alexis de Tocqueville (1805-59), who first coined the term 'individualism' in its modern sense. The son of conservative country aristocrats, Tocqueville faced a crisis in 1830 when the reactionary regime then ruling France was overthrown for a few months by revolutionaries, in whose wake a more politically moderate, economically minded king came to power. Most of Tocqueville's class retreated to their estates or withdrew from public life, making an *émigration intérieure*; the young Tocqueville chose instead to travel to America in 1831 with his friend Gustave de Beaumont, ostensibly to study prison conditions. In fact, Tocqueville was seeking hints in America for what European culture might look like in the future.

The result was the first volume of *Democracy in America*, published in 1835. It seems to be not at all about individualism, rather about 'equality of condition', by which Tocqueville meant to trace the American consequences of the proposition that all men and women are born equal, consequences for politics mostly, but also in the ways people live. Tocqueville thought the new doctrine was just, because it gave all people freedom, but he worried about the tyranny of the majority, the mass actively oppressing minorities and demanding conformity. The demand for conformity he traced to society rather than to politics; Raymond Aron, Tocqueville's great modern interpreter, thinks that Tocqueville is the prophet of mass culture.[17] Social mores seemed to Tocqueville to become equal in the sense of homogeneous, even as material inequalities might remain or increase; put in today's terms, the janitor and the business executive will share a common culture of consumer desires, of family or community life. To Tocqueville, America appeared a society governed by conformity; he wrote to his friend John Stuart Mill that American society aroused deep anger at people who don't fit in.

When Tocqueville came to publish the second volume of *Democracy in America*, in 1840, he shifted gears. Now he was more concerned about withdrawal from civic participation than about pressures on misfits to conform, or in politics on suppressing minority opinion. Tocqueville coined the word 'individualism' to name the condition of a withdrawn person. Here, in his evocative prose, is what individualism feels like:

> Each person, withdrawn into himself, behaves as though he is a stranger to the destiny of all the others. His children and his good friends constitute for him the whole of the human species. As for his transactions with his fellow citizens, he may mix among them, but he sees them not; he touches them, but does not feel them; he exists only in himself and for himself alone. And if on these terms there remains in his mind a sense of family, there no longer remains a sense of society.

This individualized withdrawal seems the perfect recipe for complacency: you take for granted people like yourself and simply don't care about those who aren't like you; more, whatever their problems are, it's their problem. Individualism and indifference become twins.

In writing his second volume Tocqueville did not forget the first; he had to connect individualism and equality. To do so, he developed the idea modern social science now calls 'status anxiety'. Tocqueville's individual suffers from status anxiety whenever he or she becomes uneasy that others do not share his or her tastes, as consumers, in family life or in public behaviour. By being different they seem to be putting on airs, or somehow – you can't explain how – putting you down. You perceive an insult: 'different' becomes translated into better or worse, superior or inferior, a matter of invidious comparison. The celebration of equality, for Tocqueville, is really anxiety about inequality. Now, as then, *ressentiment* expresses the conversion of difference into inequality. Though *ressentiment* knows no national boundaries, there's certainly much of it now in American life, as when people who call themselves ordinary, God-fearing Americans accuse those who beg to differ of being elitists.

Yet rather than make the effort to stamp them out or suppress them – which is an impulse of the tyrannical majority – individualism drives the person who feels affronted even further within him- or herself, seeking a comfort-zone; he or she seeks to 'hibernate'. Why withdraw rather than repress? Why did Tocqueville write a second volume?

The answer in his own time had to do with France rather than America. The new regime of Louis-Philippe was not as repressive as the old; everything was allowed in private life so long as a person didn't rock the boat politically; in return, Frenchmen – whom we Anglo-Saxons tend to think so contentious – turned inward, absorbed in their private affairs, more disengaged from public life than noisily disgusted by it. Tocqueville took this as a first sign of individualism in Europe, the individual who 'exists only in himself and for himself alone'.

There's another sort of answer we could give now, one focused on the impulse to withdraw. For a long time, modern psychology has coupled disengagement and dissociation; psychoanalysts like Kohut represent one line of work, social psychiatrists like Lifton another. Behavioural psychologists have sought to lift the idea of numbing out of Lifton's consulting room and study it in the laboratory. They've probed, for instance, what is called the 'Csikszentmihalyi diagram': this diagram is a pie-shaped picture of the links between anxiety, worry, apathy, boredom, relaxation, control, flow and arousal.[18] Anxiety-reduction occurs through the neutralization of stimulation: apathy, boredom and relaxation can all neutralize arousal.

Boredom in particular plays a powerful role in relieving anxiety; animals as well as human beings will seek it out. Researchers have constructed a 'boredom proneness scale' to indicate degrees to which humans and other animals are attracted to boredom.[19] The idea behind this may seem counter-intuitive, though shouldn't be. A man eating his thousandth industrial hamburger can't be much excited by the taste, but, because it's familiar, it's comforting. It's the same for the couch potato, soothed when half-watching programmes that don't really hold his attention. Both will score high on the 'boredom proneness scale'; they want familiarity which holds no surprises. Boredom differs from apathy in being more selective; the apathy of a clinically depressed person is a global, total disengagement, while boredom attaches to particular activities. Mihaly Csikszentmihalyi himself thinks, perhaps oddly, of boredom as entailing a certain level of skill; you have to become adept in filtering out disturbances. Rather than depressing, then, as the involuntary boredom of an assembly line is, boredom of this voluntary sort gives the comforting reassurance of low stimulation. Here, then, is a psychological logic consonant with Tocqueville's idea of the individual who 'may mix among [other people], but . . . sees them not; he touches them, but does not feel them'.

Of course, Tocqueville was writing on a much grander historical and social scale than the laboratory psychologist. He put to his readers the large argument that individualism will grow in modern society as old bonds of tradition and social hierarchy decline. He wasn't alone in arguing along these lines; many conservatives of his parents' and his own generation regretted the breakdown of the ties of the past. But his American travels cured Tocqueville of nostalgia. He became convinced that deference was gone for good, as in the deference that tied workers to masters on country estates like that of his parents. More, he saw in America a counterweight to individualism. This was the voluntary association: the church group, the charitable society, the local sports club. His hope was that since anyone could join, different sorts of people would come to be included and that difference would lose its anxious edge; cooperation in voluntary associations could counter individualism. Tocqueville was one of the first aristocrats in the nineteenth century to appreciate 'associationism', the path that would lead eventually to the settlement house, the cooperative bank and the local credit union. Americans, he thought, were good local organizers, and Europeans could learn something from them about getting organized. Still, his view of voluntarism was limited; unlike later associationists he did not think of countering economic distress or oppression.

What gives voluntary withdrawal its psychological weight, then, is the desire to reduce anxiety, particularly the anxiety of addressing needs other than one's own. Narcissism is one way to reduce such anxiety, complacency is another. In everyday language, the first is a matter of vanity, the second of indifference. Both psychological forces deform character, understood as a matter of acting responsibly toward others, or submitting to a demanding code of honour. Can cooperation weigh heavier on the scale? That's the question before us now as it was for Tocqueville nearly two hundred years ago.

LIGHTWEIGHT, WEAK COOPERATION

The evidence assembled in Part Two of this book suggests that cooperation does not weigh heavily today against individualism; institutional forces tip the scales. Inequality affects children's lives once they enter school. The internal distribution of wealth in a society, as described in the Unicef report, creates different sorts of adult–child relations in different social classes. Contrasts in behaviour among children begin to appear as a result; children in relatively egalitarian societies are more likely to trust in one another and to cooperate; children in societies marked by great disparities are more likely to deal with others as adversaries.

We wanted to know how children absorb these imposed inequalities inside themselves. The evidence is complicated, as Juliet Schor cautions; materialist they may be, but children do not invariably draw invidious comparisons with others based on their possessions. Still, inequality is absorbed in the ways children and adolescents buy and use technology in social networks. By the age of eight or nine, children know they are not all alike in social status, and this awareness makes a difference in their experience of cooperation. Research on the social lives of children points to something Tocqueville got wrong. This is his view that modern society is tending towards social and cultural homogenization, a view he framed as an 'equality of condition' in America that would spread to Europe. Early in their development, American youngsters learn that shared values have different consequences, depending on a child's circumstances.

We took another tack in studying adults at work. Now we sought to see how cooperation is connected to experiences of trust and authority. These connections can be made informally, overcoming to some extent the formal inequalities and isolation between people in the workplace. After the Second World War, American workers were well situated to create informal social triangles of this sort. The bonding experiences of the war and the stability of factory life made it possible for people to make connections between earned authority, leap-of-faith trust and cooperation when operations went wrong in the workplace.

Short-term time transformed these experiences in the workplace, due to a new figuration of global investment and shareholder value. Wall Street at mid-century shared some of the same social characteristics as factories, but then became the epitome of short-term time. It produced a lightweight form of cooperation, embodied in teamwork; leap-of-faith trust diminished as the Wall Street back-office workers became more technically competent than executives in the front-office; during the financial collapse on Wall Street, these executives eschewed authority rather than tried to earn it. Since Tocqueville largely neglected the subject of work, and indeed paid little attention to economics, he could not be a prophet of these changes. Yet his writings do characterize one result. Faced with a weak, lightweight and unreliable social order, people retreat into themselves.

These are the forces which tip the scales in modern society so that withdrawal weighs heavier in people's experience than cooperation. The philosophers Amartya Sen and Martha Nussbaum believe society should enlarge and enrich people's capabilities, most of all their capacity to cooperate; modern society instead diminishes it. Or to put the matter as a Chinese might see it: America and Britain lack *guanxi*. With the exception of the cowboy warrior, the lines between desire and fear, will and submission, are confused in withdrawal behaviour. That confusion, too, is part of the disminishment of character.

As a coda to the account I've given of the social psychology of withdrawal, I want to consider, briefly, a counter-case: a kind of withdrawal which does not aim to decrease anxiety, but rather embraces it. This is obsession.

OBSESSION

In exploring the consequences of the Protestant Reformation on work and economic life, the sociologist Max Weber (1864–1920) became, without intending it, a great analyst of obsession. The famous 'work ethic' Weber described is all about the obsession to 'prove oneself' through one's work. Used casually, the 'work ethic' just means the desire for success. Weber gave it a different meaning, one linked to his own travels in America, in 1904, the year he published *The Protestant Ethic and the Spirit of Capitalism*. He went at the height of the Gilded Age, when the Vanderbilts had dinners for seventy served by seventy powdered footmen. Ostentatious consumption of the Vanderbilt sort did not seem to Weber to explain what drives a man or woman to sacrifice family life, hobbies, relaxation with friends, or civic life, for work; love of luxury can't explain why every day might feel like a personal test. Weber could have asked just these same questions about many of the executives on Wall Street a century later.

To explain the self-denying obsession with work, Weber went back to its Reformation roots, particularly to Puritanism of the austere Calvinist sort. John Calvin was obsessed by theological questions of who is elect, of who will be saved in the afterlife rather than condemned to Hell. This question, Weber asserted, travelled in the course of time from theology to secular labour: the workaholic is also trying to prove him- or herself worthy. But a further ingredient is necessary: ascetic solitude. 'Christian asceticism,' he wrote in a famous passage,

> at first fleeing from the world into solitude, had already ruled the world which it had renounced from the monastery and through the Church. But it had, on the whole, left the naturally spontaneous character of daily life in the world untouched. Now it strode into the marketplace of life, slammed the door of the monastery behind it, and undertook to penetrate just that daily routine of life with its methodicalness, to fashion it into a life in the world, but neither of nor for this world.[20]

Thus the theme of withdrawal from social pleasures appears, no longer as an escape from worldly sinfulness, but now as an intensification of anxiety about self-worth. Individuals are driving themselves because they are competing against themselves. Just as you are, you aren't good enough; you strive constantly to prove yourself by success, but no achievement ever feels like solid proof of adequacy. Invidious comparison is turned against the self. But rather than do the reasonable thing and lighten up, you can't, you are always hungry, hoping that sometime, somehow, you will feel satisfied, but you never do. It's this quality of obsession that Weber traces back to its Reformation source, to the unanswerable question: will I be saved?

A century of research has shown that many of Weber's historical facts are a mess. In a study of Dutch society in the sixteenth and seventeenth centuries, *The Embarrassment of Riches*, Simon Schama has shown, for instance, that those hard-working burghers behaved more like sensualists than ascetics, loving the everyday things they could buy; Albert Hirschman found that early capitalists considered their labours a calming and peaceful activity rather than requiring inner struggle; the historian R. H. Tawney cast doubt on the very connection between religion and capitalism.[21] Weber has erred by projecting the 'driven man' of the present onto the past.

Weber has been rescued and, I think, trivialized by students of consumer behaviour who draw upon his concept of worldly asceticism. The research points to the undoubted fact that young consumers are inculcated into thinking more about what they lack than in enjoying what they own. Similarly, adult consuming passions focus on anticipation, on what a product promises; the delivery and subsequent use is a short-lived pleasure; the adult tires of the object, and begins again the quest for something new, unpossessed as yet, which promises real fulfilment. What this kind of research doesn't get at is the reasons for asceticism based on self-competition.

What we now know about obsession, as an emotion, is that it can have three elements. The first is repetition compulsion, the impulse to do something again and again, even though the act gets nowhere; unlike rehearsing music, in which hand-behaviour changes as it is repeated, a repetition compulsion is static. Weber's 'driven man' pursues deals, piles up cash, time after time without feeling he is really achieving anything. That sentiment only makes sense if, secondly, what psychology now calls perfectionism drives the individual. There is an ideal state which is the only reality; halfway measures, partial victories, never feel good enough; what the psychoanalyst Roy Schaeffer once called the 'crystal-clear image of who one should be' teases people, an ideal to which the mess of actual lived experience never measures up. Thirdly, 'the driven man' suffers from ontological insecurity. Ontological insecurity is a failure of trust in everyday experience. Ordinary life is experienced as a minefield. Encountering new people, the person suffering ontological insecurity is likely to focus on the threats they pose, the injuries they might inflict, becoming obsessed by their power to hurt.

This third element is what I think Weber meant in part by describing the driven man as not 'at home in the world', daily life seeming denuded of pleasure and filled with threat. Relentless hard work will seem a weapon to ward off the dangers posed by others; you withdraw into yourself. The work ethic diminishes the desire to cooperate with others, especially others you do not know; they appear, *avant la lettre*, hostile presences bent on doing you harm.

I recognize that these psychological accounts of obsession can also trivialize the titanic struggle against oneself, the metaphysical anxiety, which gives Weber's essay its enduring power. Perhaps Weber is best met on his own grounds in the last book of the American writer Lionel Trilling, *Sincerity and Authenticity*.[22] Trilling thinks of sincerity as a report made to others about oneself; the report, to be good, has to be precise and clear. Authenticity is not concerned with making oneself precise and clear; instead, it is an inner search to find out what one 'really' feels, and contains a strong narcissistic trace. But this search is elusive; one never arrives at really knowing one's authentic feelings. Authenticity of the sort Trilling criticizes is perhaps best represented in the social sciences by the 'Maslow paradigm', named after the social psychologist Abraham Maslow, who devoted a lifetime to developing the idea of 'self-actualization'. Trilling's view was that, unhinged from other people, other voices, the search for authenticity becomes self-defeating. This was precisely Max Weber's view of the Protestant Ethic: it turns people inwards in an impossible quest. Other people have no place in the obsessional struggle to prove oneself; at most they count as instruments, as tools to be used. Cooperation with others will certainly not salve inner doubts, it will have no value in itself.

Part Two has explored the weakening of cooperation in three realms, those of childhood inequalities, adult labour and the cultural formation of the self. This loss is not fatal, however; it can be repaired. In the next part of this study we explore how to strengthen skilled, complex cooperation.

PART THREE

Cooperation Strengthened

7

The Workshop

Making and Repairing

The hope embodied in the Hampton and Tuskegee Institutes was that practising technical skills together could strengthen the ex-slaves' social bonds. This chapter investigates that hope. I will try to show how physical labour can instil dialogical social behaviour.

Technical skills come in two basic forms: making and repairing things. Making may seem the more creative activity, repair appearing lesser, after-the-fact work. In truth, the differences between the two are not so great. The creative writer usually has to edit, repairing earlier drafts in later ones; an electrician sometimes discovers, in fixing a broken machine, new ideas about what the machine should be.

Craftsmen who become good at making things develop physical skills which apply to social life. The process happens in the craftsmen's body; social-science jargon makes this link between the physical and the social by using the ugly word 'embodiment'. In this chapter, we will look at three of these embodiments: how the rhythms of physical labour become embodied in ritual; how physical gestures give life to informal social relations; how the artisan's work with physical resistance illuminates the challenge of dealing with social resistances and differences. Couched in the jargon of 'embodiment', these links must seem abstract; I'll try make them concrete.

The theme of repair has implications outside the workshop, just because modern society is now in urgent need of repair. But repair work is a complicated matter; there are conflicting ways for fixing broken things, and these strategies lead in conflicting social directions. If repair in the workshop is to serve as any sort of guide to change, we need, again, to delve into the concrete work repairmen do.

Though we want to learn what physical work might suggest about

strengthening social bonds, we don't want to commit the error of imagining that people who are good at this kind of labour necessarily
become good at social life. Physical skills of making and repairing do
no more or less than provide insight into social relations. I think it fair
to say that the reformers who gathered in Paris a century ago for the
Universal Exposition, all of whom wanted to make the lives of everyday workers better, were not much attuned to how work actually
works; they just wanted to bring large social values like justice and
fairness into the workplace. The process of reform can be reversed, by
applying experiences inside the workshop to society.

RHYTHM AND RITUAL

Let's imagine that a scalpel lay among the objects on the table in Holbein's *The Ambassadors*. The surgeon's scalpel was just coming into
its own during the early sixteenth century; its metallic composition
was resolved but the tool's form was variable and the use of it not
well understood. How would the barber who doubled as a surgeon go
about improving his hand skills?

There is a rhythm which governs the development of human skills.
The first stage involves ingraining a habit. The barber-surgeon learns
to pick up the scalpel knife without having to think each time, 'grip the
shank but don't squeeze too hard'; he wants fluency, self-confidence in
using his tool, he wants to take his grip for granted. He achieves this
by repeating the grasping gesture over and over until, without dither-
ing, he feels the grip is firm but not tense.

In a second stage, skill expands by questioning the established
habit. In the case of a hand skill, the mostly instinctively comfortable
grip is the enclosed grasp, one which wraps the fingers around a ball
or rod as much as possible so that the object is secured in the palm.
But the human hand is constructed to perform many other kinds of
grips, for instance by holding an object at the fingertips with the
thumb beneath the object, or just using the four fingers curled in on
the palm with the thumb passive. The barber-surgeon about to cut
into a patient will find the instinctive cupping grasp of the scalpel too
insensitive to break the skin cleanly; this grip slashes, like a sword. He

is going to have to think about this grip to work more sensitively, experimenting with the tips-of-fingers grip and also the angle of the wrist. To improve, he will study his hand consciously.

Once he does so, a third stage ensues; the new skin-cutting grip has to become re-inscribed as a habit of the hand, so that he regains fluency and confidence. A rhythm thus appears: ingraining habit, questioning the habit, re-ingraining a better habit. An important aspect about the barber-surgeon's new hand skill is that it adds to rather than erases the grip he used before. For some deep-body surgical tasks, the rigid grip will still be necessary. It's true that in much physical skill-development we correct moves made before which prove inefficient or tensing, but development is more than getting just one gesture right; we want a quiverful of skills, each particularly suited to performing a particular act.

The 'quiver' is an important image in skill development. Sometimes it's imagined that becoming skilled means finding the one right way to execute a task, that there is a one-to-one match between means and ends. A fuller path of development involves learning to address the same problem in different ways. The full quiver of techniques enables mastery of complex problems; only rarely does one single right way serve all purposes.[1]

The rhythm of building up skill can take a long time to produce results. By one measure, about 10,000 hours are required to develop mastery in playing a sport, performing music or making cabinets; this works out at roughly four hours a day of practice for five or six years. This was the time required for an apprentice in a medieval guild to learn his trade (10,000 hours is too neat a number, but roughly accurate). Just putting in the hours will not ensure that you become a competent soccer player or musician, but if you do have innate talent to begin with, the long-term work builds up the security of your practice. Sometimes you might get a procedure just right the very first time you do it, but the happy accident may not occur the next time. Moreover, you can command a quiverful of skills when you first begin; that too takes time to develop.

The quiver can sometimes be too full, provisioning too many possibilities, too much complexity. In the 1920s the composer Igor Stravinsky subscribed to the doctrine 'simplify, eliminate, clarify', a doctrine rephrased a half century later by Arvo Pärt as 'make it new by making it simple'. Albert Einstein's reply to this impulse was, 'Everything should be made as simple as possible – but not simpler.'[2] Achieving simplicity in art is a highly sophisticated event. There's nothing naively innocent about Stravinsky's *Pulcinella*, for instance; it's full of comment and irony about the simple classical motifs it uses.[3] The listener's perception of simplicity may be art's greatest illusion.

In more prosaic forms of craft-work, 'type-forms', address this problem. The craftsman starts with the model, the type-form, of what cutting out a tumour or making a cabinet should be or look like; the type-form provides a simple point of reference. The barber-surgeon or carpenter then draws on the quiver of skills to give the operation or cabinet a distinctive character in smaller details – the way the surgeon ties sutures, the varnishes used by the cabinet-maker – stamping something of him- or herself on the procedure or object. In dealing with complexity this way, the artisan's technical command also produces individuality.

The rhythm of skill-development becomes a ritual, if practised again and again. Faced with a new problem or challenge, the technician will ingrain a response, then think about it, then re-ingrain the product of that thinking; varied responses will follow the same path, filling the technician's quiver; in time, the technician will learn how to impress his or her individual character within a guiding type-form. Many craftsmen speak casually about the 'rituals of the shop', and these rhythms, I think, stand behind that casual phrase.

Are these rituals within the workshop or inside a laboratory comparable to rituals outside? Do they share anything in common, say, with religious rituals? Religious rituals certainly have to be learned, and the practitioners of any religious ritual have to become fluent in its words and gestures. But it might seem that the self-aware phase of craft skill would be absent in a religious ritual, that self-consciousness impeding belief. During the Reformation, conscious consideration of established rites, and self-consciousness about performing them, intruded. The result of reflection could indeed diminish formal ritual, as among Quakers, but not always; other Protestant sects re-formatted rather than abandoned baptism.

During the Great Unsettling in the sixteenth century, the issue of skill in performing a ritual became contentious. The High Middle

Ages had refined religious ritual so that only the most skilled professionals were truly in command of it, as in the evolution of the ritual
of the Eucharist. Luther rejected ritual based on special skill, which is
why he translated the Bible into the language parishioners spoke and
simplified hymns so that anyone could sing them. To this great
reformer, faith is not a craft.

It might be simple to connect workshop ritual to secular social practices. Certainly this link applied to the practices within diplomacy during the sixteenth century; as the profession of diplomacy progressed,
young diplomats were schooled in resident embassies to behave fluently in public, employing both formal speech and informal talk in
dealing with foreigners; both formalized speech and informal diplomatic chit-chat took on the character of rituals, recognized by others
as established and quite specialized forms of behaviour. Resident
ambassadors tutored their young protégés in how to perform these
rituals well; behind closed doors, the performers were subject to conscious scrutiny. The two young envoys in Holbein's painting, sent to
deal with the crisis over Henry VIII's divorce, were not particularly
skilful; the retinue attached permanently to the resident ambassador
were more so, though not even these pros were a match for Henry's
voracious sexual desires.

If professionals, these diplomats were still an elite; if a kind of social
workshop, the embassy seems, as an institution, far removed from the
street. So we want to frame the issue of secular, skilled, social rituals
more broadly.

One way to do so lies in the very idea of the social 'role'. The sociologist Erving Goffman explored how people usually learn roles at
home and work, as well as in the special settings of mental institutions
or prisons.[4] The 'presentation of self in everyday life', as Goffman
calls it, is in fact a work in progress. It begins when people's adjustments
to one another become ingrained habits. Social actors can then suffer
from 'role dissonance' if circumstances change and old roles prove
inadequate. Role dissonance arises, for instance, between parents and
children in the wake of a divorce; single parents are now under the
gun to contrive new, easy ways of playing with, educating and talking
to children. To adapt, they have to think explicitly about their exam-
ination of behaviour; the aim, though, is to alter or expand roles so

that they can be practised fluently and unselfconsciously again. If they achieve this, Goffman says, people become more 'expert' in everyday life; more, they have organized bits of behaviour into a ritualized form.

A fine-grained study of such rituals appears in the remarkable researches done by Michel de Certeau and his colleagues in Lyons, particularly in the Croix-Rousse neighbourhood. Because the community is so poor, its resources wax and wane; housing and schools are sometimes repaired, sometimes left to decay; people become bricoleurs of work, patching together whatever jobs they can; they are in constant jeopardy. Their goal is to inscribe order through seemingly small rituals so that people can get along as harmoniously as possible. To do so, they have to become adept in practising rituals, in everything from how to manage eye-contact with strangers on the street to how to behave with propriety in dating an immigrant. Just because the community is so unstable, de Certeau found that people are obliged continually to re-format their shared behaviour. As in a divorce, at these testing moments people in Croix-Rousse scrutinize their shared habits, discussing them together, so that 'the logic of unselfconscious thought [can] be taken seriously'.[5] Since the sheer fact of order is important for them, shared rituals hold this very poor community together; necessity drives them to become 'experts' of the street.

There's nothing surprising about the fact that people alter rituals. As described in Chapter 3, religious rites like Communion have been a centuries-long work in progress, but since these rites seem to emanate from a divine source, people are not focused on themselves as makers or revisers. In secular rituals, self-conscious pauses for reflection come forward; these questioning pauses do not spoil the experience; they can be embraced if people feel they are adapting, expanding and improving their behaviour. As in the workshop, so in the family or on the street, the rhythm of skill development makes this possible.

INFORMAL GESTURES

To explain the embodiment of informality in physical gestures, I'm first going to write a dense paragraph:

Like ritual, the social triangle is a social relationship people make. In the craftsman's workshop, this three-sided relation is often experienced physically, non-verbally; bodily gestures take the place of words in establishing authority, trust and cooperation. Skills like muscular control are required to make bodily gestures communicate, but gesture matters socially for another reason as well: physical gesture makes social relationships feel informal. Visceral feelings are also aroused when we gesture, informally, with words.

Let's unpack this paragraph:

A London stringed-instrument shop (the clinic for my temperamental cello) has moved to new quarters, the new shop thoughtfully laid out by a young architect. She's decided just where each of the various activities in the shop should occur, where each of the tools should be placed, from the cutting machines and big clamps down to small boxes and holders needed for each job. She's also dealt with glue and varnish smells – the shop uses old-fashioned recipes which stink – using a clever set of overhead fans. On opening day, all seems clean and crisp; I find the three male and two female luthiers standing like soldiers on parade by their benches.

Eight months later it all looks different. Few of the tools are now in their assigned boxes; the cutting machines have been yanked into different positions; the fans have been switched off (evidently they hummed in B-flat, a jarring note for people professionally attuned to the pivot tone of A-natural). The shop is still fairly clean but no longer schematically ordered. Still, the five luthiers move agilely in the jumbled space, weaving and ducking, sometimes executing swivels like dancers around the cutting saw now shoved into the centre. These changes have happened in bits and pieces, from month to month, as people adapted the clear architectural design to their more complicated bodily gestures at work.

The bedding-in process here occurs in many working spaces, and if the physical environment is flexible it's easy. Even in rigidly defined work spaces people will bed-in through making smaller gestures, as in a frown which sends the warning 'This is my space' or a smile which invites 'Come in'. Gestures come from sounds as well as faces; in this workshop, for example, a luthier at the cutting table sensed both by the rustle of sound and out of the corner of her eye that someone was next to or behind her; she drew in her rump while continuing to cut.

Gestures of movement, facial expression and sound endow the social triangle with sensate life; in the stringed-instrument shop earned authority, leap-of-faith trust and cooperation under duress translated into physical experiences. The five luthiers pride themselves on their competence in the most demanding of jobs, cutting and shaping the plates which form the front and back of stringed instruments; they've all earned their authority at the cutter. When someone is at the cutting machine, he or she commands the shop, handing off discarded wood without twisting around, expecting others to be there and to take the discards without comment. In this workshop, people seldom need to blow up, because the others have a similar mastery. Leap-of-faith trust appears when someone carrying hot, potentially scalding, glue assumes that other people will get out of the way without having to be asked; his or her hunched back and hands cupped around the glue-pot make the gesture he or she trusts they will understand. Cooperation under duress appears when, for instance, someone discovers unsuspected small knots in blocks of wood; I've noticed that when a luthier raps on the edge of his or her bench to test soundness, the rapping sound works like a wake-up call to others, who leave their own benches to offer advice or just to commiserate.

Though this miniature, physical version of the social triangle may seem trivial, it contains some pregnant features. The first concerns gesture. Though the luthiers enact gestures in the new space based on what they had done before, these gestures evolved from those in the old, cramped shop, and entirely new gestures appeared. Formerly, for instance, the cutting operation took place at the same bench where gluing and varnishing occurred; other craftsmen saw immediately what the cutter was doing; there was no need to manoeuvre behind his or her back. I asked the man who looks after my cello about changes like this; he looked around the messy studio where people bobbed and weaved around, a bit surprised. 'I guess it just happened.' He spends his entire working life making cellos, but it seemed odd to him that he was making working-space with these gestures as his tools.

Gesture might seem just a built-in, involuntary reflex. It certainly seemed so to Charles Darwin. In a late work, *The Expression of the Emotions in Man and Animals* (1872), Darwin argued that human gestures are based on such involuntary reflexes in all living creatures; no single creature or group of animals can, by an act of will, drastically alter them.[6] Darwin's argument was in part a response to the painter Charles le Brun; in the *Conférence sur l'expression des passions* (1698), Le Brun asserted that gestures are made rather than found.[7] We might say that for Darwin, old reflexes travelled with the instrument makers when they moved to new quarters, whereas for Le Brun, passing the cut wood behind you was a creation pegged to new circumstances; to take Le Brun a step further, he might have argued that life in the workshop was made richer by this new gesture.

Modern anthropology takes Le Brun's side, showing that culture makes a big difference in shaping those gestures Darwin believed to be involuntary reflexes. Andaman Islanders strictly regulate when to start or stop crying; professional mourners in Korea used to wear a particular species of weed on their heads, carrying just the right foods placed on a special small table, when they cried on behalf of families.[8] So, too, culture makes a difference in smiling; Jean-Jacques Courtine and Claudine Haroche, historian-anthropologists of smiles, observe that eighteenth-century Maoris smiled at news of a death, while we Westerners, even if learning that distant Aunt Cecile's death has left us rich, have learned to frown; Courtine and Haroche believe, indeed, that the lips are the most culturally flexible features of the body.[9]

If gesture is under our control, how do we develop it skilfully? In craft-work, visual display often counts for more than verbal instruction. Though visual thinking often can't be translated into words, it is indeed thinking – as when we rotate objects mentally, judging the important of near and far bodies or assessing a volume. This sort of mental-visual work allows us to learn from the displays other people make to us when gesturing. In a carpentry shop, the correct way to hold a saw can be conveyed by taking wood away from the neophyte, and showing the apprentice how a saw should sit in the hand and arm so that it cuts with just its own weight. Do-it-yourself instructions inevitably prove maddening when they fail to show the gesture required to take each step; we need to see the bodily gesture to understand the act. In learning, 'show rather than tell' is seldom entirely voiceless, since the person shown a gesture is likely to ask questions, but showing comes before explaining.

Moreover, gestures can inflect the rhythm of making, suspending and remaking habits in time – shrugs, for instance. 'Shrugs,' the psychologist Jürgen Streeck believes, 'are compound enactments', which suspend 'active involvement with things'.[10] The momentary raising of the shoulders can serve as a voiceless cue to another person to step back, doubt, or at least think about what he or she is doing. Both before, when an action has been inscribed as a habit, and after, when it is enlarged or added to, the rhythm is confirmed by gestures which express for us, and signal to others, that we are confident in what we are doing.

Gestures, finally, are the means by which we experience the sensation of informality. In part, the very gap between showing and telling can make a gesture seem informal: the physical act we see cannot be wrapped up neatly in words, it's not so tightly bound. Informality has an easy visceral character, opposed to the tensed stomach muscles or tight breathing produced by anxiety. Even speech can be infused with that visceral feeling, as in open conversations, more relaxed, more pleasurable, more sensate in their flow than competitive arguments. Yet the sensation of informality is also deceiving, if we imagine 'informal' to be the same as 'shapeless'. The settlement-house workers knew this not to be true when they gave a shape to informal language classes and dramatic performances; we know also in our bodies that informality is shaped, when we gesture appropriately to our circumstances and gesture well.

This, then, is my knotty initial paragraph unpacked. The informal social triangle is a social relationship we make; gesturing is one way to enact the relationship; the gestures which bond are learned behaviour rather than involuntary reflexes; the better we get at gesture, the more visceral and expressive informality becomes.

WORKING WITH RESISTANCE

The third embodiment relates the artisan's encounters with physical resistance to difficult social encounters. The artisan knows one big thing about dealing with resistance: not to fight against it, as though making war on knots in wood or heavy stone; the more effective way is to employ minimum force.

Let's go back to our barber-surgeon to understand this way of working with resistance. Medieval surgery was very like a battlefield in the surgeon's address to the patient's body. With dull knives and bone-saws with few teeth, the barber-surgeon hacked into the body, struggling to cut through muscle and bone. The advent of better tools meant he had to fight less; if the surgeon developed more varied and delicate skills, he could work even less aggressively. One result was that he was now able to study various deep organs, since they remained intact under the knife. We can see this result in the great anatomy treatises produced by Vesalius in the sixteenth century; thanks to more refined, precise tools, the surgeon could assess minute differences in resistance his scalpel encountered between the membranes encasing an organ and the denser mass of the organ itself.[11]

The optical instruments displayed on Holbein's table both resembled and differed from the barber-surgeon's new scalpel. Like the scalpel, these were refined instruments which enabled a person to look more clearly, and further, than could the naked eye. Unlike the scalpel, the more clearly people saw, the more puzzled they became by what they saw – previously unknown moons in the solar system, the hint of stars and galaxies further away – all of which resisted understanding. Johannes Kepler (1571–1630) confronted this issue in 1604 when a supernova (a gigantic gaseous ball) suddenly became visible in the skies; astrologers using magical formulas explained why it should exist, but not its puzzling lines of movement, which Kepler observed through the telescope.

Resistance arises, then, in physical matter itself and also in making sense of matter, the second kind of difficulty often spawned by better tools. In fighting against resistance we will become more focused on getting rid of the problem than on understanding what it is; by contrast, when working with resistance we want to suspend frustration at being blocked, and instead engage with the problem in its own right. This general precept came to life in the London luthiers' shop just at those moments when an instrument-maker began banging a block of wood against the bench, suspecting there was a knot within. She'd then hold the block in different ways, trying to locate by different banging sounds just where the knot was; once she started cutting, she didn't seek to gouge out the knot, rather to shape instrument-plates by cutting around the knot's contours, feeling the presence of the knot's edge in slight resistances to her own hand when pushing the block, a delicate sort of cutting in which the as-yet-unseen knot guided her. She thus worked with the resistance.

Applying minimum force is the most effective way to work with resistance. Just as in working with a wood knot, so in a surgical procedure: the less aggressive the effort, the more sensitivity. Vesalius urged the surgeon, feeling the liver more resistant to the scalpel than the surrounding tissues, to 'stay his hand', to probe tentatively and delicately before cutting further. In practising music, when confronted by a sour note or a hand-shift gone wrong, the performer gets nowhere by forcing. The mistake has to be treated as an interesting fact; then the problem will eventually be unlocked. This precept applies to time as well as to attitude; practice sessions that stretch out hour after hour will leave the young musician exhausted, playing ever more aggressively and with ever less focus. A Zen rule says that the skilled archer should stop struggling to hit the target and instead study the target itself; accuracy of aim will eventually ensue.

Using minimum force is tied to befriending one's tools. When hammering, the novice's first impulse is to put his or her whole body into the effort. Master carpenters will let the weight of the hammer do the work, rather than using their own force from the shoulder down. The master will have developed so thorough an understanding of the tool that he knows how to hold it to use minimum force – the hammer gripped lightly at the end of the shank, thumb extended along the shank top; the hammer can then do the work for him.

In one way, the application of minimum force follows a basic rule of engineering. Machines conserve energy by using the fewest moving parts and making the least possible moves; so too the stamina of a surgeon, musician or athlete depends on economy of gesture. This engineering principle aims to get rid of friction, to reduce resistance. Invariably following the engineer's rule would, though, be counter-productive for the craftsman; the puzzling movements of the supernova of 1604 stimulated Kepler to ponder the meaning of parallax lines, whereas the astrologer got rid, magically, of that mental friction. In the instrument shop, a particularly good cutter remarked to me, 'You always learn about softer wood by exploring knots.'

This approach to resistance matters particularly in dialogical social behaviour. Only through behaving with minimum self-assertiveness do we open up to others – a political as well as personal concept. Totalitarian movements do not work with resistance. This precept also applies to warfare. Napoleon's precision tactics emphasized the application of force on the field of battle at a localized point, whereas the Nazi blitzkrieg on the Eastern Front failed by being unfocused, massive power indiscriminately applied.

Less extreme, the zero-sum game requires competitors to think about resistance with nuance. By its very nature, competition breeds resistance, since the loser doesn't want to lose. Competition must embrace the loser's share in the exchange. As Adam Smith argued, winner-takes-all markets – the economic equivalent of the apex predator's dealings with other creatures – can destroy the incentive to compete at all; in a zero-sum game, winners have to pay attention to what the loser will have left in order to play again, and so to keep the exchange going. This attention is one version, in economic competition, of working with resistance.

The use of minimum force comes to the fore dialogically in the differentiating exchange. Obviously so in the dialogic conversation, in which a person refrains from insisting or arguing in order to take in someone else's point of view. Aggressive verbal force is also minimized by deploying the subjunctive mood, whether in ordinary conversations or diplomatic exchanges. Self-imposed irony of La Rochefoucauld's sort 'stays the hand' psychologically; in diminishing overbearing pomposity, it invites other people to engage. The value Castligione placed, in *The Book of the Courtier*, on *sprezzatura*, on lightness in gesture and speech, is also a social expression of minimum force. Finally, the indirect procedures used by community organizers fall within the frame of minimizing force. They are light, preferring the nudge to the command; in community organizing practised on the Near West Side of Chicago, the light touch was inseparable from the goal of attuning residents to the complexities of the community.

These dialogic social experiences are all forms of embodied social knowledge. 'Embodiment' here is more than a metaphor: like making a social gesture, behaving with minimum force is a sensate experience, one in which we feel easy with others physically as well as mentally, because we aren't forcing ourselves on them. This sensation is perhaps why, when Castiglione sought a word for civility, he recurred to *sprez-zatura*, an old word meaning originally in Italian just 'springy'. Pleasure of that sort comes to us socially in lightening up.

Under all its varied names, the experience of minimum force in social relations contrasts to the reduction of anxiety explored in Chapter 6. Anxiety-reduction aims to diminish outside stimulation; it does so by individual withdrawal. Whereas in deploying minimum force, both physically and socially, we can become more sensitive to, more connected with, more engaged by the environment. The things or people that resist our will, the experiences which resist our instant understanding, can come to matter in themselves.

Here then are three modes of making things full of social implication. The rhythm of developing a physical skill can embody ritual; gestures between people can embody the informal social triangle; using minimum force can embody response to those who resist or differ. How might all three be put to use in improving social relations? How might these embodied skills strengthen cooperation in particular?

These are questions about social repair. We'll pursue the issue of social repair throughout the concluding chapters of this study. To do so we need first to understand the work of repair in itself.

REPAIR

There are three ways to perform a repair: making a damaged object seem just like new, improving its operation, or altering it altogether; in technical jargon, these three strategies consist of restoration, remediation or reconfiguration. The first is governed by the object's original state; the second substitutes better parts or materials while preserving an old form; the third re-imagines the form and use of the object in the course of fixing it. All repair strategies depend on an initial judgement that what's broken can indeed be fixed. An object beyond recovery, like a shattered wineglass, is deemed technically a 'hermetic object', admitting no further work. Cooperation is not like a hermetic object, once damaged beyond recovery; as we have seen, its sources –

both genetic and in early human development – are instead enduring; they admit repair.

The social and political implications of each become clear if we explore the repair work on a particular damaged building.

'Just like new' repair work is embodied by restorers of porcelain, whose challenge is to leave so little trace of the craftsman's labours on the object that you would never know it was broken. Restoration of this sort is self-effacing work, but the restorer is hardly mindless; rather he or she is crafting an illusion, and that craft is demanding, succeeding only by strict attention to detail. The skilled restorer of porcelain will collect not only the visible chips of a broken pot but also the dust on the table where it rested; these micro-bits hidden in the dust are then used in re-compounding the materials.

The illusion created by the self-effacing restorer requires also a decision about what time the restorer wants to re-create. Is the 'authentic' state of an old object the moment it was first made? In restoring paintings, this is a huge issue. Recent work on the Sistine Chapel, bringing the frescos back to the colours they had when first painted, was a nightmare to many viewers, not only because the original colours look garish, but also because, as Ernst Gombrich observed about this kind of restoration, 'the viewer's share' has been eliminated from the painting; over the centuries, people's experience of the Sistine Chapel has been shaped by the way the object aged.[12] The illusion of 'original' can thus be contested; other restorers would have brought the chapel back to a different point in its past, still provoking in the viewer the sense of seeing more of the original.

For all this, the act of reconstruction requires a certain modesty in the craftsman: intruding his or her presence is not the point of the work; the restorer thinks of him- or herself as the past's instrument. 'Authenticity' is a subject for discussion, certainly, but the discussants are not, in principle, focused on themselves.

Remediation is a technique of repair which more emphasizes the repairer's presence. Remediation preserves an existing form while substituting old parts for new and improved ones. Today's violin restorers, for instance, sometimes use different woods for pegs and sounding posts than the materials employed in Stradivarius's day.

These are, in many cases, a real improvement; Stradivarius was a genius but is not a shrine. Still, though there are detectable changes, the object has the same purpose and can be used in the same way as before.

Remediation requires inventory skill, which is knowledge of the alternatives available for substitution and the ability to insert these possible applications into an existing object. This kind of repair work also requires a searching judgement about the object's own resilience in time. When faced by the need to replace fire-prone straw thatch on a roof, the repairer may decide for fireproof synthetic thatch; the new material can also be the top slice of a sandwich of insulating materials which make the roof more energy-efficient. Here, the judgement call in remediation relates substance to function.

This is to say, remediation challenges the repairer to consider different means to achieving the same end; the original design or maker chose just one. The social equivalent of the repairer in this process is no visionary; rather, he is a fixer, and inventory skills are the fixer's stock in trade; he or she knows of the alternatives.

Technically, reconfiguration is the most radical kind of repair. The broken object serves as an occasion to make the object different than it was before, in function as well as in form. These are the repairs on which Chipperfield's team dwelled. An industrial example appeared recently in the mechanical arm used in modern bakeries to manipulate bread in the oven. Originally just a shovel-like tool to push loaves through the oven, the arm's crudeness meant that some loaves would burn, others half-cook. In the 1980s the technology of the arms improved greatly; bakers could now manipulate the dough during the actual baking process – turned over, stretched, incised – with the unforeseen result that the machines could now bake many different kinds of bread at the same time.

Improvisation is the key to radical repairs of this sort; they most often occur through small, surprising changes which turn out to have larger implications. Improvisation occurs in exploring the connections between small repairs and their large consequences. On Holbein's table, this was the story of navigation instruments, in which small changes in fabricating metals made for more precise measuring instruments that scientists then discovered they could put to new uses. Incomplete specification makes reconfiguration possible; if not every detail of the repair is specified in advance, there is more room for radical experiment.

Improvisation and incomplete specification connect this kind of technical repair to more radical social experiment. By design, the settlement houses and the community organizing which followed them in Chicago were incompletely specified. The aim of allowing improvisation was to generate new ways of cooperating, while conserving people's established sense of being capable and competent. Cooperation over small details set in motion this process of metamorphosis; the communities were meant to do their own repair work, rather than rely on an expert repairman, a fixer.

Opponents of this kind of repair/reform counter that, while it may feel good, destabilizing changes of this sort produce incoherent results. To give the opponents their due, in the technical realm this is a real issue. Incoherent reconfiguration is immediately apparent in computer word-processing programs which have gradually strayed from the purpose of writing, due to the addition of innumerable bells-and-whistles, making the programs slow and inefficient to use. Incoherence in reconfiguration arises when the craftsman forgets there was a problem to solve in the first place.

Which is more largely a challenge in all repair work. The repair worker has to treat breakdown as a caution as well as an opportunity. When an object goes wrong we need to think about what was wrong as well as right about it in the first place. As with objects damaged by time, so with people; they are survivors whose biographies have left them damaged, but the beginnings of their life stories were not necessarily mistakes. An incoherent repair can provide the sensation of change but may sacrifice the value of the initial act of creation.

In 1943 British bombing of Berlin destroyed the roof and central staircase of the city's archaeological museum; fifteen months later a second bombing shoved in the north-west part of the building. Though the treasures had been moved, the building lay in ruins for forty years; in 1980 its great columns were still scattered in a courtyard, rain poured in through gaps in the ceilings and into windows crudely boarded up; the walls had been pockmarked by machine-gun damage, testimony to street-fighting during the violent capture of Berlin by the Russians at the end of the Second World War.

In the mid-1980s the East German government began to protect the building by shoring up its foundations and installing an emergency roof. After the reunification of Berlin in 1989 the effort to rebuild suddenly had more cash at hand, but the money raised a large question: just how should this damaged icon be repaired? Should it be restored to its initial glory when the museum – an enormous, complicated architectural maze – first opened in 1859? Should it instead be razed to the ground and a truly new museum built in its stead? Or should restoration somehow register, preserve, narrate the trauma through which the building had passed? Many damaged monuments, such as Coventry Cathedral in Britain, destroyed by German warplanes on 14 November 1940, have posed questions of this sort, but in Germany itself, wracked by Nazism, then by post-war Communist tyranny, the questions were deeply unsettling. How much did Berliners want to remember, how much did they want to forget? All three technical skills of repair figured in debating how much to remember.

A strong local faction of Berliners wanted the museum to be a perfect copy of the building at its nineteenth-century unveiling, 'just like new'. Near the Neues Museum, the illusion of untouched time was planned for the Stadtschloss, a Baroque confection damaged in the Second World War and pulled down in 1950. There's nothing particularly German about making modern buildings look old: in Britain, the Prince's Trust has in the last twenty years built 'historic' villages from scratch; in America, the restoration of places like Colonial Williamsburg seeks to create the illusion of places which time forgot. In Berlin, however, wilful amnesia has that strong political purpose, the blotting out of trauma.

Amnesia comes in many forms. It can be made by rejecting repair altogether, clearing a site to make an entirely new building or, indeed, whole districts – just what the Chinese have done to their own cities and history in Shanghai and Beijing, where old, characterful courtyard architecture has been destroyed and replaced by the sort of neutral towers that are built all around the planet today. The Beijing hutongs were cramped, dirty and unsanitary; a good case could be made for forgetting them as a civic guide. The good case for erasure was compelling in Berlin during the 1990s for different reasons; in an earlier era West Berlin had erected some notable buildings, such as Hans Scharoun's Philharmonie, constructed from 1956 to 1963; many people saw the Neues Museum as an opportunity to make an entirely new museum of matching innovation.

But this was not just any building site. When the museum opened in 1859, it represented Germany's ambition to bring ancient world culture into the German present. The building was a monument to cultural imperialism, certainly; the objects themselves are, however, amazing and have been beautifully kept or restored. As in the British Museum in London, the authorities argued that these objects now belonged to world culture. A new building would still serve the objects' integrity, and could declare their neutrality politically.

A new building would still, in repair terms, be a remediation, a new form serving an old intention. The programme would remain just what it was in 1859: display. A new, improved, neutered building would still be in purpose a treasure-house.

Thus the architect chosen to rebuild the Neues Museum, David Chipperfield, faced considerable public pressure either to make the new building just like the old, or to make it entirely new in form. The politics of nostalgia are strong in a city and country that lived through so much trauma, yet it was inconceivable that this most inventive of architects could build a fake building; the gremlin of his own creativity would have subverted that strategy, and he would most likely have quit or failed. Professional colleagues instead urged Chipperfield to let rip with something entirely fresh, as did younger Berliners, who hated what this museum's past stood for.

These contending pressures disposed both the city fathers and Chipperfield to seek some sort of middle ground, but the work his team eventually produced escaped the confines of compromise, becoming something quite different; the idea of the museum itself was re-imagined in the course of repair, so that the building tells its own story, apart from any of the objects it houses. This story incorporates Germany's historic debacle; rather than just displaying that trauma, as in a display case or a set of photographs, the architect made people coming to the museum feel it in their own bodies. This was a drastic reconfiguration of the idea of a museum, its purpose modulating in the repair of its parts.

Reconfiguration may seem to require an analytical, theoretical rethink, which is certainly and generally true, but in craft-work meta-morphosis of this sort usually is spurred by quite detailed issues. In the decade Chipperfield spent on the project, beginning in 1998, he dwelt on how to mix old and new stone fragments in the terrazzo flooring, or how to paint walls of the same basic colour but of differ-ent tint from the old paint. In some rooms he literally restored war damage, so that it becomes possible to see the effects of bombing; in others he showed objects in a way not usual in museum displays, as in a room where sculptural treasures stand in front of glass walls, so that outside the rooms the viewer can see the back of the heads and bodies, an emphasis on the form-in-the-round which reflects changes in modern knowledge of ancient Egypt, differing from the frontal under-standing of these sculptures which prevailed from the mid-nineteenth century to the Second World War. In still other rooms, entirely newly made, he opened up space for activities never imagined by the original designers as occurring in a museum; the choreographer Sasha Waltz has used these rooms, for instance, as stages for modern dance.

The building exhibits its own process of transformation: new ele-ments are added, new activities become possible, but the building's troubled past remains evident; you walk on that record, you see it on the walls; your jerky progress through many of the building's spaces reinforces the visceral experience of a building no longer one coherent whole.

In his writings and interviews about the Neues Museum, Chipper-field has emphasized the close connection between making and repairing. In solving some problems, like repair of the floor-work, he had seen new ways to texture some of the walls, both in materials and in paint. The project demanded his team work with resistances, rather than fight against them, and in many parts of the building this bred a minimalist approach, as little self-dramatizing 'architecture' as pos-sible, even in the great entrance hall, where the architect refurbished a monumental staircase: the staircase itself is Chipperfield the mod-ernist, while the walls of the entrance hall seem not touched by the dramatizing gesture.

Is this a social statement? I'd judge it is so, though the architect, being an architect, prefers to talk about mortar techniques. The rebuilding embodied dialogical thinking. The results convey an ethical message about damage and repair. Wandering the museum's rooms, the visitor never forgets its painful history, yet this memory is not closed, self-contained; the spatial narrative moves forward, suggesting an openness to different possibilities from just like new or entirely new. Its politics are those of change, encompassing historical ruptures without becoming fixated on the sheer fact of injury.

This is just what we want to be experienced in the repair of cooperation. Cooperation is not like a hermetic object, once damaged beyond recovery; as we've seen, its sources – both genetic and in early human development – are instead enduring; they admit repair. The reconfiguration of this building provides a guiding metaphor in thinking about how to repair cooperation.

We've moved – or is it strayed? – from porcelain chips, roof thatch and bakery arms into philosophy, but with reason.

In sum, the processes of making and repairing inside a workshop connect to social life outside it. The pregnant word 'embodied' helps make those connections. 'Embodied social knowledge' is usually used, in the jargon of the social sciences, as a floating metaphor; though metaphors and analogies of course enable understanding, the word 'embodied' seems to me to work harder by being made more direct and concrete. I may insist on this because, philosophically, I doubt the separation of mind and body; so too, I cannot believe that social experience is disconnected from physical sensation. I've wanted to explore how the rhythm of physical technique inside the shop can be felt in the rhythm of rituals outside. Informal gestures inside the shop relate and bind people emotionally; the power of small gestures is felt, too, in communal ties. The practice of using minimal physical force inside the shop resonates sensibly outside in the conduct of differentiating verbal exchange. Even if these connections are left as analogies, I hope they freshen the sense that social relations are experiences in the gut.

Repair work suggests other ways to relate the physical and the social. Restoration, whether of a pot or of a ritual, is a recovery in which authenticity is regained, the damage of use and history undone; the restorer becomes a servant of the past. Remediation is more present-oriented and more strategic. The repair work can improve the original object by replacing old parts with new; so too, social

remediation can make an old purpose better if served by new programmes and policies. Reconfiguration is more experimental in
outlook and more informal in procedure; fixing an old machine can
lead, when people play around with it, to transforming the machine's
purpose as well as its functioning; so too, repairing broken social relations can become open-ended, especially if pursued informally. Of the
three, reconfiguration is the most socially engaging. As we shall now
see, it proves the most effective in renewing cooperation.

8

Everyday Diplomacy

Reformation Conversations Put to Practical Use

Everyday diplomacy is one way people deal with people they don't understand, can't relate to or are in conflict with. To meet these challenges, people in communities, at work or on the street proceed in ways analogous to making and repairing things in the workshop. They use minimal force; create social space through coded gestures; make sophisticated repairs which acknowledge trauma. It's often said that indirection is the essence of diplomacy, and it's true that all these efforts rely on suggestion rather than command. But more pointedly, everyday diplomacy puts the dialogic conversation to work practically. One result is skilled conflict management.

We could imagine, and rightly, that in all cultures people learn how to relate to one another through deploying tact or giving hints, while avoiding blunt statement. As we've seen, though, in Europe cultural codes of indirection took a new turn during the late Renaissance and early Reformation; professional diplomats and courtiers formulated new rituals of behaviour, drawing on new ideas about civility.

This chapter explores that heritage in ordinary life. Though civility on the modern street looks little like the courtesy so elaborately deployed in old embassies and salons, the organizing principles of secular ritual have endured.

INDIRECT COOPERATION

We left the Wall Street back-office workers in Chapter 6 in urgent need of repairing their fortunes, as they hunt for work at the employment centre. Everyday diplomacy appears in the ways job counsellors respond to this need by cooperating indirectly with clients.

The job counsellor's task is daunting. Prolonged unemployment among middle-aged workers correlates with increasing alcoholism, marital violence and divorce; these correlations begin in the fourth and fifth months of unemployment and thereafter become steadily tighter.[1] The social damage caused by long-term unemployment appears visibly in job centres among those people who sit silent and withdrawn, bottled up in anger or shame. I'm thinking, for instance, of a woman clerk without family ties and much attached to her job, who is at risk of becoming a long-term, discouraged worker. She seethes with anger at being let go after thirteen years of doing a good job; in the course of four months, with no boss to reproach – he too had disappeared from the brokerage – she has turned both on the job counsellors and on herself; a rather bouncy person when I first encountered her, after a half-year she has become listless.

How can the job counsellor respond to and rouse such discouraged employees? Jane Schwartz (as I will call her) is a particularly adept practitioner of indirect cooperation. Grey-haired, with a rasping, steel-cutting Bronx accent, she has, when faced with a silent client, mastered the art of being herself quiet; slumped in her chair, chewing gum, her gaze wandering, she seems unfazed by anything clients throw at her. She is not motherly; when she does speak, her guidance consists of gradually inducing her bottled-up clients to laugh at the follies of their employers, or at the fact that a hundred other clients are applying for the same job. I once asked Mrs Schwartz why this seemed to help, and she said, 'I have a whole collection of jokebooks,' as though this answered my question – which, in retrospect, I realized it had.

'They have to lighten up, even if they are under a lot of pressure,' another job counsellor remarked. 'Employers are shitty; if they pick up any sign you are really uptight, they are going to turn off.' Advising some-one to 'Get a grip on yourself!' is not likely to help. Telling jokes is a classic way to lighten up any tense situation, but in the job centre it has a strategic rationale: clients long out of work are usually economically desperate, a truth which can overpower them emotionally; in the job interview, however, they need to display a relaxed attitude; they need, as this second counsellor remarked, to learn how to 'deal with a weak hand'.

Seemingly small rituals aim to inculcate in clients the application of minimum force when they go for interviews. Clients are urged to drop past achievements and experience casually into the conversation rather than boast of them up-front; the idea is to create a rhythm of question and response which imparts to the interview a participatory tone. The successful job interview has to focus on 'it' rather than 'me', a successful candidate showing interest in and knowledge about the post. Never, clients are cautioned, should they hammer home to the prospective employer their own need for a job. Both sides may know the candidate is desperate, but the fiction has to be maintained that you are having an objective discussion about the work itself; this fiction will ease social tension. Conveying 'I can take it or leave it' is role-playing required of people playing a weak hand. This lightness of tone is *sprezzatura* applied to the job interview, analogous, in a workshop, to lightness of physical force and to focus on the object rather than on oneself.

The work ethic so deeply rooted in modern society makes wearing this mask difficult; the Protestant Ethic described by Weber converts work into a symbol of self-worth; it's hard to lighten up on such tests. Job candidates long without jobs know interviews are big tests they have failed several times before; the interview becomes increasingly a super-charged psychological event for discouraged workers.

The counsellor has to hope that, against the driving power of the work ethic, he or she can counter by drawing on one aspect of the client's mundane experience of working. This is stepping back from a task in order to get a new view of it, an experience so ordinary most workers don't think about it. Stepping back punctuates the middle phase of the rhythm of skill. In social relations, stepping back is not mundane, it enables a person to see differently, but it is also a suspension of truth; by stepping back one can imagine oneself a more self-confident person at ease, even as in reality the bills pile up.

The hope in job centres is that counsellors will provide clues about how to behave more easily with prospective employers. There are indeed job counsellors who rigorously lay down behavioural rules in minute detail, such as 'Look me in the eye when you shake my hand', or 'If I ask a question, answer it succinctly before explaining your answer'. But too many such imperious commands will prove counter-productive, by making the candidate only more nervous in trying to remember the etiquette. The aim of a job-interview ritual, like any ritual, is to put in practice behaviours you have absorbed, behaviours which have progressed beyond self-consciousness.

This was brought home to me when I first began to study employment offices in the 1980s, a time when job counselling was weighed down by psychotherapy. A counsellor in a first-class centre showed me a thick book, meant for job seekers, explaining the emotional ins and outs of the interview-encounter, and emphasizing introspection. Take the book to heart and you'd conclude you need psychoanalysis rather than a job.[2] Best-practice models today are less freighted. Suggestions are given, but not too many; the best-practice counsellor hopes the client will infer from these easy encounters ways to behave elsewhere.

As with behaviour, so with decision-making. A scene I witnessed several times in a private job centre embodies how the light touch works. A conference table in the small meeting room is covered with documents about starting and financing one's own business. Many of the private centre's clients think of starting their own businesses, as consultants working out of home, or in small-company start-ups within the dense crinkle of New York's knowledge economy. At the extreme, a very few urban romantics dream of that total transformation, starting an organic farm. Yet in good times the chances of an American start-up business lasting two years are about one in eight, and starting a small organic farm is, statistically, almost certainly a recipe for ruin.

On the table, the counsellor has provided the documents about these prospects but leaves their interpretation up to the client, who hovers over the bumf, frowning like a buyer being offered a dubious second-hand car. When asked about a specific issue, the counsellor tells what he or she knows factually, but no more. The procedure is meant to convey the counsellors' trust that their clients can work out what is best for themselves. This procedure, like the joke, avoids the warning 'Be realistic!' Its cunning lies in presenting the facts about new small businesses as though the client might indeed want to go ahead, trusting that in time the client will decide not to. In this staging, the job counsellors apply minimum personal influence, saying as little as possible about what the clients should decide, seeking instead to turn them outward, oriented to an objective reality beyond personal desires.

The counsellor's self-restraint invites clients to look at the relation between problem-solving and problem-finding. It contrasts with the self-contained, isolated problem-solving which occurs within corporate silos. Moreover, the practice of indirect, light-touch, outward-oriented cooperation serves community organizers as well. As described in Chapter 1, the light touch differentiates the community organizer from the labour organizer. Indeed, focusing people outward rather than inward is necessary for any difficult form of sociability. Particularly, as de Certeau and his colleagues found, people faced with daunting material circumstances.

Though many job counsellors of my generation have had training in psychotherapy, they are not psychotherapists. Advisers like Jane Schwartz avoid behaving like priests hearing confession; the point is not to get inside the client's psyche, rather, to turn the client outward. If a client succumbs to domestic violence, for instance, they can't deal with that problem on its own; it is not part of their remit. Time-pressure also rules this aloof behaviour. Most counsellors deal with hundreds of clients; experienced counsellors correct novices who become overly sympathetic, too involved, spending too much time on individual cases. Because of time-pressure, they can focus only on the first steps in rousing a discouraged worker, or staging a quick drama to bring dreamers up short.

An interesting fact about job counselling – at least to judge from the stack of feedback evaluations piled up at the Wall Street centre – is that successful clients value the coaching but don't become very emotionally involved with their coaches; in psychoanalytic jargon, there's little transference left once these clients are re-employed. 'I almost never hear from them after,' Mrs Schwartz remarked, and she doesn't sound too unhappy about it: 'I barely have time for my friends; very, very busy now . . .' The counsellor has exercised empathy rather than sympathy; by avoiding 'Poor you, I feel for you', he or she wants to deflect the answering response 'Poor me'.

There's nothing remarkable about indirect cooperation; it can occur on the streets of Croix-Rousse, or appear among labourers, like those I studied in Boston, who were able to build an informal social structure over mechanical labour. But it could reasonably be asked whether this practice makes much difference in finding a job, that is, whether the repair works.

The labour market in both Europe and North America is becoming transformed structurally. It's a commonplace that, from the beginning of the 1980s ever fewer workers in Europe and North America have been engaged in mass manufacturing; that shrinkage has extended today – as in computer programming and engineering – to skilled professional work which can be done elsewhere in the world more cheaply.[3] It's a fantasy, in my judgement, to think that new creative or green economies can do much to offset the massive drift in jobs away from the West. The trend within white-collar work is for more lower-level service work, as in retail sales and in care-work for the aged, service labour subject to the short-term time-frame explored in Chapter 5. Of course, some face-to-face professional services will not shrink – you won't want a lawyer in India to handle your divorce by email – but Western economies face the paradox of high productivity without full employment. We face the prospect that it will seem 'normal' for 15 to 18 per cent of the labour force to be without full-time work for more than two years; among young people in their twenties, these percentages will rise to 20–25 per cent.[4]

The employment centre will thus loom ever larger as an institution in the lives of ever more people. It will not be the only such institution. Britain is currently seeing the rise of 'job clubs', community-based, mutual-support groups that are especially important to people out of work for long periods in keeping their spirits up and providing word-of-mouth leads. Yet the structural problem, both for professionals and for community groups, is the increasingly difficult task of matching applicants to scant available jobs. In the middle classes, this means lowering expectations; professional job counsellors and job-club organizers alike need to become skilled in handling disappointment. These counsellors and organizers are society's realists; politicians promising a return to full employment of the sort our parents' generation knew are society's fantasists.

That said, the employment centre cannot be just a school of misery. Indirect cooperation can indeed school job seekers about how best to behave if they manage to get through an employer's door. More, people need to believe they can make something of their lives; few employment counsellors would stay in their own jobs if they functioned as professors of disappointment. The value of the effort to both job seeker and adviser is that they've reconfigured what the repair involves, socially and personally rather than economically; the task is to stay engaged with others even if one feels rotten inside. The hard-boiled rationalist who slights this task as just a 'feel-good factor' ignores the stakes involved. The discouraged worker has to learn how to be a survivor: that's the goal that keeps good job counsellors at their posts. How can you transcend the feeling of being the prisoner of job statistics?

The power to resist adversity is a sweeping personal and collective issue to which the people in the employment centre offer one perhaps special but still resonant answer. Repair occurs in part by resisting economically induced withdrawal. This is not withdrawal of the Tocquevillian sort, voluntary and anxiety-reducing. It is rather withdrawal of the sort described by Max Weber, being the negative side of the work ethic, an isolation which increases anxiety as the person focuses ever more on his or her insufficient self. The point of the repair is staying socially connected to others – a task that, paradoxically, requires lowering the emotional temperature. Job counselling provides a small but still evocative picture of how these repairs can be attempted through indirect cooperation.

CONFLICT MANAGEMENT

Good advisers are always on their clients' side. Much social exchange between people is more adversarial, either as the zero-sum game or a winner-takes-all struggle. We might imagine that appeasement is the role everyday diplomacy plays in these situations, indirection soothing the combatants. But everyday diplomacy can do more. To understand how, we need to delve into the way of expressing conflict can sometimes bind people together so that they cooperate better.

One example of this expression comes from the former British Prime Minister, Margaret Thatcher, in her dealings with Cabinet ministers. Simon Jenkins describes her style of conducting meetings as follows: 'She argued and shouted. She invited [ministers and senior officials] to stand up to her and then battered them with a mix of trivial knowledge and the authority of her office.' One of her aides 'calculated that she would talk for 90 per cent of the time at meetings. She would state her conclusion at the start and challenge anyone present to disagree.'[5] Yet people who did stand up to her often came away feeling that the meetings were productive. A less elevated example has already appeared in these pages; foremen in the Boston bakeries got on well with their men even though they often swore at and abused them.

This is the storm-cloud version of exchange, the storm which clears the air. The sociologist Lewis Coser thought this kind of expression the general model for productive conflict. People learn the limits beyond which others will not yield, the points on which they will not compromise; the storm then passes, people emerging with their honour intact and more bonded than before.[6] According to this view, Thatcher's Cabinet meetings were not so different from many family arguments. Cooperation is strengthened not just by blowing off steam; trials of strength establish lines not to be crossed in the future.

The storm cloud can also make for very dangerous weather, confrontations so embittering the participants that they want to have nothing further to do with one another. The professional mediator has for this reason to do more than simply soothe tempers. Labour mediators, like diplomats, have, for instance, to learn when to bring parties in conflict together and when to keep them apart. Shuttling between the rooms in a negotiation where the warring beasts are separately caged, the skilled mediator will judge quite finely when the moment has arrived to bring them together; one labour mediator says that moment occurs when he judges that the parties in conflict have become sick of their own arguments.[7]

In a conference room, once the warring beasts are together, soothing tempers may still be necessary, but again will not be enough. A more searching technique was first developed by the Duc de Joinville in the nineteenth century for diplomats and has been used to great effect by American labour negotiators like the late Theodore Kheel.[8] The technique draws on the formula 'in other words, you are saying that . . .', but does not in fact just repeat back; the negotiator embeds some of the concerns or interests of the opposing party into the rephrasing, thus establishing a common ground for negotiation. Joinville called this procedure 're-pairing', which is an apt *jeu de mots*; the repair of conflict, like a workshop repair, re-formats an issue so that it becomes changeable.

We've earlier touched on cooperative listening skills in terms of understanding and responding empathically to what another person is saying. Ordinarily the phrase 'in other words . . .' is used to clarify what that person is saying; for Joinville as for Kheel the goal is to distort the message somewhat. The negotiator practising Joinville's technique mis-hears on purpose so as to introduce new, bridging elements. Joinville must have been a clever reader as well as a skilful listener, for he claims this technique can be traced back to Plato. In Plato's dialogues, Socrates constantly rephrases other people's arguments in ways which are different from what they themselves said and meant; Socrates mis-hears to open ideas up.

But what if there is no mediator? Is the storm then likely to lead to devastation? Do the beasts become insatiable for blood? Under certain circumstances, conflict management can occur without mediators; here, damage can be repaired by reconfiguring the balance of silence and speech.

Wall Street was once all of New York. Early on, immigrants established specialized businesses just above what is now the financial centre, in Tribeca or along Canal Street; these were small services or manufacturers, run from the late nineteenth century onwards by Jews, Slovaks, Italians, Poles and Asians, family-owned and -operated, near to where the families lived in the Lower East Side. This immigrant belt of specialized businesses still survives, though its geography is shrinking, knit tight by long-standing relationships with suppliers and customers. As in all small-business communities, competitors tend to cluster together; one single street in Chinatown currently contains, for instance, eight wholesalers of restaurant-sized woks.

Driven by civil war and economic turmoil at home, Koreans started to migrate in large numbers to the United States in the mid-1970s, going to large cities, especially to New York and Los Angeles. In New York they were like, and not like, immigrants who came before. Like other migrants, they were desperately poor. They differed because many of the Korean migrants were highly educated, but found no market for their skills as doctors or engineers in the United States; their situation compares best, in Europe, to the highly educated Vietnamese who came to Paris in the 1960s, as Vietnam convulsed.

In New York, Koreans also differed because they broke out of the traditional city-centre immigrant belt. They set up shops in places where they were alien presences, making a niche for themselves by creating small stores open twenty-four hours a day, seven days a week, selling prepared food and flowers as well as packaged goods to people who were not Korean; their customers were either wealthy Manhattanites, or poor blacks in communities scattered throughout the city where no large grocery stores operated. Taken for granted today by New Yorkers, the Korean shops were an innovation forty years ago. In one way the Koreans resembled the Chinese who had come before them by establishing revolving credit organizations to finance their stores; prosperous businesses pushed some profits back into the credit funds to help other newcomers. In the beachhead generation, social bonds were also tight; within the Korean shops, adults who were not working were expected to baby-sit for others, often caring for children in the back of the stores.[9]

Cooperative among themselves, the Korean grocers faced in a particular way the dilemma we have underlined throughout this study, that of getting along with those who are different. This dilemma became a confrontation for the beachhead generation in dealing with poor African-American customers. Language barriers of course stood in the Koreans' way, but more, some of these customers became their adversaries, feeling exploited by the prices the Koreans charged; some also harboured jealousy of the financial resources standing behind each shop. For their part, the Koreans viewed with disdain these poor customers whose lives seem unmended and disordered – and worse, Koreans occasionally let their contempt for these customers show.

This had violent consequences: in 1992, rioters in Los Angeles destroyed about 2,300 Korean businesses; in New York, Korean grocery stores had been long subject to rock-throwing incidents and, since 1984, organized boycotts. The Koreans' response was both to organize for self-defence and to deal with representatives of the

African-American community. The Korean Association of New York and the Korean Merchants Association made contact with professional community organizers from the African-American community, organizers who had been honing their skills since earlier riots in the 1960s directed at the white establishment. The government in New York had also developed a cadre of skilled mediators.

Like all professional efforts at conflict-resolution, these encounters began with mutual accusations, declarations and demands. It took a long time for the exchanges to get anywhere – only after five years did accusatory confrontation develop into procedures for managing potential violence. Progress occurred through achieving what Theodore Kheel calls 'symbolic cover'; cooperation on the small issues moves forward to symbolize that something can be done; large, irreconcilable issues are deferred, perhaps permanently.[10] The formal negotiations focused, for instance, on which government agency would pay for shop-front damage, and buried the holding of any violent customer to account.

There was no practice of reconciliation, in the sense that shopowner and customer came to a better understanding of each other; no rapprochement. By 1992, the year when formal mediation was finally making progress, a study of Korean merchants found that 61 per cent believed blacks are less intelligent than whites, a similar percentage were convinced that blacks are less honest, and 70 per cent believed blacks to be more disposed to commit crimes than whites.[11] These views were a compound of pure racism, actual experience of robbery and, equally, sentiments which reflect the Koreans' own history of vulnerability. Formal mediation had not blown away these storm clouds, any more than actual conflict had. But both Koreans and their customers did find a solution, of sorts. They lightened up the conflict by silence, by a tacit agreement to push anger and prejudice into the background. Like job seekers, they learned to practise emotional distance.

That is only half the story. The other half lies in the Koreans' dealings with their own employees. As the shops expanded beyond the Koreans' capacity to staff with Koreans, these employees became almost exclusively Latinos, another strange ethnic group for the immigrants but with whom they had quite different relations than with their

African-American customers. The Latino employees also harboured resentments, based on low wages and abusive working hours; these resentments bred strikes, though in New York little physical violence against the shopkeepers. Koreans and Latinos had professionals at hand to address these conflicts, but the two ethnic groups pursued a dual path: one which used professionals to mediate outside the stores, the other inside the shops where mediation occurred without mediators, enabled by everyday diplomacy.

Outside the shops, union organizers in Local 169 fought to force Korean grocers to observe labour laws and wages and working hours, but this fight itself took a social turn; the organizers and the State of New York began offering seminars on labour law, and issued certificates of education to Korean grocers who attended them; in Flushing, a neighbourhood at the edge of the city, about 250 Korean grocers 'graduated' from this one-day university. The point was to change their attitudes as much as to teach them the law.

Like Boston factory workers in an earlier generation, the Latinos – mostly Mexican – were long-term employees. Since so many of these Mexicans were illegal immigrants, the owners could simply have menaced them with exposure to keep them in line, but the relations of Koreans and Latinos had over time become personally close. The ethnographer Pyong Gap Min found that the Koreans sensed, and admired, an ethic of working hard among the Latinos very similar to their own. Prejudice did enter the picture: whereas the Koreans viewed African-American customers as criminals, the owners felt paternal about these Latino employees and that they would be obedient if led firmly. A woman grocer told Pyong Gap Min, 'All of them work hard and cause no trouble at all. I feel like they are my own children. It hurts me to think about their miserable situation.'[12]

Instead, the Latinos wanted the Koreans to treat them as adults. Because the two ethnic groups worked intimately, day in and day out, over the years, that change occurred slowly but effectively. Like Thatcher's Cabinet ministers, the Latinos argued back, in the back-rooms of the stores during cigarette breaks and sometimes even while serving customers.

This is no story of healing, however; the tensions remain today, two decades after they erupted. But they have been managed – without mediators – because these two groups are mutually dependent; the Koreans need people willing to work as hard and long as themselves, the Latinos need employers willing to shield them from the law. In time, the two have acknowledged this shared dependency, but they have also, as in a family, established lines which cannot be crossed. The Mexicans cannot go on strike and not expect the owners to call in the authorities; the Koreans cannot treat these long-serving, hard-working employees as children doled out money-treats.

Professional mediators seek to arrange the conditions in which the storm blows over and a productive result emerges; mediation without mediators can produce this same result, but not so methodically and generically; the sources of tension remain in the repair. Either way, the balance between speech and silence, on both sides, will be reconfigured.

It could be said that this rebalancing creates civility of a sort. In his late philosophy, Ludwig Wittgenstein's rule was that you keep silent about things that lie beyond clear and precise language. In practising social civility, you keep silent about things you know clearly but which you should not and do not say. This was the rule Koreans, Latinos and African-Americans began to apply in their dealings with each other.

PROCEDURES

For all the virtues of indirection and silence, the nub of cooperation is active participation rather than passive presence. Tocqueville took up this proposition in idealizing the local New England town meetings or voluntary organizations where everyone had his or her say. This rosy prospect often becomes an experience of torture, as twenty people discuss to death a decision which an individual could take in a min-ute; worse, skilled torturers know just when to make the killer point or summarize 'the sense of the meeting', a consensus to which others agree only because they are exhausted. On such occasions anyone, like Denis Diderot, may exclaim, 'The man of sensibility obeys the impulse of nature and gives nothing more or less than the cry of his very heart; the moment he moderates or strengthens this cry, he is no longer himself . . . '[13]

The challenge of participation is to make it worth people's time. In meetings, that depends on how they are structured. Were they structured like the luthiers' workshop, they would create consensus through bodily gestures. Were they structured like a laboratory-workshop, they would proceed openly yet produce a tangible result, steering between the Scylla of the fixed agenda and the Charybdis of aimless rambling. The fraught meeting, as in a reconfiguring repair, would acknowledge the pains and troubles which brought people to the table, avoiding the fantasy of 'settling matters' once and for all. In all such meetings, participants would develop rituals of talking better and more fully to one another, via the tacit-explicit-tacit rhythm of skill.

Sounds good? It seems an exercise in fantasy. We want to know whether and how it might in practice become more a reality. To do so, we need to touch on a seemingly boring subject.

Formal and informal meetings

In a study of 'the development of modern meeting behaviour', Wilbert van Vree has traced the history of the procedures which today structure meetings – rules of procedure, of note-taking, of speaking in turn and yielding the floor.[14] This is the formal meeting which regulates participation and discourages informal exchange. So familiar now are the numbing procedures van Vree details that we might think it has always been thus, but it wasn't, at least in the business world. Medieval commercial meetings were often violent occasions, people moving easily in negotiating a contract from exchanging words to exchanging blows. The guild system kept order partly by emphasizing hierarchy, since superiors always spoke first and masters were obliged to speak among themselves in order of age. Rank is the governor of the formal meeting, establishing when it is someone's turn to speak. In the sixteenth century, however, European commercial culture opened up an alternative practice.

In part, the change occurred due to the advent of printing. In an age when printed texts – formal contracts, published double-entry bookkeeping accounts and the like – began to shape business, spoken discussion became necessary to interpret mass-produced documents.

Such discussion weakened age-grading; the elder might be no better at making sense of the impersonal printed page than the bright young assistant, who could be as good as, or better than, anyone else at reading or calculating numbers. Interpreting printed documents helped unsettle the authority implicit in rank. But the numbers in these documents were no replacement for personal authority in conducting business meetings.

On Holbein's table, Peter Apian's book *On Mercantile Calculations* asked its readers to think about accounting procedures. Then, as now, people sought the reassurance that something was a hard fact if it could be represented by a number. Apian, one of the first methodical accountants, knew otherwise; numbers are representations which need to be discussed. The historian Mary Poovey has argued, indeed, that the rising of double-entry book-keeping and of literary criticism were intertwined in the early modern era, as both numbers and words seemed equally in need of critique.[15] Thus the rigidly formal business meeting began to prove counter-productive.

The more open meeting derived also from new forms of power. Due to its colonizing reach during the sixteenth and seventeenth centuries, European business became ever more complex, and complexity spawned the need to meet. At its origin, for instance, Britain's East India Company had a rudimentary structure and few formal meetings; as the company grew globally, its departments met more frequently to sort out turf battles and allocate the colonial spoils; the more powerful the Company became, the more it intersected with government, requiring yet more meetings. Bureaucracy sought to push back against this imperative for open communication; against the open meeting it sought defence in the written report, the report which achieves the bureaucratic sanctity of an official document defeating open discussion. The official document is bureaucracy's formal version of the silos discussed in Chapter 5; conflict between the official document and the need for free discussion appeared in the early modern period in diplomacy as in business, the diplomat's back-channels and vernacular speech set against the formalities of negotiation in official documents. By the eighteenth century, when Frederick the Great reformed the Prussian civil service, he was pulled between these forces: he wanted the state apparatus formally fixed in documents yet understood that departments work poorly if they rely for coordination solely on paper reports.

A third side of the open meeting's history was bigger and less dry, one of the consequences of the weakening of inherited position. In medieval armies, the son of a regimental commander could look forward to inheriting his father's regiment (a situation which lasted in Britain up to the nineteenth century); so too could sons of government officials. Birth was authority enough, the idea of earned authority was weak. Inherited office began to be challenged in the early modern period; the shocking thought was that, instead, the holders of office should earn their jobs by actually being good at them. Ability should rule, rather than birth or seniority.

One way to discover talent lay in behaviour at meetings. The diaries of Samuel Pepys (1633–1703), a 'new man' making his way by his own abilities in the Admiralty, show him to be a master of meetings, disputing the formal dictates of his superiors without putting their backs up, getting warring departments to sit down and talk, disputing and discussing the financial numbers given to the Admiralty by the Crown's financial masters. These discursive talents provided a different forum for civility from the salon; mutual pleasure was not the point. Nor was Pepys a split-the-difference appeaser; in meetings he fought his corner but without making other participants feel cornered. This skill in meetings sends an important signal now, as it did to his contemporaries.

We often imagine compromisers as the people skilled at meetings and the act of striking a compromise to be enabled by formality. Not so. The compromiser assumes that beliefs and interests are just bargaining chips, which supposes that the people holding these views aren't firmly committed. Oddly, many people do believe what they say to others; meetings which chip away at these beliefs in the name of compromise often leave engaged participants with the sour sense that they've been sold out by the meeting, or, worse, that they've sold themselves out. More, the committed compromiser, as it were, seeks to diffuse conflict, assuming that conflict will spiral out of control. Rather than behave like the Korean grocers, who manage violent conflict through silence, committed compromisers want an explicit resolution. For the sake of this, they often give away their own position in advance before any conflict has begun, hoping to show others how 'reasonable' they are.

The real virtue of the formal meeting is that it can avoid this vice of appeasement. If a written record of talk is kept, people can put their views as strongly as they like, knowing that these will be preserved. The record makes for official transparency, and more, if the meeting does wind up with a compromise, the participants can still feel that they have not been personally compromised; it's on record that they put on the table what they really believed.* Formality allows for inclusion, if all participants follow the same code of speaking in turn or yielding the floor.

Yet formality is not a solution, by itself, to the problem of transparence. This is in part due to the behaviour of the chairman. In an analysis of how people chair formal meetings, the Dutch sociologist P. H. Ritter argued some time ago that 'Every meeting has the tendency to adjust its behaviour to the chairman. The chairman is the example for the meeting.'[16] People at the meeting become fixated on the chairman's approval, by judicious nods of the head, say, trying to catch his attention and the recognition he gives for their valuable, pertinent, etc. contribution.

More, a formally fixed agenda inhibits evolution of a problem from within. In a workshop, shared labour follows where the materials and tools at hand lead; there is an overall goal but getting to the end may take different routes, following alternative scenarios to see which is best; such workshop labour is a narrative. A formally fixed agenda is not a narrative. Even the contribution of clear comments and positions can freeze a formal meeting. The odd thought may have struck someone, a thought ill-formed but well worth pursuing, but such a *coup de foudre* will have less weight than the carefully thought-out contribution. Formality favours authority and seeks to prevent surprise.

The open meeting, in principle, seeks by contrast more equality and more surprise. The issue is how the open meeting might create an

---

* During the Blair regime in Britain, the Prime Minister practised 'sofa politics', informal dealings with his ministers on his prime ministerial sofa which left no trace. After he left office, many of these ministers claimed they really didn't believe in what he was doing – but who knows? There is no record.

alternative to demeaning compromise. That issue turns on how people negotiate the borderline between formality and informality; it is a liminal zone, one in which some of the skills of indirect cooperation are put to a severe test.

The liminal zone

Professional diplomats have a bible for negotiating this borderline condition. It is Sir Ernest Satow's *Satow's Diplomatic Practice*, originally published in 1917, now in its sixth edition; non-English versions and variations of this work are in use globally.[17] Satow saw himself as a scribe, writing down practices which had crystallized since the time of Wotton's resident mission in Venice. The genius of this work is to show how informality, indirection and mutuality can be injected into even the most stiff meeting. Four of Satow's counsels are particularly useful.

The first explains what to do if two sides in conflict want to test a possible solution without actually taking ownership of it on the record: in this case, Satow counsels passing a *bout de papier* silently across the conference table. This unsigned piece of paper contains versions of the formula, 'If you felt able to propose . . . I should be prepared to try it on my government'; the diplomat thus behaves as if he or she is then responding to an adversary's position rather than asserting one of his or her own.[18] Say the diplomat is negotiating a treaty of surrender on behalf of a victorious country: the *bout de papier* might help the defeated save face, and so push the negotiations forward more quickly; the great diplomat Talleyrand served Napoleon in just this way. The ritual of the *bout de papier* creates a space of deference from a position of power; it is an exercise in applying minimum force.

The *démarche* in one way extends the *bout de papier*; it is a document which floats a set of ideas and talking points for circulation, without the authors actually asserting they think or believe what's in the document; American diplomatic practice now calls this the 'front-channel cable'.[19] The *démarche* can invite a subtle kind of participation: rather than declaring, 'This is what I want or my country wants,' the talking points, the document – the 'it' in workshop parlance – floats freely so that all parties can engage equally in discussion. I'll give a personal example. When I worked with UNESCO, the United Nations' cultural arm, almost all discussions about listing monuments as World Heritage Sites were floated as *démarches*; diplomats took no personal ownership over any particular recommendation in order that each could be considered freely and impersonally. The ritual of the *démarche* differs from the *bout de papier* in eschewing agency, rather than enacting deference, and is useful to the weak as well as the strong.

These diplomatic practices are alternatives to split-the-difference appeasing, since they can put strongly held positions on the table, but not as self-interested declarations. By stepping back, the parties can then work towards accepting or rejecting another view without necessarily having to compromise their own. The exchange is liminal in the sense that it creates ambiguity, yet it would be wrong to scorn this kind of diplomacy as ineffective; the *bout de papier* and the *démarche* seek to make the meeting between the strong and the weak a win-win exchange. In everyday life, both practices translate as what we have called deployment of the subjunctive mood.

Diplomatic protocol is nothing so subtle as the *bout de papier* or the *démarche* but can also be structured to make diplomacy more liminal. In the seventeenth century the English diplomatic William Temple declared, 'ceremonies were made to facilitate business, not to hinder it.'[20] He was referring to ceremonial protocols of placement; at a formal dinner, the guest of honour is always placed next to the host or spouse of the host; this protocol is indeed formal and rigid. Protocol of a more ambiguous sort shapes seemingly casual meetings.

Diplomatic receptions and cocktail parties are occasions for the relentless exchange of non-controversial observations about sports or pets; in the flow of these inanities, the diplomat will 'casually' drop into the conversation something meaty about a government's plans or personnel, knowing that the conversation will be minutely dissected, if it hasn't actually been covertly recorded; the casual comment will later be fished out and acted on. The diplomatic craft, for the speaker, requires making sure the message gets through without too obviously dropping the hint; the skill of the listener lies in seeming not to notice. This ritual of casualness is, so professional diplomats say, very hard to get right, a demanding form of light touch; it is most often used for issues too explosive to be put on paper. Satow rightly views these cocktail-and-canapé occasions as meetings in disguise.

The fourth skill of indirect diplomacy which applies to the meeting concerns friendliness. Satow echoes the warning of the Earl of Malmesbury in 1813, to beware of foreigners 'eager to make your acquaintance and communicate their ideas to you'. Friendliness of this seemingly open sort is usually a trap.[21] No one is expected to be without guile, so the rituals of casualness, like the ritual of deference in the *bout de papier*, establish a particular social zone in diplomacy. Casualness can send a signal of trust – that the person to whom the diplomat is speaking will pick up the dropped clues.

This is not friendliness of the sort appearing on Facebook, where the adolescent point is to display as explicitly as possible all the details of one's daily life and little is left to the viewer's imagination. The casual hint is disguised and requires interpretative skill to be read right. The oblique diplomatic hint is most usefully an unfriendly warning encased in the rituals of sociable pleasure. Rather than appeasing, the indirect expression of the warning, engaging the listener suddenly, is meant to be more telling in its force. We know this practice in everyday life, but usually do not analyse dropped hints as methodically as do professional diplomats.

The prospect of violent conflict puts to an extreme test all four diplomatic skills, and often they fail to meet the case. In the confrontation launched in 1991 against the Iraqi regime of Saddam Hussein, the American letter announcing war was delivered to the foreign minister, Tariq Aziz, who was allowed to leave it unopened on the table while discussing its contents; the long-established ritual of the unopened letter is meant to allow the parties to continue talking, and to look for solutions, up to the very last moment. Similarly, in 1939, the first paragraphs of a British letter raising the prospect of war against Germany were full of expressions of respect for relations between the two countries; given these boilerplate expressions, if the Hitler regime had genuinely wanted peace, his diplomatic response might have focused on these niceties.

Such failures reinforce the common view that diplomatic ritual does not answer to the realities of power. The wily diplomat today certainly commands little public respect. Perhaps, though, we are looking in the wrong place to assess the value of these practices. Just as the Korean grocers learned to refigure the relation between speech and silence, so professional diplomats employing these tools refigure the liminal relation between clarity and ambiguity. By doing so, they enable the practice of what the political analyst Joseph Nye calls 'soft power'.[22] Softening the divide between informal and formal exchange can enable people to meet productively; it can keep people connected even when hostile to one another; it can provide behavioural alternatives to split-the-difference conduct.

In turn, we should look at them more as critical standards for everyday conduct. We need diplomatic skills in everyday meetings whenever a complex issue cannot be managed through decision-making. Rather than dropping the issue, people need to stay connected to one another; thorny issues seldom go away. The four diplomatic procedures establish rituals for the conduct of everyday meetings which accomplish just that. As appeared in Chapter 5, something like these diplomatic rituals appears in the formation of the informal social triangle, but changes at work are today making it harder for people to develop and practise these skills. While the socialist wants to make a large-scale critique of capitalism, the professional diplomat – certainly unwittingly – serves as a critic of those social practices at work which disable people who differ from working well together.

One thread runs through this chapter's themes of indirect cooperation, conflict management, diplomatic technique and meeting behaviour. All are performances of a sort, performances which differ from the self-serving drama Mazarin staged for Louis XIV. The dancing king dramatized his distance from, his domination over, his subjects. Mrs Schwartz, the Korean grocers and Satow's diplomats dramatize their engagement with other people by wearing a sociable mask.

THE SOCIABLE MASK

As was described in Chapter 1, Simmel took the city-dweller's cool and impassive demeanour to hide his or her inner, aroused response to the stimulations of the street. La Rochefoucauld thought of the mask as a metaphor for seeming other than one really is: 'each person puts on a pretended look and outward appearance to make him seem what he wants people to think him.'[23] Masks of the concealing, protective sort are found in all corners of social life; the job seeker needs to wear one at interviews, as did Theodore Kheel in labour negotiations, or German diplomats at Versailles negotiating the terms of defeat after the First World War; the Koreans in New York wore the mask of silence. The concealing mask need not be intended for self-protection; courtesy and tact are behaviours which mask feelings that might be hurtful to others.

Because the concealing mask is so ubiquitous, it's perhaps hard to imagine another sort, the sociable mask which makes people more aroused, their experience more intense. But if we consider the mask as physical object, this possibility makes more sense. The mask is one of culture's oldest stage-props, connecting stage and street.

The domino is a simple eye-mask, most familiar from old images of masked balls. The domino came into fashion in Europe in the fifteenth century, derived from *commedia dell'arte* performances given on the streets from the thirteenth century. In society, the domino has served as a sexually arousing mask. At balls, women donned coloured satin masks, cut to fit above the cheekbone up to the eyebrow, with slits for the eyes; the eye-mask sent the signal that a man or woman was up for pleasure; in street celebrations before Lent, the domino particularly gave women liberty to wander from place to place, flirting with strangers. The flimsy piece of cloth enabled a fiction: 'You don't know me,' even though the identity of a woman wearing it was barely disguised; 'I'm free,' the mask suspending bodily decorum, artifice making pleasure anonymous.

A more sober physical experience appeared in those masks worn by Jewish doctors in Venice from the fourteenth to the seventeenth century. These strange, dried-paste, painted objects began above the lips, covering the entire upper face. The mask was made to look half-human, half-bird, an enormous beak covering the nose but very wide slits exposing the recognizably human eyes and eyebrows. Most Christians shrank from physical contact with Jews and most doctors in Venice were Jewish; this mask was meant to bridge that fear. When a doctor donned the bird-mask, his patients relaxed about being touched, pushed and prodded physically by a Jew; some strange creature instead seemed to make physical contact.

Some masks provide one-sided, often vicious stimulation. As in Abu Ghraib prison during the recent war in Iraq, masking another person's body can excite the torturer; photographs from Abu Ghraib show hooded but otherwise naked victims disoriented or in pain, while surrounding them are young, clean-cut Americans smiling and laughing. The hooded figure has an older, less vicious provenance in the magician's costume, images of hooded magicians appearing as early as the eleventh century in France. At its medieval origins the magician's hood was, in an odd conceit, supposed to conceal the magician from the sight of God yet expose him to the influence of darker cosmic forces. As the historian Carlo Ginzburg has shown, during the black mass hooded celebrants signalled that they had left the realm of human feeling.

Domino, bird-mask and hood signal the mask's stimulating powers, but there is another kind of mask which has a more general social reach; this can be, oddly, a mask whose features are neutral. It can be arousing, if worn skilfully.

When France was liberated in 1944, the very young actor Jacques Lecoq had a fateful encounter. Performing in Grenoble, he met Jean Dasté, a great actor and animateur who wanted to free actors from all traces of pomposity and bombast, to act more simply and so more forcefully. To accomplish this, Dasté created painted papier-mâché masks whose features were neutral, wearable on stage by men or women, young or old. Lecoq was struck by the result. 'With an actor wearing the neutral mask, you look at the whole body,' he observed; 'the "face" becomes the whole body.'[24] Deprived of facial gesture, the actor has to communicate through body gestures and through the play of the voice.[25]

Inspired, Lecoq asked the sculptor Amleto Sartori to fashion leather masks for him (leather was used in the original *commedia dell'arte* masks). Lecoq then enlarged the eye-holes, and stretched the lips horizontally, neither smiling nor frowning; he made the chin an abstract bar and painted the mask white. Lecoq eventually founded a school to teach masked actors how to communicate without facial expression. The Lecoq 'method' involves in fact a demanding discipline, since, as it were, an emotional limb has been cut off. The extreme of this practice is mime, where no sound issues from the mouth; the tongue also cut out. The actor's hands then have to work hard to convey shock, pleasure or grief, and the craft of doing so does not come easily; simply donning a mask will not release the performer's body. The dominoes women wore at balls communicated one thing only: 'I'm available.' The masked actor has to express much more varied sentiments.

'Neutrality' is of course a many-sided experience. The neutral physical spaces in modern cities – those big glass-and-steel boxes surrounded by a bit of green which are everywhere and anywhere – are dead spaces, and many social relationships resemble the inert box. But Lecoq wanted his neutral mask to prompt the actor to behave expressively and directly: 'the mask will have drawn something from [the actor], divesting him of artifice.' Lecoq discovered that 'when the actor takes off the mask, if he has worn it well, his face is relaxed'.[26]

We want to pause on this. Alexis de Tocqueville created from his American travels the figure of an individual, the individual who takes comfort in a neutral, homogenized society, who seeks to avoid the anxiety of difference, and who, therefore, practises withdrawal. Lecoq's masked actor turns around these terms: the neutral mask relaxes the performer's body, but its purpose is to make him more expressive to his audience. The job counsellor and job applicant, the Korean grocer and the diplomat may actually act expressively in just the way Lecoq's actors do: by neutralizing some aspects of their behaviour, other aspects come to the fore. The neutral mask may increase stage presence in ordinary social behaviour.

At least this is a possibility which should be pursued a bit further. Professional actors, whether in Lecoq's mould or not, certainly have to suppress their own anxieties in order to express themselves forcefully on stage. To shed excess tension or stray energy from the body, the performer will concentrate on specific, focused and above all small gestures. Focused detail releases tension – the same goal as in masking. The actor Laurence Olivier proved a master of the small focused gesture, his arms and hands only rarely making sweeping movements; the same work on detail is part of the secret of the stage presence of great dancers like Sylvie Guillem or Suzanne Farrell, dancers who convey to audiences an enormous, stage-filling presence through focused detail, as in the sudden turn of a foot or flip of the hand.

This observation takes us a step further in making the comparison between stage and street. Cooperation also becomes a more expressive experience when focused on small gestures; many of these binding gestures are, as appeared to us in the luthiers' shop, physical and non-verbal. Again, one dimension of ritual lies in choreographing gestures both physical and verbal so that they can be repeated, performed again and again. Focused stage-work suggests why we can behave expressively in these social practices; we are feeling less tension physically, and so relaxation can prove stimulating rather than numbing.

The neutral masks on stage contrived by Dasté and Lecoq were meant to be impersonal in the sense that the same mask could be worn by a man or a woman, a short, fat actor or a willowy actor. They are thus freed from being typecast; indeed, when I've watched performances given by Lecoq's acolytes, it's striking how much more audiences engage with what the actor does rather than what the actor is like; the audience shares with the impersonal performer in the character of an act. This is an outward turn – just the turn required in complex forms of cooperation with people one may not like or know. Lecoq thinks of his theatre as a cooperative space, and that description makes sense socially.

In sum, social masks can enable expression, in addition to providing protective cover. There's a danger in thinking of everyday diplomacy, which in its varied forms makes use of the neutral mask, as mere empty manipulation of others. On the contrary, if we are not focused on revealing or characterizing ourselves, we can fill a shared social space with expressive content. Lecoq's theatre aims to efface the star performer, and, indeed, he claims that he has created democracy in the theatre. His method certainly lies at the opposite pole from Louis XIV's self-dramatization on stage, and his social claim is not extravagant, though it's not at all what Tocqueville meant by 'democracy'. The neutral, impersonal mask is one way to turn the actor outward, and so create a common space with the audience; complex cooperation needs to take that outward turn, to create a common space; everyday diplomacy is a crafting of expressive social distance. Concrete political consequences follow from this abstract precept.

9

The Community

Practising Commitment

In the first chapter of this study, I mentioned briefly the settlement house in Chicago where informal cooperation helped provide a social anchor for poor children like myself. At the study's end, I want to visit this scene again. Cooperation's difficulties, pleasures and consequences appeared among the people who passed through this dilapidated, bustling building on the city's Near West Side. Or so it seemed to me, when decades later I returned to share a weekend, sponsored by the settlement house, with thirty or so African-American adults who had grown up in this small corner of the Chicago ghetto.[1]

Memory played the same trick on my childhood neighbours that it does on everyone; the experience of years of change can be compressed in the memory of a face or a room. The black children I grew up with had a compelling reason to remember in this way. They were survivors. Their childhoods disorganized by poverty, doubting as adolescents that they had much of value in themselves to offer the larger world, they puzzled later in life about why they survived while so many of their childhood mates had succumbed to addiction, crime or lives lived on the margins. So they singled out a person, place or event as a transforming experience for themselves, as a talisman. The settlement house became a talisman, as did the strict local Catholic school and the sports club run by an organization called the Police Athletic League.

My childhood companions were not heroic; they did not rise from rags to riches, becoming racial exemplars of the American Dream. Only a few made it to university; most steadied themselves enough to get through secondary school, thereafter taking jobs as secretaries, firemen, store-keepers or functionaries in local government. Their gains, which might seem modest to an outsider, were to them enormous. Over the four days of our reunion, I went to visit some of their homes, and recognized domestic signs of the journey we had all taken: tidy backyards with well-tended plants, unlike the broken-bottle-strewn play areas surrounded by chain-link fences we had known as children; domestic interiors stuffed with knick-knacks and carefully brushed furniture, again a contrast to the bare, scuffed interiors which before had counted for us as 'home'.

At the settlement-house reunion, people spoke with wonder at what had happened to the neighbourhood since we had all left. It had sunk further than any of us could have imagined, and was now a vast archipelago of abandoned houses, isolated apartment towers in which the elevators stank of urine and shit, a place where no policemen responded to telephone calls for help and most adolescents carried knives or guns. The magic talismans of a place or a face seemed even more required to explain the luck of escape.

The administrators of the settlement house, like the elderly cop representing the Police Athletic League, were of course happy to hear these testimonials to their saving presence, but too realistic to believe entirely in their own transforming potency: many kids who banged on instruments in the settlement house or played basketball on a nearby paved court eventually wound up in jail. And the past remained unfinished business for the survivors; issues they faced as children they continued to face as adults. That unfinished business falls under three headings.

The first concerns morale, the matter of keeping one's spirits up in difficult circumstances. So simple to state, morale was less clear to explain in practice, since my neighbours had every rational reason to succumb to low spirits as children, and even now could still wake up at night, when worried about an unpaid bill or a problem at work, thinking the whole edifice of their adult lives might suddenly collapse like a house of cards.

The second issue concerns conviction. At our gathering, people declared they had survived thanks to strong, guiding convictions – all were devoted churchgoers, and all had faith in family writ large. Though the African-American adults had passed through, and benefited from, the American civil rights upheavals of the 1960s, those political gains didn't figure so much in their own thinking about their personal survival; if a door opens, you do not automatically walk through it. Yet when we got down to the grit of discussing our own children's adolescent angst, few people applied Scripture to that perennial, particular hard case. So too at work; rather than moralizing, people think flexibly and adaptively about concrete behaviour. On the job, for the first time, many of these young African-Americans were working side by side with whites, and they had to feel their way. Even twenty years later they had to do so, as when my childhood next-door neighbour became the supervisor of a group of mostly white subordinates in the motor bureau of Chicago.

And then there was the matter of cooperation. As children, the 'fuck you' version of cooperation dominated our lives, since all gangs in the community subscribed to it, and the gangs were powerful. In the immediate post-Second World War era, gangs dealt in petty theft rather than in drugs, as they would a generation later; small children were sent to 'front' shoplifting, since, if these children were caught, they could not be sent to jail. To avoid being sucked into gang life, kids had to find other ways of associating with one another, ways that flew under the radar-screen, as it were, of the gang's control. This meant hanging out in bus shelters or other places than those marked out as gang turf, or staying late at school, or heading directly to the settlement house. A place of refuge meant somewhere you could talk about parents, do homework together, or play checkers, all intermissions from 'fuck you' aggression. These intermissions in retrospect seemed enormously important, since the experiences planted the seed for the kind of behaviour, open rather than defensive, which had served people to make their way outside the community.

Now some of those who had survived by leaving wanted to 'give something back', in the words of a childhood neighbour, a foreman in the city's sanitation department, but the youngsters in the project a generation later were hostile to people who offered themselves as helping hands, as 'role models'. As always, the message 'If I can do it, so can you' can be turned around: 'If I made good, why aren't you succeeding? What's wrong with you?' So the role model's offer to give something back to the community, to reach out, was rejected by the young people in the community who most needed help.

All three of these issues – the fragility of morale, conviction, cooperation – were familiar to me, but for me as a white boy they cut a different way. My mother and I moved to the housing project when my father left in my infancy and left us penniless, but we lived there only about seven years; as soon as our family fortunes returned, we moved out. The community posed dangers for me but not mortal dangers. Perhaps thanks to this distance, the reunion sparked in me the desire to understand how the three pieces of unfinished business among my childhood friends might be seen in a larger context.

THE QUEST FOR COMMUNITY

As housing projects like Cabrini Green began to sink into misery during the 1950s, the conservative sociologist Robert Nisbet (1913-96) conceived a classic book, *The Quest for Community*, first published in 1953, the book becoming a bible for the group known as 'the new conservatives'.[2] These were American and English heirs to Tocqueville who stressed the virtues of local life, of volunteering and voluntary organizations, to which they contrasted the vices of the big state, especially the welfare state. The 'quest' for community is more, in Nisbet's writing, than a metaphor: he traces the struggle required for people to form face-to-face relationships, when state bureaucracies get in the way. Nisbet and his colleague Russell Kirk were 'new' conservatives in the 1950s because they actually cared about the social lives of the poor, whereas small-government advocates in the Great Depression of the 1930s had dwelled just on taxes, free enterprise and property rights. These new conservatives were also 'old' because the belief that poor people can fulfil themselves in local life traces back to the eighteenth-century philosopher Edmund Burke.

They were also prophetic. What is called in Britain today 'modern conservatism' dwells on the virtues of local life, the poor in communities being supported by volunteers rather than by welfare-state bureaucrats; this localism the Prime Minister David Cameron calls the 'Big Society', by which he means big in heart, though short of state funding. In America, some elements of today's Tea Party movement are communal conservatives who share the same vision; rather than merely selfish individualists, these conservatives want neighbours to help each other out.

The proverbial visitor from Mars might think that little distinguishes conservatives of this stripe from the heirs of the social Left, those legions following in the steps of Saul Alinsky also engaged in community service and fighting big bureaucracy. This visitor thinks she (he? it?) hears exactly the same language on the Right and Left, that of resisting the state and of empowering the people. But there is a huge difference. Nisbet's view was that small communities can be self-supporting, while the social Left doubts that such communities can sustain themselves economically. The social Right believes capitalism will provide for local life, the social Left thinks not.

Left and Right are talking about two different kinds of small communities. The social Right's model is the village or the town, with locally owned shops and banks; even if small-town life was never in fact self-sufficient, the social Right wants to make it so now. The social Left's engagement with small communities has occurred in big cities, cities filled with chain stores, giant corporations and globally oriented, locally insulated bankers. Of course the capitalist monster has to be resisted, but the realistic Leftist knows it will not be slain at the corner store.

Though Nisbet had grown up in a small town, he was interested in cities. He stressed that, before European and American cities began their great growth-spurt in the nineteenth century, a close connection existed between where people worked and where they lived; though one might not work in the same street where one lived, labour, family and community were still linked geographically. The advent of big factories changed this compactness; factories required vacant, cheap land; cheap land lay in most cities far from the crowded centre.[3] The development of train networks prompted the spread of another sort, working-class and lower-middle-class suburbs far away from the grime of the factories or the office beehives of the central business district. In fact, sprawl was not an invariable rule: in New York, for instance, garment workers on the Lower East Side in 1900 lived a fifteen-minute commute by subway from the garment distinct uptown; in the East End of London, sizeable factories were mixed into the fabric of local housing.

Nisbet hoped that local virtues could be strengthened by increasing the density of cities, and by returning their geography to a more compacted, linked condition. He slighted, in this hope, the power of the forces that had split the city apart. These powerful facts now seem obvious, facts which render local communities ever less self-sufficient.[4] The retail commerce in most British high streets is now conducted by large non-local firms, and the profits from high-street, brand-name shops do not stay in the community. A telling American example of the same loss is that, in 2000, only about five cents of every dollar spent in retail commerce in Harlem remained in Harlem. Small, locally based enterprises have trouble getting financing, especially from big banks, and these businesses are obliged to charge more than chains like Walmart, weakening their customer base. The result of these familiar evils is, as the urbanist Saskia Sassen argues, that local retail economies now function as colonial natural-resource economies once did, generating wealth that is extracted and exported.[5]

The social conservative's hope to replace the welfare state by local volunteer action suffers from a kindred economic fact. When money is stripped out of a local community, it becomes ever harder to get people to volunteer.[6] The reason for this is straightforward: cash-strapped local organizations are continually obliged to make cuts and, as the mantra has it, 'do more with less'; service-provision becomes more stressful for the providers; volunteer providers are put off, not just by the pressure but also by the fact that charities or grass-root groups can't do the job they are asked to do. Leaders of these groups, whether paid or not, spend much of their time scrounging for donations rather than concentrating on the substance of the work. When conservatives like Nisbet hark back to Tocqueville's celebration of the volunteer, they ignore what impressed Tocqueville in the prosperous America through which he travelled: sufficient money existed in each community to make volunteer effort work and seem worthwhile. For this reason, I think it's fair to liken the 'Big Society' idea of David Cameron to economic colonialism as Sassen describes it: the local community, like the colony, is stripped of wealth, then told to make up for that lack by its own efforts.

The challenge faced by local community organizers on the social

Left is how to strengthen communities whose economic heart is weak. That sluggish organ can't be resuscitated locally, as economic-justice groups in the United States like ACORN or DART have found; they've had to grow into national organizations, abandoning the path of local 'associationism' which oriented the social Left in Paris a century ago. Certainly, there are organizers who have accepted the economic facts of life yet insist on the value of community. The American, British and Dutch followers of the Brazilian educator Paulo Freire (1921–97) do so; the groups they have formed dwell on reform of local schools as a point of entry to mobilizing people locally.[7] They know the poor have suffered an economic wound; they want people to recover from that wound by making a fresh start in another aspect of their lives. This quest is about lifting the poor from dwelling on their weakness; the quest is complicated just because they are likely to remain, in modern capitalism, poor and marginal. How can morale be built up on these tough terms?

MORALE

The Victorians were rather stern about morale. 'Pick yourself up!, stop wallowing and get on with it!' In this spirit, the rabbi of my local synagogue remarked to me, 'Whenever a moment of metaphysical doubt descends on me, I clean out the garage.' Morale differs from commitment in being a sentiment of immediate well-being; commitment has a longer prospect in time: raising your children well, starting your own business or perhaps writing a novel. Can people suffer from weak morale even as they feel strong commitment? On the face of it, certainly. Raising children is frequently demoralizing but that doesn't weaken the commitment of most parents to their children: you get on with it. Novel-writing, which demands enormous commitment, seems a pleasure only to people who have never written a novel. But modern society seems to counter the Victorian imperative differently, believing that morale is an all-important fact. Morale is contained in our phase 'well-being'.

A recent World Health Organization study argues that low morale, framed as depression, has reached epidemic proportions, with nearly a quarter of the population in the developed world suffering from it, and 15 per cent of the population in those countries taking medication for it.[8] (As noted in Chapter 4, children are now targeted consumers for these pills.) The psychoanalyst Darian Leader is sceptical of the WHO statistics, believing that the epidemic of depression reformats the sadness and injustice which attend real life into a disease.[9] Still, the experience of depression is a neurochemical reality; in its bodily state, depression diminishes energy, and at its further reaches makes any demanding action seem impossible. True clinical depression is no temporary feeling, and it destroys the capacity to commit.

Cooperative activity is sometimes recommended as a therapy for the clinically depressed. The complexity of cooperative experience is itself demeaned when used as therapy in this way. Visiting in a hospital a friend whose depression had reach suicidal dimensions, I found the clinic's staff trying to engage her in simple singalongs and kitchen clean-ups with others. She could engage in these tasks but nothing more complicated; an abyss separated their very simplicity from the depths inside her. Surprisingly, in time she got better on her own. We owe to Freud one explanation of why this should have occurred; clinical recoveries of her sort led him to frame in a larger way the meaning of morale.

Early in his researches, Freud took aim at the popular idea of depression simply as low self-esteem. The depressive, he argued, is instead full of rage and anger at the world for failing him or her; this anger is then turned on him- or herself; self-reproach is safer, more controllable, than confronting others. In *Totem and Taboo*, a work that took shape in 1912, Freud wrote that 'in almost every case where there is an intense emotional attachment to a particular person we find that behind the tender love there is a concealed hostility in the unconscious'.[10] Depression, he argued, masks anger against parents, spouses, lovers or friends: the anger which dare not speak its name.

These early views are the Freud many of us dislike; the psychic machine grinds on relentlessly, no matter what the circumstances. Perhaps Freud himself sensed that his account was too mechanical, or perhaps the horrors of the First World War with its millions of deaths spoke to him; for whatever reason, by the end of the war he had enlarged his understanding of depression. An essay published in 1917, 'Mourning and Melancholia', draws a distinction between two forms of low morale in terms of time. Depression, 'melancholia', is a steady-state, a dull drumbeat which repeats again and again, whereas mourning contains a narrative, one in which the pain of loss for a parent or a lover is gradually acknowledged as irremediable, the lost one is accepted as gone and the desire to go forward revives; in Freud's clinical language, 'reality-testing has revealed that the beloved object no longer exists ... [in time] respect for reality carries the day ... the ego is left free and uninhibited once again after the mourning-work is completed.'[11]

By the end of the First World War, then, Freud found in the experience of mourning a way to depict the natural rhythms of life, death and survival. Mourning fits the case of my friend, whose lover had decamped, taking their adopted children with her; in time my friend accepted the sheer fact that they were gone. In a different register, mourning is built into Chipperfield's Neues Museum: the city's painful history is inscribed into the building's fabric, becoming a solid object rather than a hovering black cloud. Again, Freud's distinction explains why some of the unemployed people I interviewed on Wall Street have indeed sunk into depression while others have not. If Freud is right – unlike the legions of pop psychologists who invoke 'healing' – the sentiment of loss never heals, but rather is accepted, a contained experience in itself.

Most of all, his view of mourning shaped Freud's belief in work. Work issues a call to return to the world, outside of the worker's own emotional history. Answering the call, morale returns in the form of personal energy; physiological as well as psychic weight lifts. Rather than promising 'well-being', work promises re-engagement. Yet this is not a social re-engagement; cooperative acts in themselves don't figure much in Freud's way of thinking.

We might think of mourning as a kind of repair work. The forms of repair explored in Chapter 7 can make this thought more precise. Freud didn't view the traumas in a life as a china restorer would view a shattered vase. The depressive who longs to reattach to everyday life knows he or she cannot just set back the clock. This knowledge applies to every refugee who survives exile well – mourning the past, certainly, but avoiding the iron grip of nostalgia, as Hannah Arendt put it, in order to make a second life elsewhere.[12] Theologically, Adam and Eve knew they could not return to the Garden of Eden. Mourning is thus a reconfiguration, coming from within.

These observations are one way to make sense of the survivors of Cabrini Green. The littered streets and broken-windowed tenements in which they had grown up were to them disorders neither erased nor denied; indeed, they felt sentiments of a somewhat positive sort about these scenes; they had been children here, played amid the garbage, fought one another to no purpose, and survived. They mourned the ghetto realm of their childhood, in the way Freud speaks of mourning. The past was in them, still disturbing but no longer a governing history; the trauma strengthened the convictions they possessed about how now to lead their lives.

To Freud's picture we want to draw a sharp contrast. It lies in the classic sociological version of low morale made by Émile Durkheim (1858–1917), an explanation which emphasizes the role of social institutions and sociable cooperation in restoring morale. Durkheim was a generation older than Freud, and that difference of a generation counts. War played little role in Durkheim's thinking; the institutions Durkheim put on the couch were the seemingly permanent factories, government bureaucracies and political parties of Europe in the last decades of the nineteenth century.

In one way, Durkheim's view of morale is simple: strong attachment to institutions stiffens morale, while weak attachments erode it. He would have made straightforward sense of the back-office workers on Wall Street in just this way; though strongly motivated to do good work, their morale was low because the workplace bred little loyalty. An 'institution' meant more to Durkheim than a formal bureaucratic structure; institutions like the army or the government ministry embody traditions and mutual understandings, rituals and civilities, which can't be pinned down to an organizational chart; to Durkheim we owe the concept of institutional culture. This culture can make detachment a demoralizing experience.

One of the most striking passages in Durkheim's famous study of suicide focuses on the fate of the 'driven man' who makes good.

Durkheim found that the suicide rates of such upwardly mobile individuals are nearly as high as those of people whose fortunes collapse and plunge downward.[13] He pondered this statistical fact, and came to a more general explanation. The upwardly mobile are often cut adrift, ill at ease with new-found wealth or power, because institutional cultures do not allow them to feel they belong. Upwardly mobile Jews in France were a touchstone for Durkheim, himself a Jew. The French army took in Captain Alfred Dreyfus, but, even before spewing him out during the infamous Dreyfus Affair, never allowed Dreyfus to feel 'one of us'. So, too, the higher reaches of the French government; while Jews had had equal rights for a century, since Napoleonic times, in 1900 high Jewish officials were still treated as outsiders. Nor could upwardly mobile businessmen buy their way in by money alone; the Jockey Club – that most elite of Parisian social clubs which made an exception for Charles Haas (on whom Proust based his character Charles Swann) – prided itself on leaving Jewish applicants in limbo for years, or decades.

Durkheim then applied his explanation more generally. People who are kept out of institutions, whether they are upwardly mobile Jews or, way down the economic scale, workers whose voices are unheard by foremen – people who are shut out, unrecognized – then suffer anomie, which was Durkheim's term for loss of morale. Anomie is a sentiment of rootlessness, of being cast adrift. In couching anomie in these terms, Durkheim sought to dig deeper into the consequences of exclusion; people can internalize exclusion to feel that, indeed, they really have weak claims on others, that the exclusion is somehow justified. The internal rebound is evident in those upwardly mobile people who feel they are faking in their new circumstances; in American literature, Jay Gatsby in Fitzgerald's novel suffers from anomie in this form. But Durkheim believed this sort of internalized rootlessness was much more widespread. The culture of institutions has judged you and you really don't fit in. Suicide, so extreme a state of despair, opened for Durkheim a window on the more ordinary consequence of detachment that the individual inwardly absorbs as self-doubt.

Among the poor, as in Cabrini Green, gang life can be a solution to the problem of anomie – and an effective one. Sudhir Venkatesh, a sociologist who has studied gang life in my childhood community in depth, shows how it has provided children and adolescents with a way to feel that they fit in and belong. The gangs which now deal drugs, so immensely profitable in the short-term for kids, also solve the upward-mobility puzzle of anomie Durkheim explored far up the social scale in another country; gangs make young people feel they belong through elaborate rituals of initiation and promotion; a young person rising up the gang ladder feels ever more bonded to his or her peers.[14] By contrast, community organizers seeking to get young people out of gangs have risked creating anomie – at least in neighbourhoods like Cabrini Green – since the alternative institutional culture they seek to create is relatively weak.

Put largely, anomie and mourning are the two sides of morale, on one side detachment, on the other reattachment. This two-sided coin differs from and is more complex than thinking in terms of solidarity. And between the two, mourning is more complex emotionally than anomie. Mourning is framed in terms of the passage of time; in the mourning process one reattaches to a new condition. It lifts the spirits in a different way from simply offering people the prospect of fitting in. But morale, boosted either by the passage of time or by simple adhesion to a familiar group, has limits. A moment arrives when people have to make a judgement: is the institution worth one's attachment? One of the effects of mourning, indeed, is to sharpen that question; people reconsider how they want to live. Thanks to the work of Elijah Anderson and Mitchell Duneir, as well as that of Sudhir Venkatesh, we know many young gang members indeed begin asking the question, 'Is this what I want to do with my life?' when they hit their mid-twenties.[15] It is a question, indeed, for which all people have to find an answer, an answer which can appear by testing commitment in different ways.

TESTS OF COMMITMENT

Commitment can be tested in a straightforward way: how much are you prepared to sacrifice for it? In the scale of social exchange presented in Chapter 2, altruism represents the strongest sort of commitment; Joan of Arc going to the stake for her beliefs, the ordinary soldier dying in battle to protect his buddies. At the other end of the scale, among apex predators, whether alligators or bankers, self-sacrifice does not figure, and so the test does not arise. In the middle human zones, the sacrifices entailed by commitment are more mixed. The win-win exchange of a business deal requires all the parties to give up some particular interest for the sake of an agreement beneficial to all; so too a political coalition requires a similar calibration. The differentiating exchange, the illuminating encounter, involves no self-sacrifice, but neither does it entail besting another person, requiring them to give up something.

A brutal test of commitment, on just these terms, arose in communities like Cabrini Green in the 1960s. That was the decade in which the black middle class began to expand; should people beginning to rise stay in the places where they grew up? Nearly a century earlier, Booker T. Washington had imagined the upwardly mobile craftsmen in the Institutes would return home to improve the lot of others. But now it was a zero-sum game, real sacrifice was involved if the upwardly mobile remained, for in the 1960s poor black communities were becoming more socially disorganized, as the drug trade entered the ghetto, the numbers of adolescent single mothers rose and government efforts to improve material living standards fell short. Did the upwardly mobile have a duty to sacrifice themselves on this altar? Only the privileged can answer that question easily.

Another way to measure commitment is in terms of time, short-term and long-term commitment. In Chapter 5, we contrasted short-term teamwork in some businesses on Wall Street with Chinese *guanxi*, a long-term connection: the short-term weakens commitments between the different ranks within an organization, while *guanxi* strengthens them outside institutions. Short-term commitments can be particularly destructive of the sentiments of obligation and loyalty. Short-term time does not, though, invariably produce these dire consequences. Serious communication online, like that attempted in GoogleWave, can be both brief and strongly bonding; the people in my GoogleWave group became so mutually committed that we boarded aeroplanes to meet when the program failed us.

One of the threads between poor people that is not so visible to outsiders is long-term commitments made through extended family ties. These ties mark African-Americans as much as Korean Americans, and obtain elsewhere, as among Turks and Moroccans living in Western Europe. Legal definitions of family tend to dwell on blood kin who live in the same house; further, social policy tends to focus on the nuclear family of parents and their immediate children.[16] For the poor, immigrant or not, house-based, nuclear ties do not measure well the web of supportive commitments on which people draw. Each household may be an insufficient foundation economically; socially, the passing of young people from household to household is a way of strengthening ties in a large circle and across the generations – a domestic version, if you like, of *guanxi*.[17] In moving up and moving out of the ghetto, some of my childhood friends found that commitments of this sort contracted; social mobility meant that the long-term frame of commitment shrank to the nuclear family.

Reliability is a third way to test commitment. We can think of this test as belonging to the realm of what can be predicted to happen, the most predictable behaviour seeming predetermined. Bees do not decide to dance; the urge to do so lies in their genes. Commitment becomes less reliable, the more it entails making a decision; changed circumstances and desires cause us to take back commitments. All primates, in groups as well as individually, are capable of withdrawing from commitments. Humans moralize this withdrawal as betrayal, or frame it emotionally as disappointment – but, as adults, we know we will at times fail others and that they will fail us; the commitments formed in adult experience cannot have beelike certainty.

The community reunion in 1980 sparked in me, as it did for the sanitation foreman, the desire to give something back. Life had turned out well for me; I had become a solid bourgeois. Occasionally, when in Chicago, I returned to Cabrini Green but also began spending the odd Saturday at a housing project in Spanish Harlem in New York; what I had to give back was what I knew best, helping kids learn to play music. But 'giving back' inspired in them great anxiety: what if I didn't show up because I was too busy, or wanted to do something else that day? It was, after all, my choice. And because giving something back was my choice, I was, in their eyes and rightly so, unreliable, even though I did my best to appear regularly. Gradually I felt burdened by their anxiety, by the question of my reliability; the desire to give something back then eroded in me.

VOCATION

Self-sacrificing, long-term, wilful and so fragile: these measures of commitment make it an experience inseparable from the ways we understand ourselves. We might want to reframe the experiences I've described by saying that strong commitment entails a duty to oneself. And then shift again the oppressive weight of that word 'duty' by thinking of commitment as a road map, the map of what you should do with your life.

Max Weber sought to explain this kind of sustaining commitment by the single German word *Beruf*, which roughly translates into English as a 'vocation' or a 'calling'. These English words are saturated with religious overtones from the time of the Great Unsettling.

The medieval Catholic imagined a religious vocation as the monk's decision to withdraw from the world; for others, remaining engaged in society, choice didn't enter the picture in the same way; faith was naturalized behaviour, taken for granted, beelike, though programmed culturally rather than genetically. Lutheran theology changed this. Drawing on the experiences of early Christianity, particularly on St Augustine's struggles to believe, Luther portrayed faith as an inner, active decision, a 'commitment to Christ' which has to be renewed again and again in the course of a believer's lifetime. The Protestant trauma lies in knowing what you should do with yourself, in the world. Judaism, Islam and Catholicism all provide life-designs external to the self; Protestantism of Luther's sort provides less of a design and stresses more the self.

A vocation can be made simple, framed just as strategic personal planning; when business gurus like John Kotter give motivational pep talks, they speak of inventing 'life-pursuit strategies' – all the Protestant pain of not knowing your purpose in life is rather hygienically removed in that advice.[18] Searching for a life-purpose more deeply serves us as self-criticism; a commodity-trader on Wall Street who became a schoolteacher observed to me, 'I guess I was meant to do something else.' This observation might apply as well to the upwardly mobile people in Cabrini Green; they were meant to do something else in their lives than remain rooted in poverty. But do any of us have an inner core of self waiting to be realized through our actions? Can convictions alone constitute that inner self? What has kept all my childhood friends going is their religious convictions, which seem to realize that inner core in themselves, even when these convictions don't translate literally as guides for everyday behaviour.

Weber pondered vocations which were more commanding – commanding in the political sense. His essay 'Politics as a Vocation' focuses on the 'ethic of conviction'. That 'ethic' can solve the riddles of self propounded by the Protestant Ethic, when command over others becomes a personal life-purpose. In part, this is not an original idea; both Arthur Schopenhauer and Friedrich Nietzsche believed that the exercise of power cures sickness of self. But Weber focused more sharply on politicians who are genuine believers, politicians at the opposite pole from Machiavellian schemers, politicians who believe what they preach. Weber feared committed politicians because they are likely to force others to pay obeisance to the convictions which have saved the political believer from his or her own inner confusions. We saw in Chapter 1 a concrete example of what worried Weber: the declarations of solidarity displayed on the walls of the *musée social* in the Paris Exposition. 'Solidarity' was for Weber a cover for the process of purifying the will, of reinforcing its certainties, and so warding off inner doubt. In Weber's view the 'ethics of conviction' must always exclude or punish difference; once admit disagreement and conviction itself will collapse.

What then of the alternative to the ethic of conviction? In Paris in 1900 an alternative was put on display in documents about settlement houses, communal associations and workshops; the organizers of these groups certainly had both convictions and commitments, but a different sense of vocation. Community itself had become the vocation, a vocation in which cooperation became more an end in itself, fulfilling the selves of the people who lived or worked in the community. My childhood neighbours in Cabrini Green, who had an early and profound engagement with a local community, did not develop that sense of community as an adult vocation – nor did they follow Weber's trajectory of power over others to confirm the self. Nor did mourning the past guide then about the vocation of 'giving something back'.

What, then, does the vocation of community entail? Put aside the romantic overtones of fulfilling one's destiny in a vocation; the issue then becomes how one might develop a sense of inner purpose by communal cooperation. Our study ends with three versions of community as a vocation made by the heirs to the Parisian community organizers, each compelling, each ambiguous and each still, now, unfinished business.

COMMUNITY AS A VOCATION

Faith-based community

The Catholic Worker movement has embodied one kind of communal vocation. This movement in the 1930s was small, like most Leftist groups in America, though it would later come to inspire radical priests throughout Latin America and South East Asia, in concert with changes in the Church occurring during Vatican II. At the time of its founding the American movement had echoes among members of the Netherlands Catholic Workers Party and among small, anti-Nazi Catholic groups in Germany. Throughout its history the Catholic Worker ministry has focused on the lives of the poor; in America, the movement did so in its 'hospitality houses' – an evolution of the settlement house open to anyone, native or foreigner, who was poor – and in its monthly newspaper the *Catholic Worker*, animated by Peter Maurin and Dorothy Day.[19]

The hospitality houses in New York, Chicago and other cities provided shelter and also helped people find work; the movement has done the same on farms it runs. The newspaper resembles an online blog more than traditional reporting, filled as it was, and is still, with readers' submissions and comments. The houses, farms and newspaper are open, in the sense of being open to anyone in need. The practical activities differ from Booker T. Washington's two Institutes in providing tasks for people without emphasizing their skill or fitness; the hospitality houses were and remain casual in tone.

The American Catholic Worker group defined the issue of commitment in terms of living one's own life as simply as possible. Caritas is the foundation of this radical, faith-based commitment. In Christian theology, the Latin word *caritas* means the free gift of concern for other people; it is opposed to strategic sociability, the cunning, calculated arts of getting along well with other people in order to gain something for oneself. *Caritas* also differs from 'altruism', at least as that word is used by students of animal behaviour, for it does not imagine self-sacrifice for the sake of the group's advantage, like soldier ants or humans willing to die fighting. For this reason, Dorothy Day became ever more uncomfortable about versions of a militant, organized class struggle; she thought of struggle as Gandhi did, the practice of non-violence transforming the oppressor and the oppressed alike.

The foundation Caritas has posed a particular problem about paternalism for the Catholic Workers, since their religion is based on the elaborate, paternal hierarchy of the Church; cooperation in a giving, equal spirit cannot easily be separated from submission to Church officials. From the 1830s on, French 'social Catholics' had viewed their religion as a counter and antidote to nascent capitalism, but the medicine of transcending the economic system had to be taken under the strict guidance of religious authority. Towards the end of the nineteenth century, Leo XIII's papal encyclical *Rerum Novarum* proposed that the Church directly address issues of labour and capital when governments failed to support workers. Mother Cabrini, one of his most fervent emissaries, was sent to Chicago to work among immigrant Italians and Poles; the community centres she founded, though described in the local press as cooperatives, were in fact not so. Face-to-face collaboration was to Mother Cabrini a means, a tool, for strengthening one's faith in, and one's place within, the Church.[20]

The Catholic Worker movement can be said – with all respect – to have finessed the problem of equality versus submission. 'The Aims and Means of the Catholic Worker' is a credo that 'our inspiration [comes] from the lives of the Saints', making no mention of guidance by the Church hierarchy; the statement celebrates instead 'personalism', the 'freedom and dignity of each person as the basic focus and goal of all metaphysics and morals'.[21] On a peace mission to Rome in 1963, Day noted that the elevation of the Pope, carried aloft through the crowd at St Peter's, serves a practical end ('how could any have seen him if he were not conducted in this way?') rather than acting as a symbol of his superiority.[22]

Day's belief in a local, open community turns on the role religion plays in getting people to commit to one another, to feel it their vocation to cooperate. Faith, she says, is the most reliable 'spur' for social engagement. About faith's power to do so, she shares something in spirit with the American philosopher William James. In *The Varieties of Religious Experience*, James observed that religious conversions are often preceded by profound periods of depression and by detachment from other people. The individual believer can emerge from this trauma feeling twice-born, a new person born out of the ashes of the old. This interpretation of conversion differs sharply from Freud's idea of mourning, mourning which retains attachment to what once was. James was more American in outlook; he believed the transforming moment boosts morale, commitment and conviction all at once; as he writes in *The Varieties*, we have to feel we are someone different in order to engage.[23] Day shared his faith in the sheer power of conversion.

This has produced a problem in the Catholic Worker community, a divide between its believer and non-believer activists that started in Day's time and is still continuing. The Catholic Worker movement has drawn many non-Catholics, indeed some non-Christian and agnostic activists. It has done so precisely because the movement is open, and has no hidden agenda; it concentrates upon the moment of connection, on committing to one another. Though the social commitments are similar among believers like Dorothy Day and the non-believers whom her movement has attracted, there is unease with one another as well. The Catholic Worker community has persevered in radical action in the same spirit as they have prayed. My mother got to know Dorothy Day through their mutual friend Mike Gold, author of *Jews without Money*; when she left the Communist Party in the late 1930s, the Catholic Worker movement was her first port of call. She once described to me the 'eerie experience' of watching others believe. Faith in a higher good has driven the believers, rather than belief in social life as an end in itself, and for this reason non-Catholics working in the hospitality houses often feel that they are mere spectators.

A very old divide from the Reformation appeared again among this militant group, the issue of spectacle, explored in Chapter 3. This divide translated in the daily life of the community into the matter of ritual, especially ritual prayers. Though no one was obliged to pray, the believers needed to do so. Ritual is not necessary for militant, faith-based social action; as also appeared in Chapter 3, Quaker activists dispense with ritual while retaining faith. And, as in the American Elks clubs or those British guilds which have become today's charities, it's common to combine ritual and secularity in a fraternal organization. But the spectators in the Catholic Worker movement have been in an uneasy condition: the non-Catholic praying to God for the sake of cooperation would commit a terrible fraud.

The Catholic Worker movement embodies a more general problem in faith-based radical action, a problem which can be cast in purely social terms. It's the problem of equality of conviction. Faith-based militants may draw no invidious comparisons – those in the Catholic Worker movement certainly do not – but others cannot help doing so. The non-religious members are watching as through a window what they lack; put crassly, they risk becoming consumers of the believer's commitment. Put another way: for the believer, helping one's neighbour should arise from belief in an Other which transcends the human, whereas for the non-believer the point is other people. From this arises a paradox: within the sphere of faith-based radicalism, the believer may have entirely inclusive impulses, but the non-believer, in good conscience, can only conclude that he or she does not belong.

The simple community

A well-thumbed book on our family bookshelf was a collection of the writings of A. D. Gordon, a Russian visionary who lived from 1856 to 1922.[24] He had a somewhat therapeutic view of community: commitment to others can and should solve inner psychological problems. But he was neither a follower of Max Weber not a psychologist; instead, Gordon provided the philosophical vision for the kibbutz, a community based on shared identity in which cooperation becomes an end in itself.

In one way, the kibbutz is a Jewish descendant of the nineteenth-century Institutes of ex-slaves, Gordon believing that in the kibbutz its members could restore their self-respect, and so draw closer to one another. His enemy was the convoluted social intricacies of everyday diplomacy. Jews had been obliged to practise this diplomacy in order to survive in Europe; in the kibbutz, Gordon hoped, they would take off the mask which they wore in Europe to accommodate to a hostile society.

The kibbutz took root in Palestine at the end of the nineteenth century; its original design began to fade in Israel during the 1960s. At its beginnings, the kibbutz was a rural work cooperative, emphasizing hard and often unskilled manual labour; in this latter respect, it differed from the Institutes. And it was explicitly socialist, rearing children communally, minimizing private wealth, the community sharing as a whole in the proceeds of their labour.

Gordon was well prepared for the rigours of this all-encompassing communal life when he migrated from Russia to Palestine in 1904. Related to the powerful Günzberg family in Russia, his father managed a forest for them; Aaron David (his full names, which he did not use as a writer) himself worked for the Günzbergs on another estate. He knew how to farm; the reflections of this most philosophical of farmers turned in part on the fact that most Jews of the time did not.

In most parts of Eastern Europe, most Jews could not legally own land; nature was a foreign territory. Gordon believed that Jews in Europe, whether lowly merchants and traders or prosperous doctors and lawyers, had further lost contact with physical labour itself because they did not work with their hands. Gordon's facts were faulty; there were large numbers of Jewish industrial workers throughout Eastern Europe by 1914. Still, his dislike of landless, non-physical labour was as sharp as Henry David Thoreau's, after the American sage moved to Walden Pond: people who could not trust themselves in nature were not truly self-reliant; they were alienated from themselves.[25] Gordon's is a harsh judgement which flies in the face of thousands of years of Jewish persecution and survival, but softened, perhaps, because of the spell cast over Gordon, as over many others, by Leo Tolstoy.

It's hard, a century later, to convey the hold Tolstoy's communitarianism had on the imaginations of liberally minded Russians in the 'Silver Age' – those twenty years or so before the Russian Revolution. His followers believed that Russia had sickened in ways which extended beyond Tsar Nicholas II's oppressive rule; the tissues of community holding Russians together as one people had withered. As a result, personal character had become damaged. Tolstoy had in mind a specific vocational remedy; he argued that privileged people needed to recover their roots by working on the soil, doing ordinary labour in the company of ordinary people; this argument is built into Levin in his novel *Anna Karenina* (1873-7), an aristocrat who makes himself a healthy man by returning to the land. (One of my own most vivid childhood memories is of an elderly, elegant, penniless lady, a survivor of the Revolution, reading to me passages from *Anna Karenina* on the virtues of the old peasantry.) Gordon knew many passages of the novel by heart, but they meant something special to him because he was a Jew. Jews should renew themselves outside Europe by turning to physical labour and regaining bodily strength: the doctor driven from Europe should recover pride in building a house in the kibbutz with his own hands, tending his own vines, preparing the communal meal. Tolstoy in the kibbutz meant that people came to be in touch with their working bodies.

Cooperation as a vocation of simplicity has a long pedigree; some Franciscans – though not St Francis himself – subscribed to it, and believed that monks should therefore revel only in the rudest tasks in the monastery, since in sweeping halls or cutting grass they could recover *agapé*, the fellowship of the early Christians. Many modern crimes have been committed in the name of hard work as personality reform, from Nazism to Mao's Cultural Revolution, but in his celebration of the return to the simple life Gordon might seem to be more travelling in the company of Jean-Jacques Rousseau.

An astute commentator on Gordon's thought, Herbert Rose, makes an important distinction here: 'Gordon never asserted that man was naturally good . . . Nature does not represent for Gordon innocence but the source of vitality.'[26] Hebrew tries to convey the contrast between lethargy and vitality in two words. *Tsimtsum* implies both egotism and inner division; when the two combine, vitality ebbs. The remedy is *histpashtut*, the natural desire to give to others and so make oneself whole. This may seem close to Dorothy Day's ideal of *caritas* but again there is an important difference. The experience of *histpashtut* is all about what you do here, how you behave right now; there is no transcendence in Gordon's philosophy. Nor is there suspicion, cynicism or resignation, traits which Gordon thought had defaced Jewish culture in the Diaspora. Each act of cooperation has an immediately healing effect on the self, whereas in Christian theology of

Day's sort it can be only a step toward healing, which occurs, if at all, in another life. Thus the simplicity of kibbutz life meant something different to him than did the life of voluntary poverty and service to others Day pursued.

Reading Gordon now is difficult because of the path Zionism took long after he died. Like the theologian Martin Buber, Gordon believed Jews and Palestinians could and should share the same land as equals; Gordon was convinced Jews ought never to forget the lesson learned during the three thousand years of the Diaspora, that those who differ should be treated with justice.

Gordon is vexing in part because of his conviction that simple cooperation can mend the heart. But he is important to us because of his emphasis on shoring up identity through communal cooperation. Many activists in oppressed communities subscribe to this logic; it's the local descendant of the more national or international versions of solidarity which moved the political Left in 1900. In becoming local, though, the nature of shared identity changes, coming to depend on direct references to the experience of other people whom you know well. Instead of appeals to Jewishness or to the African-American experience, a shared identity is built by the history shared by you and me.

The idea that community should be based on simplicity is hardly unique to Gordon as the philosophic father of the kibbutz; many community activists accept this precept without thinking much about it. But it leads to the same problem as in the Catholic Worker movement: that communication with those who differ becomes elusive. The virtue of both lies in stressing local, open cooperation built freely from the bottom up. Gordon's own reproach to the Bolsheviks was that they conflated socialism and nationalism; to him, there could never be a Five Year Plan for cooperation.[27] Yet still, the social question of how to live locally in a complex society remained unanswered.

The pleasures of community

The American who most sought a solution to this problem was Norman Thomas (1884–1968), the leader of the Socialist Party of America for much of the twentieth century. He sought to marry European social democracy with the American preference for local action. The tool he used to do this was informality, both in his own behaviour and in his views of community. He aimed to make the communal experience of cooperation a sustainable pleasure.

His commitment was tested by the fact that he had little chance of winning elections. When he was a candidate for the American presidency during the 1930s and 1940s he saw Roosevelt's liberal New Deal draw ever more troops away from his own party, while Stalin's Communists sniped at him from the far Left.[28] The vocation of politics therefore took another turn for him; he sought to put the social back into socialism.

Like many American radicals, Norman Thomas moved from religion to politics. He began public life as a Christian pastor who left the ministry to represent and write about workers. The 1930s were his formative era; the League for Industrial Democracy which he led became the Socialist Party of America, with him as its new head. Thomas conceived of the Socialist Party of America more as a clearing house of information for Leftist union members and grass-roots organizers than as a controlling centre: a Party designed for civil society. Thomas's radicalism came from his vision of America as a civil society of displaced peoples. He thought the 'melting pot', in which people lose their past histories, was an illusion: the actual or symbolic memories of migrants are too important ever to be erased. The same was true of race: amnesia is no recipe for racial harmony. And, more subtly, he argued that class inequalities are experienced as a kind of displacement, the American white working class treated as invisible, just part of the background, not figuring in the upwardly mobile ethos of the post-war years.

The challenge, as Thomas saw it, lies in getting people who have no place in the American Dream to want to look outward, beyond their limits, and so cooperate with one another. Informal sociability is a radical means to this end, or so Thomas thought, because the more experienced people become in getting along without guiding rules or rulers, the more they will come to value one another.

Thomas was sometimes said to be a charismatic speaker, but many of his listeners did not find him so. His voice was harsh, his gestures awkward, the views he presented in public little more than well-meaning clichés; he spoke of economic equality, good welfare state care, racial justice and, after the Second World War, support for the United Nations. His usual listeners could recite these themes by heart.* His genius lay rather in his behaviour; he was informal, and genuinely so. Roosevelt was also easy in public, but *de haut en bas*, an American aristocrat assuring and guiding the masses. Thomas spoke as one among many; he was perfectly content to say boring things, and managed to wrest trust from others through his very ordinariness.

It might seem that his lack of theatrical presence, his absence of charisma on-stage, disabled him as a politician. I would say instead that he was skilled at informality. For instance, he always placed his own seat in the middle of a group, a circle if possible, rather than holding meetings where the chairman sits elevated at the front in a room. At the end of a speech he never called for raised hands, but sought out, by an intuition he could never explain, those people too shy to speak up. After meetings, he usually spoke to people while gripping them by the forearm, and he didn't let go when they talked.

In small meetings, he ignored the logic of the agenda, even if one had been distributed; an item Thomas wanted to get done would be attached to the name of someone in the room, often surprising them, since they hadn't thought about it one way or another. He seldom moved beyond items 1 or 2 on an agenda; he let matters develop and metamorphose from within. Thomas's *démarche* often consisted of a newspaper clipping or extract from a report – by an enemy – that was meant to provoke outrage or discussion in equal measure.

All these procedures, aimed at stimulating informal problem-solving and problem-finding, drove colleagues like the labour leader Walter Reuther crazy, colleagues who wanted to get business done quickly and efficiently. Once a meeting started, it could last late into the night; counter-productive certainly if the point was reaching a decision, highly productive if the point was to accustom different people to being together. In this, Thomas was canny. Since he was trying to accommodate people of very different and often conflicting interests, he turned on its head the saying attributed to Oscar Wilde

* My family knew him quite well; out of friendship, they frequently attended his speeches, though the prospect of hearing these set pieces yet again filled them with dread.

that 'the trouble with socialism is that it takes too many evenings'. Settling down, bedding-in, suspending pressure, spending time with other people for its own sake, all added up to increasing by informal means commitment to the collective project.

Thomas used a quite Rochefoucauldian irony about himself to invite participation. At his eightieth birthday celebration, admirers gave him a cheque for $17,500; his response was, 'It won't last long . . . every organization I'm connected with is going bankrupt.' In meetings, he similarly refused to present himself as more capable than anyone else in the room, eschewing any hint of the Chairman.

All of which left him, President of the Socialist Party of America, powerless. If commitment is judged by gaining power, Thomas's commitment to socialism, like that of Dorothy Day or A. D. Gordon, is meaningless. But Thomas put into practice the idea of knowing the limits of reality but refusing to define oneself by those limits. In doing so, he set a social example for the Left. His ways of dealing with others served as a kind of conscience for the labour unions of his time, unions engaged in power struggles and playing by other rules. Thomas challenged union leaders to reflect on why, as the unions became more structured and bureaucratic internally after the 1930s, the life drained out of them. Union leaders knew how to act formally in the name of their members, but not how to engage with members informally, with the practical result that voluntary membership dropped off. Be more radical, he urged – which means not asking for more but behaving differently. This same provocative critique he issued to other American liberals.

Of the three forms of communal commitment, Thomas's was the most oriented to informal pleasure. And for all that his politics were doomed to fail in the larger America, Thomas's lasting example lies in how he practised commitment to others, rather than in the subject of what he preached.

These, then, are three versions of commitment to community among children of the Great Depression: faith-based, simplicity-based and sociably-based. These three speak to issues of cooperation which transcend their own times, and are not unique to the Left: communal cooperation focuses us on how quality-of-life issues count in everyday experience.

Our theme throughout this study has been that cooperation enhances the quality of social life. The local community seems the setting for the pursuit of a good quality of life, but it is a complicated setting. I've dwelled in this chapter on communities of the poor, in part for auto-biographical reasons but also because they are the hard cases. They are places that people like my childhood friends have had to survive, and if they do survive, will be disposed to leave. They are also the places that the 'new conservatives' are abandoning to a resource-less fate. Complicated issues appear in the lives of the people who are survivors, issues of morale, of attachment, loss and mourning; issues also of the vocations which sustain people in the struggle for survival. No simple promise of happiness answers to these lived realities.

Could community itself become a vocation? Faith, identity and informal sociability suggest ways in which community among the poor or the marginalized can be sustaining, but not entirely so. When Freud was asked for his recipe for a good-quality life he famously replied, 'Leben und Arbeiten' (love and work). In this advice, commu-nity is missing, the social limb is amputated. Hannah Arendt embraced community life as a vocation, but not the sort of community most poor people experience first-hand; hers was an idealized political community in which all the actors have equal standing. We want to imagine, instead, community as a process of coming into the world, a process in which people work out both the value of face-to-face rela-tions and the limits on those relations. For poor or marginalized people, the limits are political and economic; the value is social. Though community cannot fill up the whole of a life, it promises pleasures of a serious sort. This was Norman Thomas's guiding prin-ciple, and it is, I think, a good way to understand the value of community, even if you do not live in a ghetto.

Coda

Montaigne's Cat

At the end of his life, the philosopher Michel de Montaigne (1533–92) inserted a question into an essay written many years before: 'When I am playing with my cat, how do I know she is not playing with me?'[1] The question summed up Montaigne's long-held conviction that we can never really plumb the inner life of others, be they cats or other human beings. Montaigne's cat can serve as an emblem for the demanding sort of cooperation explored in this book. My premise about cooperation has been that we frequently don't understand what's passing in the hearts and minds of people with whom we have to work. Yet just as Montaigne kept playing with his enigmatic cat, so too a lack of mutual understanding shouldn't keep us from engaging with others; we want to get something done together. This is the simple conclusion I hope the reader will draw from a complex study.

Montaigne provides a fitting coda to this book because he was a master of dialogical thinking. He was born the year Holbein painted *The Ambassadors*. Like Holbein's young emissaries to Britain, the young Montaigne had a political education as a member of the *parlement* of Bordeaux – a regional council of notables; like these two emissaries, he came to know the religious conflict between Catholics and Protestants close up. The civil wars of religion in the mid-sixteenth century convulsed the Bordeaux region, and threatened the village in which his family's own domains lay; tribalism of the religious kind led to the burning of enemy fields, the starvation-siege of towns, and random, terrorist murder. While Montaigne took the side of the Protestant leader Henri de Navarre, his heart was neither in religious dogma nor in professional politics. In 1570, two years after the death of his father, he retired to his estate, and even further within it to a tower within the south-east corner of the chateau, where he set up a room in which to think and to write. In this chamber, he began both to experiment with writing in a dialogical way and to think through its application to everyday cooperation.

Although he had retired to an intimate stage, and spent much of his time on the wine-making which supported the estate, he had not withdrawn mentally and emotionally from concern with the wider world. The great friend of his youth, Étienne de La Boétie, had written a *Discourse on Voluntary Servitude* (probably in 1553, at the age of twenty-two), a study of the blind desire to obey, and Montaigne elaborated many of its precepts in his own writings. The religious wars had implanted in both young men a horror of the craving for faith, for service to an abstract principle or to a charismatic leader. Had the two friends lived a century later, the theatrics of Louis XIV would have embodied for them the state's effort to induce passive, voluntary submission among a crowd of spectators to a leader. Had they lived in our own time, the charismatic despots of the twentieth century would equally have posed, to Montaigne and La Boétie, the threat of passive obedience. After La Boétie's early death, Montaigne continued to champion his friend's alternative idea of building political engagement from the ground up, based on ordinary cooperation in a community.

Montaigne was a seigneur who availed himself fully of his historic privileges, so that he certainly cannot be likened to a radical community organizer in the modern sense, yet he studied how the communal life around him was organized, hoping to gather from casual chats, the rituals surrounding wine-making and the care of dependants on his estate how La Boétie's project of participation built from the ground up might be realized.

Montaigne's emblematic, enigmatic cat lay at the heart of this project. What passes in the minds of those with whom we cooperate? Around this question Montaigne associated other aspects of practising cooperation: dialogic practices which are skilled, informal and empathic. Great writers usually inspire in us the sentiment that they are our contemporaries, speaking directly to us, and of course there's a danger in this. Still, Montaigne had a prophetic grasp about what these elements of cooperation entail.

Blaise Pascal singled out Montaigne as 'the incomparable author of "the art of conversation" '.[2] The 'art' of conversing is for Montaigne in fact the skill of being a good listener, as we have explored it in this book, a matter of attending both to what people declare and to what they assume; in one essay, Montaigne likens the skilled listener to a detective. He detested Bernard Williams's 'fetish of assertion' on the speaker's part. Fierce assertion directly suppresses the listener, Montaigne says; the debater demands only assent. In his essay, Montaigne observes that, in society more largely, the declaration of a speaker's superior knowledge and authority arouses doubt in a listener about his or her own powers of judgement; the evil of passive submission follows from feeling cowed.[3]

Montaigne disputes that the skilled detection of what others mean but do not say is the province of exceptional minds; this detective and contemplative skill, he insists, is a potentiality in all human beings, one suppressed by assertions of authority. The idea of everyday diplomacy would have made sense to him for just this reason; once freed from top-down commands, people require skill in keeping silent, in showing tact, in that lightening of differences which Castiglione called *sprezzatura* – at least this was so between Catholics and Protestants in the town next to Montaigne's estate when political authority collapsed as a result of the nation's religious wars; only the vigilant practice of everyday diplomacy allowed people in the town to carry on with life on the streets.

As a man moving around his local community, Montaigne enjoyed what we have called dialogic conversations more than dialectical arguments, tinged as all disputes were for him with the threat of descent into violence. He practised dialogics in his writing; his essays bounce from subject to subject, seeming to wander at times, yet the reader finishes each with the sense that the author has opened up a topic in unexpected ways, rather than narrowly scored points.

'Dialogics' is in fact a modern name for a very old narrative practice; the ancient historian Herodotus employs it, creating a mosaic of fragments which, as in Montaigne's essays, produce a coherent large form. But Montaigne was, I think, the first to deploy this literary practice with a certain cunning: narrating in bits and pieces will suppress readerly aggression. By dissipating emotional temperature in the reader, as in an essay on cruelty, he hopes, ironically, to make the vices of cruelty stand out more in their sheer unreasonableness; he hopes in this way that, as he says, the reader will 'unlearn evil'.[4] For Montaigne, this was the point of dialogics – looking at things in the round to see the many sides of any issue or practice, the shifting focus making people cooler and more objective in their reactions.

As a man of his time, Montaigne was entranced by skill of a technical sort. Rather than the elaborate astronomical devices resting on Holbein's table, Montaigne was interested in more everyday crafts, such as carpenters' lathes, new culinary tools like clockwork spits for roasting, and above all he was fascinated by plumbing; water pumps for ornamental fountains and cattle basins seem particularly to have fascinated him. These prosaic interests become incorporated into a pair of essays, 'Habit' and 'Same Design: Different Outcomes'. Habits, he says, steady a skill, but the rule of unchanging habit is a tyranny; good habits are those 'designs' left free to produce different 'outcomes'. This precept applies equally, he argues, to machines and to men.[5] It seems obvious to him, and so he leaves it as just a stray observation. We've sought in these pages to dig deeper, to show that by modulating their habits people become more interactive, both in exploring objects and in engaging with one another. The craft ideal has governed our exploration of making and repairing physical things and social relations.

Montaigne was, Sarah Bakewell observes, the philosopher par excellence of modesty, particularly the self-restraint which helps people to engage with others.[6] Modesty encapsulates Montaigne's idea of civility, but his version little resembles the account of civility given by Norbert Elias. As a man, Montaigne was easy in his body, and wrote frequently about it, going into details about how his urine smells or when he likes to shit. Modesty without shame: Montaigne's idea of civility is in part that, if we can be easy with ourselves, we can be easy with other people. In a late essay he writes of informality, 'in whatever position they are placed, men pile up and arrange themselves by moving and shuffling about, just as a group of objects thrown into a bag find their own way to join and fit together, often better than they could have been arranged deliberately.'[7] These words could have been written by Saul Alinsky or Norman Thomas; they should have guided the programmers of GoogleWave.

'Our self', Montaigne writes in an essay on vanity, 'is an object full of dissatisfaction, we can see there nothing but wretchedness and vanity.' Yet this is not a counsel to engage in Luther's anguished self-struggle: 'so as not to dishearten us, Nature has very conveniently cast the action of our sight outwards.'[8] Curiosity can 'hearten' us to look beyond ourselves. As has appeared in the course of this book, looking outward makes for a better social bond than imagining others are reflected in ourselves, or as though society itself was constructed as a room of mirrors. But looking outward is a skill people have to learn.

Montaigne thinks empathy rather than sympathy is the cardinal social virtue. In the record he kept of life on his small country estate, he constantly compares his habits and tastes with those of his neighbours and workers; of course he is interested in the similarities, but he takes particular note of their peculiarities: to get along together, all will have to attend to mutual differences and dissonances.

Taking an interest in others, on their own terms, is perhaps the most radical aspect of Montaigne's writing. His was an age of hierarchy in which inequalities of rank seemed to separate seigneurs and servants into separate species, and Montaigne is not free of this attitude; nonetheless, he is curious. It's often said that Montaigne is one of the first writers to dwell on his own personal self; this is true but incomplete. His method of self-knowledge is to compare and to contrast; he stages differentiating encounters and exchanges again and again in the pages of his essays. Frequently he is gratified by his own distinctiveness, but almost as often, as with his cat, he is perplexed by what makes others different.

Like Holbein's table, Montaigne's cat was an emblem fashioned at the dawn of the modern era to convey a set of possibilities; the table represented in part new ways of making things, the cat represented new ways of living together. The cat's backstory is Montaigne's, and La Boétie's, politics: cooperative life, freed of command from the top. What happened to these promises of modernity? In a pregnant phrase, the modern social philosopher Bruno Latour declares, 'We have never been modern.'[9] He means specifically that society has failed to come to grips with the technologies it has created; nearly four centuries after Holbein, the tools on the table remain mystical objects. As concerns cooperation, I'd amend Latour's declaration: we have yet to be modern; Montaigne's cat represents human capabilities society has yet to nurture.

The twentieth century perverted cooperation in the name of solidarity. The regimes which spoke in the name of unity were not only tyrannies; the very desire for solidarity invites command and manipulation from the top. This was the bitter lesson Karl Kautsky learned in his passage from the political to the social Left, as have too many others since. The perverse power of solidarity, in its us-against-them form, remains alive in the civil societies of liberal democracies, as in European attitudes toward ethnic immigrants who seem to threaten social solidarity, or in American demands for a return to 'family values'; the perverse power of solidarity makes itself felt early among children, reaching into the way they make friends and construct outsiders.

Solidarity has been the Left's traditional response to the evils of capitalism. Cooperation in itself has not figured much as a strategy for resistance. Though the emphasis is in one way realistic, it has also sapped the strengh of the Left. The new forms of capitalism emphasize short-term labour and institutional fragmentation; the effect of this economic system has been that workers cannot sustain supportive social relations with one another. In the West, the distance between the elite and the mass is increasing, as inequality grows more pronounced in neo-liberal regimes like those of Britain and the United States; members of these societies have less and less a fate to share in common. The new capitalism permits power to detach itself from authority, the elite living in global detachment from responsibilities to others on the ground, especially during times of economic crisis. Under these conditions, as ordinary people are driven back on themselves, it's no wonder they crave solidarity of some sort – which the destructive solidarity of us-against-them is tailor-made to provide.

It's little wonder also that a distinctive character type has been bred by this crossing of political and economic power, a character type seeking to relieve experiences of anxiety. Individualism of the sort Tocqueville describes might seem to La Boétie, were he alive today, a new kind of voluntary servitude, the individual in thrall to his or her own anxieties, searching for a sense of security in the familiar. But the word 'individualism' names, I believe, a social absence as well as a personal impulse: ritual is absent. Ritual's role in all human cultures is to relieve and resolve anxiety, by turning people outward in shared, symbolic acts; modern society has weakened those ritual ties. Secular rituals, particularly rituals whose point is cooperation itself, have proved too feeble to provide that support.

The nineteenth-century historian Jacob Burckhardt spoke of modern times as an 'age of brutal simplifiers'.[10] Today, the crossed effect of desires for reassuring solidarity amid economic insecurity is to render social life brutally simple: us-against-them coupled with you-are-on-your-own. But I'd insist that we dwell in the condition of 'not yet'. Modernity's brutal simplifiers may repress and distort our capacity to live together, but do not, cannot, erase this capacity. As social animals we are capable of cooperating more deeply than the existing social order envisions, for Montaigne's emblematic, enigmatic cat is lodged in ourselves.

Notes

INTRODUCTION

1. Lily Allen's 'Fuck You', which first appeared in 2008, was aimed at the Right; when she performed it at the Glastonbury Festival in 2009, she said it took aim specifically at the British National Party. The music video of 'Fuck You' can be accessed at http://www.lilyallenmusic.com/lily/video.
2. Aristotle, *Politics*, ed. Richard McKeon, trans. Benjamin Jowett (New York: Random House, 1968), p. 310.
3. Samuel Stouffer *et al.*, *The American Soldier* (Princeton: Princeton University Press, 1949).
4. Robert Putnam, '*E Pluribus Unum*: Diversity and Community in the Twenty-First Century', *Scandinavian Political Studies*, 30/2 (2007), pp. 137–74.
5. Bernard Mandeville, *The Fable of the Bees*, ed. Phillip Harth (London: Penguin, 1989), 'The Grumbling Hive', section H, p. 68.
6. Cf. Michael Ignatieff, *The Needs of Strangers* (London: Penguin, 1986).
7. Richard Sennett, *The Culture of the New Capitalism* (New Haven: Yale University Press, 2006), p. 95.
8. Naomi Klein, *No Logo*, rev. edn. (London: Flamingo, 2001).
9. Alison Gopnik, *The Philosophical Baby* (London: Bodley Head, 2009).
10. James Rilling, David Gutman, Thorsten Zeh *et al.*, 'A Neural Basis for Social Cooperation', *Neuron*, 35/2 (18 July 2002), pp. 395–405.
11. Jerome Bruner, *On Knowing: Essays for the Left Hand*, second edn. (Cambridge, Mass.: Harvard University Press, 1979 (1962)).
12. Benjamin Spock and Robert Needlman, *Dr Spock's Baby and Child Care*, eighth edn. (New York: Simon & Schuster, 2004), pp. 131, 150.
13. D. W. Winnicott, 'Transitional Objects and Transitional Phenomena', *International Journal of Psychoanalysis*, 34 (1953), pp. 89–97; John Bowlby, *Attachment and Loss*, vol. 2 (London: Penguin, 1992).

14. Sarah Hrdy, *Mothers and Others* (Cambridge, Mass.: Harvard University Press, 2009).

15. Erik Erikson, *Childhood and Society* (New York: Norton, 1964). Erikson's 'eight ages of man' link stages of physical and psychosocial development from the moment of incorporation – achieved through a baby's mouth on its mother's breast – shortly after birth, to ego integrity or despair as we contemplate death near the end of our lives (chapters 2 and 7). Erikson's second stage, 'elimination', is where a child physically learns to 'stand on his own feet', accompanied by emotional developments around 'autonomy versus shame and self-doubt' (pp. 251–4). In this stage the child learns to see him- or herself as an independent being with wills, desires, behaviours of his or her own, and to develop a sense of self-control and autonomy.

16. Johann Huizinga, *Homo Ludens* (Boston: Beacon, 1950); Gerd Gigerenzer and Klaus Hug, 'Domain-Specific Reasoning: Social Contracts, Cheating, and Perspective Change', *Cognition*, 43/2 (1992), pp. 127–71.

17. Erikson, *Childhood and Society*, pp. 244–6. This proposition has been challenged in the last half-century. More recent research sees individuation appearing from the earliest moment of human development.

18. Balfour Browne, KC, quoted in Geoffrey Madan, *Notebooks* (Oxford: Oxford University Press, 1985), p. 127.

19. Robert Winter, 'Performing the Beethoven Quartets in their First Century', in Robert Winter and Robert Martin (eds.), *The Beethoven Quartet Companion* (Berkeley and Los Angeles: University of California Press, 1995).

20. Richard Sennett, *The Craftsman* (London: Allen Lane, 2008), pp. 157–76.

21. Bernard Williams, *Truth and Truthfulness* (Princeton: Princeton University Press, 2002), pp. 100–110.

22. Aristotle, *Politics*, bk. 1, ch. 2, p. 28.

23. Theodore Zeldin, *Conversation* (London: Harvill, 1998), p. 87.

24. Mikhail Bakhtin, *The Dialogic Imagination*, trans. Caryl Emerson and Michael Holquist (Austin: University of Texas Press, 2004), pp. 315 ff., 361 ff. Bakhtin talks about layering voices of the different characters – including the author's – in the novel as the source of its depth and richness: 'The language used by characters in the novel, how they speak, is verbally and semantically autonomous; each character's speech possesses its own belief system, since each is the speech of another in another's language; thus it may also refract authorial intentions and consequently may to a certain degree constitute a second language for the author. . . . the character speech almost always influences authorial speech

(and sometimes powerfully so), sprinkling it with another's words ... and in this way introducing into it stratification and speech diversity. ... Thus even where there is no comic element, no parody, no irony and so forth, where there is no narrator, no posited author or narrating character, speech diversity and language stratification still serve as the basis for style in the novel. ... prose's three-dimensionality, its profound speech diversity, which enters the project of style and is its determining factor' (p. 315).

25. Adam Smith, *The Theory of Moral Sentiments* (Indianapolis: Liberty Fund Press, 1982), p. 21.

26. Sarah Bakewell, *How to Live: A Life of Montaigne* (London: Chatto and Windus, 2010), p. 1.

27. Shani Orgad, *Story-Telling Online: Talking Breast Cancer on the Internet* (London: Lang, 2005).

28. Cass Sunstein, *Republic.com 2.0* (Princeton: Princeton University Press, 2001).

29. Quoted online in 'BBC News Technology', 5 August 2010 (http://www.bbc.co.uk/new/technology-10877768).

30. Jaron Lanier, *You Are Not a Gadget* (London: Allen Lane, 2010), p. 33.

31. Martha Nussbaum and Amartya Sen, *The Quality of Life* (Oxford: Clarendon Press, 1993).

CHAPTER 1. 'THE SOCIAL QUESTION'

1. The *musée social* has been well evoked by Daniel Rogers in *Atlantic Crossings* (Cambridge, Mass.: Harvard University Press, 1998), pp. 11–17.

2. Ibid., p. 13.

3. See W. E. B. Dubois, 'The American Negro at Paris', *Atlantic Monthly Review of Reviews*, 22 (1900), pp. 575–7.

4. Georg Simmel, 'Soziologie der Geselligkeit', *Verhandlungen des ersten Deutschen Soziologentages vom 19-22 Oktober, 1910 in Frankfurt A.M.* (Tübingen: Mohr, 1911), pp. 1–16.

5. Georg Simmel, 'The Stranger', in Simmel, *On Individuality and Social Forms*, ed. Donald Levine (Chicago: University of Chicago Press, 1972), pp. 143–9.

6. Georg Simmel, 'The Metropolis and Mental Life', ibid., pp. 324–9; for the relations between Tönnies and Simmel, see Kurt Wolff, *The Sociology of Georg Simmel* (New York: Free Press, 1950).

7. Hannah Arendt, *The Origins of Totalitarianism* (New York: Harcourt Brace Jovanovich, 1968), pt. 2, 'Imperialism', pp. 136–7.

8. Theda Skocpol, *Protecting Soldiers and Mothers* (Cambridge, Mass.: Harvard University Press, 1993).

9. See Frank Henderson Stewart, *Honor* (Chicago: University of Chicago Press, 1994).

10. This sorry story turns on the figure of the truculent defeated Prime Minister, Gordon Brown. Other Labour figures, notably the business secretary Lord Mandelson, had a better sense of how to negotiate, but could not dispel the climate of menace and anger. See David Laws, *22 Days in May* (London: Biteback, 2010).

11. See Alan Rusbridger, '2010 Andrew Olle Media Lecture' (http://www. abc.net.au/local/stories/2010/11/19/307135). For other good discussions of this issue, see Robert McChesney, 'Journalism: Looking Backward, Going Forward', *Hedgehog Review* (Summer 2008), esp. pp. 73–4; Michael Schudson, *The Sociology of News* (New York: Norton, 2003), esp. pp. 38–40.

12. See Richard Sennett and Jonathan Cobb, *The Hidden Injuries of Class* (New York: Knopf, 1972).

13. For a good review of the literature, see S. Sayyid and Abdoolkarim Vakil (eds.), *Thinking Through Islamophobia* (London: Hurst, 2011).

14. Alinsky's two books were *Reveille for Radicals*, 2nd edn. (New York: Vintage, 1969), and *Rules for Radicals* (New York: Random House, 1971). A good biography is by Nicholas von Hoffman, *Radical* (New York: Nation Books, 2010). For Obama's own work as a community organizer in Chicago, see David Remnick, *The Bridge* (New York: Knopf, 2010), pp. 134–42.

15. Alinsky, *Rules for Radicals*, p. 66.

16. Jane Addams, *Twenty Years at Hull House* (Charleston, SC: Bibliobazaar, 2008).

17. A fuller description of the neighbourhood, and of Hull House, appears in Richard Sennett, *Families Against the City* (Cambridge, Mass.: Harvard University Press, 1970).

18. I've written more fully about Cabrini Green in Richard Sennett, *Respect in an Age of Inequality* (New York: Norton, 2003), pp. 5–20.

19. Manuel Castells, *The City and the Grassroots* (Berkeley: University of California Press, 1985).

20. Booker T. Washington, *Up from Slavery* (1901; New York: Dover, 1995), p. 50.

21. See Richard Sennett, *The Craftsman* (London: Allen Lane, 2008), for a fuller account.

22. Plato, *The Republic*, trans. Melissa Lane *et al.* (London: Penguin, 2007),

V.1–16; VI.19–VII.5; and Confucius, *Analects*, trans. D. C. Lau (London: Penguin, 2003), book 7, sayings 4–19.

23. The historical fortunes of the artisan are recounted in more detail in Sennett, *The Craftsman*.

24. Randy Hodson, *Dignity at Work* (Cambridge: Cambridge University Press, 2001).

25. Many readers will know about Fourier from the pages devoted to him in Roland Barthes's wondrous essay *Sade, Fourier, Loyola* (Berkeley: University of California Press, 1989). A more sober assessment of his work appears in Anthony Vidler's *The Writing on the Walls* (Princeton: Princeton Architectural Press, 1987). Gareth Stedman Jones's *Fourier* (Cambridge: Cambridge University Press, 1966) provides additional information.

26. Frances Johnston's photographs were conserved by the writer, dance impresario and photographic historian Lincoln Kirstein, who republished the 1900 display at New York's Museum of Modern Art in 1966. Frances Johnston, *The Hampton Album* (New York: Museum of Modern Art, distributed by Doubleday & Co., 1966).

27. These factory images were not in Kirstein's Museum of Modern Art exhibition. I've seen individual prints from time to time in galleries, but cannot document what I've seen; my description relies on my memory.

28. Karl Kautsky, *The Labour Revolution*, trans. Henry Stenning (London: Allen and Unwin, 1925).

CHAPTER 2. THE FRAGILE BALANCE

1. St Augustine, *City of God*, trans. Henry Bettenson (London: Penguin, 2003), book XIV, ch. 27. For St Augustine, only renewal of mankind's faith can restore natural harmony.

2. A fine modern edition of Milton's *Paradise Lost*, with full commentary, is by Earl Miner, William Moeck and Steven Jablonski (New York: Bucknell, 2004). The quotation comes from H. van Nuis, 'Animated Eve . . . ', *Milton Quarterly*, 34/2 (2000), p. 50.

3. *Paradise Lost*, book 1, lines 254–5.

4. Thomas Hobbes, *Leviathan* (London: Penguin, 1982), part 1, chapter 13, paragraph 9.

5. Steven Pinker, 'The Mind Reader', *Guardian*, profile (6 Nov. 1999), pp. 6–7.

6. Robert Axelrod, *The Evolution of Cooperation*, revised edn. (New York: Basic Books, 2006). This superb study revolves around the Prisoner's

Dilemma, a classic social problem in which an individual has to calculate the benefits and dangers of working with, or against, others.

7. T. D. Seeley, *Honeybee Ecology* (Princeton: Princeton University Press, 1985), and more technically, T. D. Seeley and R. A. Morse, 'Nest Site Selection by the Honey Bee *Apis mellifera*', *Insectes sociaux*, 25/4 (1978), pp. 323–37.

8. Bert Hölldobler and E. O. Wilson, *The Superorganism* (New York: Norton, 2009), p. 7.

9. Ibid., p. 5.

10. See James Lovelock, *Gaia: A New Look at Life on Earth* (Oxford: Oxford University Press, 1979).

11. This is Gould's theory of 'punctuated equilibrium' – which I have absolutely no competence to assess. It is presented in readable prose in Stephen Jay Gould, *The Structure of Evolutionary Theory* (Cambridge, Mass.: Harvard University Press, 2002), pp. 765–811.

12. Michael Tomasello, *Why We Cooperate* (Cambridge, Mass.: MIT Press, 2009), pp. 33–5.

13. Frans de Waal and Sarah Brosnan, 'Simple and Complex Reciprocity in Primates', in Peter Kappeler and Carel van Schaik (eds.), *Cooperation in Primates and Humans* (New York and Heidelberg: Springer, 2006), pp. 85–105.

14. J. B. Silk, S. F. Brosnan *et al.*, 'Chimpanzees are Indifferent to the Welfare of Unrelated Group Members', *Nature*, 437 (2005), pp. 1357–9. Interestingly, the authors' data also show that these primates can exhibit signs of indifference to kin when bonded to members in the group of the same sex or age.

15. See Jane Goodall, *The Chimpanzees of Gombe* (Cambridge, Mass.: Harvard University Press, 1986).

16. See Joan Silk, 'Practicing Hamilton's Rule', in Kappeler and van Schaik, *Cooperation in Primates and Humans*, pp. 25–46.

17. Natalie and Joseph Henrich, *Why Humans Cooperate* (Oxford: Oxford University Press, 2007), p. 37.

18. Richard Dawkins, *The Selfish Gene*, 30th anniversary edn. (Oxford: Oxford University Press, 2006), p. 213. The whole of chapter 12, pp. 202–33, explores this proposition.

19. Natalie Zemon Davis, *The Gift in Sixteenth-Century France* (Oxford: Oxford University Press, 2000).

20. Marcel Mauss, *The Gift*, trans. W. D. Halls (London: Routledge, 1990); Richard Titmuss, *The Gift Relationship* (New York: The New Press, 1997); Alain Caillé, *Anthropologie du don* (Paris: Desclée de Brouwer, 2000).

21. *The Talmud*, trans. and ed. Michael Levi Rodkinson, Isaac Mayer Wise, Godfrey Taubenhaus (Charleston, SC: Bibliobazaar, 2010), Bath Bathra 9b.

22. 1 Corinthians 12: 4.

23. Richard Sennett, *The Corrosion of Character* (New York: Norton, 1998), pp. 184–5; Richard Sennett, *Respect in an Age of Inequality* (New York: Norton, 2003), pp. 210–16.

24. See Richard Sennett, *Flesh and Stone* (New York: Norton, 1993), p. 183.

25. This was, for example, the belief of Edward Wilson in his early book *Sociobiology* (Cambridge, Mass.: Harvard University Press, 1975); in more recent writings, such as *Consilience* (New York: Little, Brown, 1998), he has changed his views. A balanced overview of the possibilities and limits of animal behaviour as a model for human cultures is given by W. G. Runciman, *The Social Animal* (Ann Arbor: University of Michigan Press, 2000).

26. Partha Dasgupta, Peter Hammond and Eric Maskin, 'The Implementation of Social Choice Rules', *Review of Economic Studies*, 46/2 (1979), pp. 185–216; Drew Fudenberg and Eric Maskin, 'Evolution and Cooperation in Noisy Repeated Games', *American Economic Review*, 80/2 (1990), pp. 274–9.

27. Adam Smith, *The Wealth of Nations* (1776; London: Methuen, 1961), book I, pp. 109–12.

28. Goodall, *The Chimpanzees of Gombe*.

29. See Richard Sennett, *The Fall of Public Man* (New York: Knopf, 1977), pp. 80–84.

30. Quoted ibid., p. 82.

31. See ibid., pp. 73–88.

32. Walter Benjamin, *Illuminations*, ed. Hannah Arendt, trans. Harry Zohn (New York: Harcourt Brace Jovanovich, 1968), 'On Some Motifs in Baudelaire', pp. 155–201.

33. This arcane reference is Antoine-Henri Jomini, *A Treatise on Grand Military Strategy*, trans. S. B. Holabird (New York: Van Nostrand, 1865).

34. A full exposition of his ideas appears in Herbert Blumer, *Symbolic Interactionism* (New York: Prentice Hall, 1969); see also Herbert Blumer, *Movies and Conduct* (New York: Macmillan, 1933).

35. William McNeill, *Keeping Together in Time* (Cambridge, Mass.: Harvard University Press, 1995).

36. Ibid., p. 37.

37. The event is described in Bryan Spinks, *Reformation and Modern Rituals and Theologies of Baptism* (Aldershot: Ashgate, 2006), pp. 204–5; for the quote, see http://news.bbc.co.uk/l/hi/uk/4120477.sm.

38. Clifford Geertz, *Negara* (Princeton: Princeton University Press, 1980), esp. chapter 4.

39. Eric Hobsbawm and Terence Ranger (eds.), *The Invention of Tradition* (Cambridge: Cambridge University Press, 1983); Benedict Anderson, *Imagined Communities*, revised edn. (New York: Verso, 2006).

40. Bronisław Malinowski, *Argonauts of the Western Pacific* (originally published 1922; London: Read Books, 2007).

41. Victor Turner, *From Ritual to Theater* (New York, PAJ [Performing Arts Journal] Publications, 1982).

42. See Caitlin Zaloom, *Out of the Pits* (Chicago: University of Chicago Press, 2010).

43. This view is put most fully in Roland Barthes, *Elements of Semiology*, trans. Richard Howard, Annette Lavers and Colin Smith (New York: Hill and Wang, 1967).

44. Denis Diderot, *The Paradox of Acting*, trans. W. H. Pollack (New York: Hill and Wang, 1957), p. 14.

45. See Erving Goffman, *The Presentation of Self in Everyday Life* (New York: Anchor Books, 1959); Keith Thomas, Introduction, in Jan Bremmer and Herman Roodenburg (eds.), *A Cultural History of Gesture* (Ithaca, NY: Cornell University Press, 1992), p. 1.

46. Niccolò Machiavelli, *Literary Works*, ed. and trans. J. R. Hale (Westport, Conn.: Greenwood Press, 1979), p. 139.

47. See Hannah Arendt, *Eichmann in Jerusalem*, revised edn. (London: Penguin, 1977).

CHAPTER 3. THE 'GREAT UNSETTLING'

1. The most recent, and exhaustive, study of *The Ambassadors* is John David North, *The Ambassadors' Secret* (London: Phoenix, 2004).

2. A fuller description of the invention of optical instruments appears in Richard Sennett, *The Craftsman* (London: Allen Lane, 2008], pp. 195–7.

3. The clearest discussion of Renaissance diplomacy remains Garrett Mattingly's classic *Renaissance Diplomacy* (London: Cape, 1955).

4. Ernest Satow, *Satow's Diplomatic Practice*, sixth edn., ed. Ivor Roberts (Oxford: Oxford University Press, 2009), pp. 45–6.

5. Two useful sources which chart these changes are Miri Rubin, *Corpus Christi: The Eucharist in Late Medieval Culture* (Cambridge: Cambridge University Press, 1991), and Caroline Walker Bynum, *Holy Feast and Holy Fast: The Religious Significance of Food to Medieval Women* (Berkeley: University of California Press, 1987).

6. O. B. Hardison, *Christian Rite and Christian Drama in the Middle Ages* (Baltimore: Johns Hopkins Press, 1965), pp. 35 ff.

7. The 'prop' is the language used by Andrew Sofer. I am indebted to his excellent study *The Stage Life of Props* (Ann Arbor: University of Michigan Press, 2003), pp. 31–60, for illuminating the medieval uses of the wafer.

8. Quoted in Henry Kamen, *Early Modern European Society* (London: Routledge, 2000), p. 222.

9. Benjamin Kaplan, *Divided by Faith* (Cambridge, Mass.: Harvard University Press, 2007), p. 41. I have taken the liberty of reversing Mr Kaplan's sentence order.

10. Bryan Spinks, *Reformation and Modern Rituals and Theologies of Baptism* (Aldershot: Ashgate, 2006), p. 100.

11. Romans 6: 3.

12. Martin Luther, *Luthers Werke*, ed. J. F. K. Knaake *et al.* (Weimar: Bühlau, 2003), vol. 49, pp. 128–9.

13. See Diarmaid MacCulloch, *The Reformation* (London: Penguin, 2004), p. 136.

14. Martin Luther, *Colloquia Mensalia; or, The Familiar Discourses*, ed. Henry Bell (Charleston, SC: Nabu Press, 2010), ch. 2.

15. I am indebted to my former student and now colleague Jennifer Homans for teaching me this material. Jennifer Homans, *Apollo's Angels* (New York: Random House, 2010); see also Jennifer Nevile (ed.), *Dance, Spectacle, and the Body Politick, 1250–1750* (Bloomington: Indiana University Press, 2008); Georgia Cowart, *The Triumph of Pleasure* (Chicago: University of Chicago Press, 2008).

16. Cowart, *The Triumph of Pleasure*, p. xvii.

17. Julia Prest, 'The Politics of Ballet at the Court of Louis XIV', in Nevile, *Dance, Spectacle, and the Body Politick*, p. 238.

18. Philippe Beaussant, *Louis XIV: Artiste* (Paris: Payot, 1999), pp. 23–41.

19. Homans, *Apollo's Angels*, pp. 15–19.

20. See Ernst Kantorowicz, *The King's Two Bodies* (Princeton: Princeton University Press, 1957).

21. See Richard Sennett, *The Fall of Public Man* (New York: Knopf, 1977), pp. 232–6.

22. Quotes are found in Joachim Fest, *Hitler* (New York: Harcourt, 1974), pp. 517 and 51.

23. Theodore Abel, *Why Hitler Came into Power* (New York: Prentice-Hall, 1938), p. 212.

24. For general reference about workshops, see Robert Lopez, *The Commercial Revolution of the Middle Ages, 950–1350* (Englewood Cliffs, NJ:

Prentice-Hall, 1971); Ibn Khaldūn, *The Muqaddimah*, abridged version, trans. Franz Rosenthal (Princeton: Princeton University Press, 2004); Gervase Rosser, 'Crafts, Guilds, and the Negotiation of Work in the Medieval Town', *Past and Present*, 154 (1997); S. R. Epstein, 'Guilds, Apprenticeship, and Technological Change', *Journal of Economic History*, 58 (1998).

25. The condition of medieval guilds is described in greater depth in Sennett, *The Craftsman*.

26. See Bruno Latour and Steve Woolgar, *Laboratory Life* (Princeton: Princeton University Press, 1986); Bruno Latour, *Science in Action: How to Follow Scientists and Engineers through Society* (Cambridge, Mass.: Harvard University Press, 1987).

27. The refinement in polishing is usually attributed to Eucharias Janssen (1580–1638), though many others at the time created equally refined lenses. Henry King, *The History of the Telescope* (New York: Dover, 2003).

28. Steven Shapin and Simon Schaffer, *Leviathan and the Air-Pump* (Princeton: Princeton University Press, 1989); Steven Shapin, *The Scientific Revolution* (Chicago: University of Chicago Press, 1998).

29. See Elizabeth Eisenstein, *The Printing Press as an Agent of Change*, 2 vols. in 1 (Cambridge: Cambridge University Press, 1980), p. 55.

30. Sennett, *The Craftsman*, pp. 195-6.

31. Mikhail Bakhtin, *Speech Genres and Other Late Essays*, trans. Michael Holquist (Austin: University of Texas Press, 1986), p. 7.

32. Peter Burke, *The Fortunes of the Courtier* (Philadelphia: University of Pennsylvania Press, 1996), p. 13.

33. Castiglione, *The Book of the Courtier*, trans. George Bull (London: Penguin, 1976), pp. 342-3.

34. Ibid., p. 67.

35. Ibid., p. 59; Giovanni della Casa, *Galateo*, trans. R. S. Pine-Coffin (London: Penguin, 1958), pp. 44-7.

36. See Jorge Arditi, *A Geneology of Manners* (Chicago: University of Chicago Press, 1998).

37. Norbert Elias, *The Civilizing Process*. This work comes in many versions, especially in its English translations. Originally published in 1936, as a revised version of his *Habilitationsschrift*, the book waited many decades to appear in English, and was at its English debut poorly translated. The best current version is translated by Edmund Jephcott (Oxford: Blackwell, 2000).

38. Castiglione, *The Book of the Courtier*, pp. 346-7.

39. See Mattingly, *Renaissance Diplomacy*.

40. Quoted in Douglas Blow, *Doctors, Ambassadors, Secretaries* (Chicago: University of Chicago Press, 2002), p. 143.
41. Ottaviano Maggi, *De legato*, Book 2, 64ᵛ, trans. and quoted in Blow, *Doctors, Ambassadors, Secretaries*, p. 102.
42. Niccolò Machiavelli, *The Prince*, trans. George Bull (London: Penguin, 2003), pp. 27–8.
43. Blow, *Doctors, Ambassadors, Secretaries*, p. 171.
44. Satow, *Satow's Diplomatic Practice*, sixth edn., ed. Ivor Roberts, p. 9.
45. Castiglione, *The Book of the Courtier*, pp. 284–5.
46. See Benedetta Craveri, *The Age of Conversation*, trans. Teresa Waugh (New York: New York Review of Books, 2005), pp. 27–43.
47. Vincent Voiture, *Poésies*, vol. 1 (Paris: Didier, 1971), pp. 21–2.
48. La Rochefoucauld, *Collected Maxims*, trans. E. H. and A. M. Blackmore and Francine Giguère (Oxford: Oxford University Press, 2007), maxims 204, p. 57, and 102, p. 31.
49. Ibid., pp. 276–83.
50. Jerrold Seigel, *The Idea of the Self* (Cambridge: Cambridge University Press, 2005), esp. the 'epilogue' of this extraordinary book.
51. See Sennett, *The Fall of Public Man*, pp. 80-82.

CHAPTER 4. INEQUALITY

1. Arloc Sherman and Chad Stone, 'Income Gaps between Very Rich and Everyone Else . . . ', Center on Budget and Policy Priorities, 25 June 2010, http://www.cbpp.org/cms/index.cfm?fa=view&id=3220.
2. The reader may be most familiar with this research in Putnam's most popular work, *Bowling Alone*, revised edn. (New York: Simon & Schuster, 2001). The foundation of this research was laid in an earlier study of civic traditions in modern Italy: Robert Putnam, Robert Leonardi and Raphaella Nanetti, *Making Democracy Work*, revised edn. (Princeton: Princeton University Press, 1994).
3. Putnam, *Bowling Alone*; Jeffrey Goldfarb, *The Cynical Society* (Chicago: University of Chicago Press, 1991).
4. A good summary of these debates appears in John Field, *Social Capital*, second edn. (London: Routledge, 2008).
5. The last of these attacks appears in Ben Fine, *Theories of Social Capital: Researchers Behaving Badly* (London: Pluto Press, 2010).
6. Yuan Luo, 'Guanxi: Principles, Philosophies and Implications', *Human Systems Management*, 16/1 (1997), p. 43.

7. See Douglas Guthrie *et al.*, *Social Connections in China* (Cambridge: Cambridge University Press, 2002), pp. 3–20.

8. Staff of Unicef Innocenti Research Centre, *Child Well-being in Rich Countries* (also referred to as Innocenti Report Card 7) (Florence: Unicef, 2007), which can be downloaded from www.unicef.org/irc.

9. Ibid., p. 3.

10. Richard Wilkinson and Kate Pickett, *The Spirit Level* (London: Allen Lane, 2009); see e.g. graph 8.6, p. 116.

11. Sonia Sodha and Julia Margo, *Ex Curricula* (London: Demos Institute, 2010), p. 77.

12. Unicef, *Child Well-being*, pp. 42–5.

13. Harold W. Stevenson, 'Learning for Asian Schools', *Scientific American* (Dec. 1992), pp. 71–7, and Christopher Bagley, 'Field Independence in Children in Group-Oriented Cultures: Comparisons from China, Japan, and North America', *Journal of Social Psychology*, 135/4 (Aug. 1995), pp. 523–5.

14. Jay MacLeod, *Ain't No Makin' It*, third edn. (Boulder, Colo.: Westview Press, 2009), and Pedro A. Noguera, *The Trouble with Black Boys* (San Francisco: John Wiley and Sons, 2009).

15. Twentieth-century data comes from James McNeil, *The Kids Market* (Ithaca, NY: Paramount, 1999); for a full economic picture, see Alison Watson, *The Child in International Political Economy* (London: Routledge, 2008).

16. Juliet Schor, *Born to Buy* (New York: Simon & Schuster, 2004), pp. 189–202.

17. Darian Leader, *The New Black: Mourning, Melancholia and Depression* (London: Penguin, 2009), p. 13.

18. Leonard Sax, 'Ritalin: Better Living through Chemistry?', *The World and I*, 286 (2000), pp. 1–11.

19. Mary Eberstadt, 'Why Ritalin Rules', *Policy Review*, 94 (April–May 2000), pp. 24–46.

20. See Larry Tye, *The Father of Spin* (New York: Holt, 1998).

21. Of the immense Piagetian literature, perhaps the most direct application to childhood consumption is Deborah Roedder John, 'Consumer Socialization of Children', in Flemming Hansen *et al.* (eds.), *Children – Consumption, Advertising and Media* (Copenhagen: Copenhagen Business School Press, 2002). See particularly pp. 30–31.

22. Schor, *Born to Buy*, p. 149.

23. Ibid., p. 174.

24. See Agnes Nairn, Jo Ormrod and Paul Bottomley, *Watching, Wanting, and Wellbeing* (London: National Consumer Council, 2007), p. 34.

25. Tim Kasser, Richard Ryan *et al.*, 'The Relations of Material and Social Environments to Late Adolescents' Materialistic and Prosocial Values', *Developmental Psychology*, 31 (1995), pp. 901–14; Tim Kasser and Richard Ryan, 'A Dark Side of the American Dream', *Journal of Personality and Social Psychology*, 65/2 (1993), pp. 410–22.

26. David Kirkpatrick, *The Facebook Effect* (New York: Random House, 2010).

27. Ed Mayo and Agnes Nairn, *Consumer Kids* (London: Constable, 2009), p. 171.

28. Sherry Turkle, *Alone Together: Why We Expect More from Technology and Less from Each Other* (New York: Basic Books, 2011).

29. Judy Wajcman, Michael Bittman and Jude Brown, 'Intimate Connections: The Impact of the Mobile Phone on Work/Life Boundaries', in G. Goggin and L. Hjorth (eds.), *Mobile Technologies: From Telecommunications to Media* (London: Routledge, 2009), pp. 9–22; Judy Wajcman, Michael Bittman and Jude Brown, 'Families without Borders: Mobile Phones, Connectedness and Work-Home Divisions', *Sociology*, 42/4 (2008), pp. 635–52.

30. Cf. Jo Henley, 'We're Not Socially Abnormal', *Guardian*, G2 (16 July 2010), pp. 12–15.

31. Paul DiMaggio, Eszter Hargittai *et al.*, 'Social Implications of the Internet', *Annual Review of Sociology*, 27 (2001), pp. 307–36.

32. Ibid., p. 316.

33. Mayo and Nairn, *Consumer Kids*, p. 224.

34. Ibid., p. 225.

35. Kirkpatrick, *The Facebook Effect*, p. 92.

36. Shamus Khan, *Privilege* (Princeton: Princeton University Press, 2010). see also Erik Olin Wright and Donmoon Cho, 'The Relative Permeability of Class Boundaries to Cross-Class Friendships: A Comparative Study of the United States, Canada, Sweden, and Norway', *American Sociological Review*, 57/1 (Feb. 1992), pp. 85–102.

CHAPTER 5. THE SOCIAL TRIANGLE

1. See Richard Sennett and Jonathan Cobb, *The Hidden Injuries of Class* (New York: Knopf, 1972).

2. Rob Gregory, 'Interview with Peter Zumthor', *Architectural Review*, 225 (May 2009), p. 20.

3. Georg Simmel, *The Philosophy of Money*, trans. Tom Bottomore and David Frisby, second edn. (London: Routledge, 1990), p. 179.

4. William James, 'The Will to Believe', in *Essays in Pragmatism* (New York: Hafner Press, 1948), p. 89.

5. William James, 'The Sentiment of Rationality', in *Essays in Pragmatism*, p. 22.

6. Tom Juravich, *Chaos on the Shop Floor* (Philadelphia: Temple University Press, 1985).

7. Adam Smith, *The Wealth of Nations* (1776; London: Methuen, 1961), pp. 302–3.

8. David Kynaston, *A History of the City of London*, vol. 4 (London: Pimlico, 2002).

9. Saskia Sassen, *The Mobility of Labor and Capital* (Cambridge: Cambridge University Press, 1988), pp. 4–5, 105–6.

10. Daniel Bell, 'Work and its Discontents', in Daniel Bell, *The End of Ideology* (Cambridge, Mass.: Harvard University Press, 1988), p. 233.

11. Richard Sennett, *The Corrosion of Character* (New York: Norton, 1998), pp. 41–2.

12. William H. Whyte, *The Organization Man* (Philadelphia: University of Pennsylvania Press, 2002 [1956]); C. Wright Mills, *White Collar* (Oxford: Oxford University Press, 1968); Michel Crozier, *The Bureaucratic Phenomenon* (Chicago: University of Chicago Press, 1964; repr. New Brunswick, NJ: Transaction Publishers, 2010).

13. Bennett Harrison, *Lean and Mean* (London: Routledge, 1998).

14. See Saskia Sassen, *The Global City*, second edn. (Princeton: Princeton University Press, 2001).

15. His most recent thoughts on this difference appear in George Soros, *The New Paradigm for Financial Markets* (New York: PublicAffairs, 2008).

16. Manuel Castells, *The Rise of the Network Society*, second revised edn., vol. 1 (Oxford: Blackwell, 2009).

17. Quoted in the *New York Times* (13 Feb. 1996), pp. D1, D6.

18. See Sennett, *The Corrosion of Character*.

19. *The Economist* (28 Feb. 2009), p. 27.

20. Richard Sennett, *The Culture of the New Capitalism* (New Haven: Yale University Press, 2006).

21. My thanks to Matthew Gill, who first suggested this project to me, and who has just published a study of accountants in London, *Accountants' Truth* (Oxford: Oxford University Press, 2009), which is a good induction into the world of the financial back-office; also thanks to my student Jesse Potter in London, who is conducting a study of job-change for workers in early middle age. In New York, I want to thank Sarah Kauffman, who helped me get started.

22. Job centres in New York come in three forms: those run by the State of

New York, those supported by the City of New York, and those privately funded. My contacts came through the State's Manhattan Workforce 1 Career Center, which is a partial and mixed enterprise in Varick Street, funnelling many people up to the full-service Workforce 1 Career Center in 125th Street. Uptown, people will get help finding a job, getting specific training, or long-term professional development advice. There are numerous private firms downtown, such as Wall Street Services, providing help targeted to workers in financial services.

23. Katherine Newman, *Falling from Grace* (Berkeley: University of California Press, 1999). 'Job market restructuring means that "displaced workers," those whose craft or industrial jobs have dried up or moved offshore, find themselves in a more precarious position even if they find new employment. They are often the oldest but least senior, inexperienced and entering a new field, or in new jobs with less long-term security' (pp. 24–7). Thus, even among those who manage to 'find the respectable positions they once had', many 'will have lost years in the process and will find it hard to recapture the career advances that would have been theirs had they not been displaced. In both instances (those re-employed and those permanently displaced), the damage – measured in financial or emotional terms – is lasting and painful' (p. 40).

24. American Management Association, '2002 Survey on Internal Collaboration', p. 1, http://www.amanet.org/training/articles/2002. To access this material, the reader has to sign up online to the American Management Association, but the sign-up is free.

25. American Management Association, 'Organizational Communication Survey 2005' (conducted jointly by the Society for Human Resource Management and Career.Journal.Com), posted 14 November 2005, http://www.amanet.org/training/articles/2005.

26. See fuller discussion in Sennett, *The Corrosion of Character*, pp. 106–17.

27. Gideon Kunda, *Engineering Culture* (Philadelphia: Temple University Press, 1992).

28. Gill, *Accountants' Truth*.

29. Chartered Management Institute, 'Better Managed Britain, OnePoll Study', issued Nov. 2009, http://www.managers.org.uk/listing_media_1.aspx?ide=. This is a survey of 3,000 adults, conducted in 2009.

30. Ludwig von Mises, *Epistemological Problems of Economics*, trans. George Reisman (New York: New York University Press, 1978), 'Malinvestment of Capital', pp. 239-42.

31. Data compiled from Jeffrey Pfeffer, 'Size, Composition, and Function of Hospital Boards of Directors', *Administrative Science Quarterly* (1988), pp. 349–64 (http://www.jstor.org/stable/2391668). Melissa Stone and

Francie Ostrower, 'Acting in the Public Interest? Another Look at Research on Nonprofit Governance', *Nonprofit and Voluntary Sector Quarterly* (2007) (http://nvs.sagepub.com/content/36/3/416). Rikki Abzug and J. S. Simonoff, *Nonprofit Trusteeship in Different Contexts* (Aldershot: Ashgate, 2004).

32. David Rothkopf, *Superclass* (New York: Farrar, Straus & Giroux, 2009), p. 31.

CHAPTER 6. THE UNCOOPERATIVE SELF

1. C. Wright Mills and Hans Gerth, *Character and Social Structure* (New York: Harvest, 1999); see section entitled 'Social Relativity of the Generalized Other', pp. 98–107, 125–9.

2. Søren Kierkegaard, *The Concept of Anxiety*, trans. Reidar Thomte (Princeton: Princeton University Press, 1981).

3. Leon Festinger *et al.*, *When Prophecy Fails* (Minneapolis: University of Minnesota Press, 1956).

4. Quoted and translated in Richard Sennett, *Authority* (New York: Knopf, 1980), p. 76.

5. Quoted and translated ibid., p. 96.

6. Reinhard Bendix, *Work and Authority in Industry* (Berkeley: University of California Press; New Brunswick, NJ: Transaction Publishers, 2001).

7. See Eric Klinenberg, *Solo* (London: Penguin, forthcoming, 2012).

8. Jean-Paul Sartre, *Being and Nothingness*, trans. Hazel E. Barnes (New York: Philosophical Library, 1976), p. 456.

9. Sigmund Freud, *Totem and Taboo*, trans. James Strachey (London: Routledge Classics, 2001); 'On Narcissism: An Introduction', in Peter Gay (ed.), *The Freud Reader* (London: Norton, 1995).

10. Heinz Kohut, *The Analysis of the Self* (New York: International Universities Press, 1971), pp. 33–4.

11. See Otto Kernberg, 'Structural Derivatives of Object Relationships', *International Journal of Psychoanalysis*, 47 (1966), pp. 236–53.

12. Morris Janowitz, *The Professional Soldier* (Chicago: University of Chicago Press, 1964), p. 112.

13. Robert J. Lifton, *Home from the War* (New York: Simon & Schuster, 1974).

14. The classic study of such bonding is Bernard Fall, *The Siege of Dien Bien Phu* (New York: Random House, 1967); see also, for the Vietnam War, A. F. Krepinevich, Jr., *The Army and Vietnam* (Baltimore: Johns Hopkins University Press, 1986). A powerful depiction of soldier bonding in the First World War appears in 'Charles Edmunds' (pseudonym of Charles Carrington), *A Subaltern's War* (London: Peter Davies, 1929).

15. Anthony Giddens, *Modernity and Self-Identity* (Cambridge: Polity, 1991).

16. Martin Heidegger, *Being and Time*, trans. Joan Stambaugh (Albany: State University of New York Press, 1996), part IV, 'Temporality and Everydayness', section 69, 'The Temporality of Being-in-the-World and the Problem of the Transcendence of the World' (pp. 321–33).

17. Raymond Aron, *Main Currents in Sociological Thought*, vol. 1 (London: Penguin, 1969).

18. See Mihaly Csikszentmihalyi, *Beyond Boredom and Anxiety* (San Francisco: Jossey-Bass, 1975).

19. R. Farmer and N. D. Sundberg, 'Boredom Proneness: The Development and Correlates of a New Scale', *Journal of Personality Assessment*, 50/1 (1986), pp. 4–17.

20. Max Weber, *The Protestant Ethic and the Spirit of Capitalism*. The standard English translation is by Talcott Parsons (New York: Scribner, 1950); the translation is more wooden than Weber's German. This passage, as translated by Martin Green, appears in Martin Green, *The Von Richthofen Sisters* (New York: Basic Books, 1974), p. 152.

21. See Simon Schama, *The Embarrassment of Riches* (New York: Knopf, 1987); Albert Hirschman, *The Passions and the Interests*, revised edn. (Princeton: Princeton University Press, 1992); R. H. Tawney, *Religion and the Rise of Capitalism*, revised edn. (London: Read, 2006).

22. Lionel Trilling, *Sincerity and Authenticity* (Cambridge, Mass.: Harvard University Press, 1972).

CHAPTER 7. THE WORKSHOP

1. See Kenneth Holyoke, 'Symbolic Connectionism', in K. Anders Ericsson and Jacqui Smith (eds.), *Toward a General Theory of Expertise* (Cambridge: Cambridge University Press, 1991), pp. 303–35.

2. The earliest known appearance of Einstein's saying is in an essay by Roger Sessions in the *New York Times* (8 Jan. 1950) (http://select.nytimes.com/gst/abstract.html?res=F30615FE3559137A93CAA9178AD85F4485.85F9), where Sessions appears to be paraphrasing Einstein: 'I also remember a remark of Albert Einstein, which certainly applies to music. He said, in effect, that everything should be as simple as it can be, but not simpler.' A more elaborate version is Einstein's 'On the Method of Theoretical Physics', Herbert Spencer Lecture, delivered at Oxford (10 June 1933); also published in *Philosophy of Science*, 1/2 (April 1934), pp. 163–9, at p. 165.

3. The reader interested in Stravinsky's sophisticated simplicity could do no better than read Richard Taruskin, *Stravinsky and the Russian Traditions*, vol. 2 (Oxford: Oxford University Press, 1996), pp. 1441–1500.

4. Erving Goffman, *The Presentation of Self in Everyday Life* (New York: Anchor Books, 1959); Goffman 'Role Distance', in his *Encounters: Two Studies in the Sociology of Interaction* (Indianapolis: Bobbs-Merrill, 1961).

5. Michel de Certeau, *The Practice of Everyday Life*, vol. 1, trans. Steven Rendall (Berkeley: University of California Press, 1988), p. xv. Readers of this English translation should know that a second volume focuses more on Croix-Rousse. This is Michel de Certeau, Luce Giard and Pierre Mayol, *The Practice of Everyday Life*, vol. 2, trans. Timothy Tomasik (Minneapolis: University of Minnesota Press, 1998).

6. Charles Darwin, *The Expression of the Emotions in Man and Animals*, centennial edn. (New York: Harper Perennial, 2009).

7. For Darwin's conflict with Le Brun, see Jean-Jacques Courtine and Claudine Haroche, *Histoire du visage* (Paris: Rivages, 1988), pp. 89–93.

8. See William Elliot Griffis, *Corea, the Hermit Nation* (New York: Scribner, 1882). Griffis was one of the first anthropologists to make mourning a special subject.

9. Courtine and Haroche, *Histoire du visage*.

10. Jürgen Streeck, *Gesturecraft* (Amsterdam: John Benjamins, 2009), p. 189.

11. See discussion in Richard Sennett, *The Craftsman* (London: Allen Lane, 2008), pp. 197–9.

12. Ernst Gombrich, *Art and Illusion* (London: Phaidon, 1950). It's worth noting that this ground-breaking study emphasized that the viewer's participation – looking at gestures, images, or objects – is as important to aesthetic experience as what is put on display to be seen.

CHAPTER 8. EVERYDAY DIPLOMACY

1. See Godfried Engbersen, Kees Schuyt *et al.*, *Cultures of Unemployment* (Amsterdam: University of Amsterdam Press, 2006).

2. The issue is explored largely by Phillip Rieff in *The Triumph of the Therapeutic* (Chicago: University of Chicago Press, 1987).

3. I'm summarizing a huge body of data here. The reader wishing to penetrate this forest might consult Andrew Hacker, 'Where Will We Find the Jobs?', *New York Review of Books*, 58/3 (24 Feb. 2011). See further Phillip Brown, Hugh Lauder and David Ashton, *The Global Auction: The Broken Promises of Education, Jobs and Incomes* (Oxford: Oxford University Press, 2011).

4. Rowena Barrett and Pooran Wynarczyk, 'Building the Science and Innovation Base: Work, Skills, and Employment', *New Technology, Work, and*

Employment, 24/3 (2009), pp. 210–14 (this entire issue is devoted to skills shifts).

5. Simon Jenkins, *Thatcher and Sons* (London: Allen Lane, 2006), p. 56.

6. See Lewis Coser, *The Functions of Social Conflict* (New York: Free Press, 1956).

7. I'm referring to my uncle, Norman Brown, who was a great labour mediator and arbitrator in Chicago. For academic references on this judgement call, see, historically, Duff Cooper, *Talleyrand* (New York: Grove Press, 2001); or, in contemporary diplomatic practices, Henry Kissinger, *Diplomacy* (New York: Simon & Schuster, 1994). Both Talleyrand and Kissinger were masters at judging when to separate and when join together warring parties.

8. Theodore Kheel (1914–2010) was a New York lawyer who became a labour negotiator in 1938, and established Automation House, a centre for labour negotiators, in the early 1960s. His book, *The Keys to Conflict Resolution* (New York: Four Walls, Eight Windows, 1999), does not quite do justice to his gritty talent for everyday diplomacy; a journalistic portrait better conveys it: *New York Magazine*, 8 Jan. 1979, pp. 35–43.

9. For a good overview of immigrant entrepreneurs, see Robert Kloosterman and Jan Rath (eds.), *Immigrant Entrepreneurs* (Oxford: Berg, 2003), in particular Pyong Gap Min and Mehdi Bozorgmehr, 'United States: The Entrepreneurial Cutting Edge', ibid., pp. 17–38.

10. Kheel, *The Keys to Conflict Resolution*.

11. Pyong Gap Min, *Ethnic Solidarity for Economic Survival* (New York: Russell Sage Foundation, 2008), p. 85.

12. Ibid., pp. 114–18; woman grocer quoted on p. 117.

13. Denis Diderot, *The Paradox of Acting*, trans. W. H. Pollock (New York: Hill and Wang, 1957).

14. Wilbert van Vree, *Meetings, Manners, and Civilization*, trans. Kathleen Bell (Leicester: Leicester University Press, 1999), pp. 256–311.

15. Mary Poovey, *A History of the Modern Fact* (Chicago: University of Chicago Press, 1998).

16. Quoted in van Vree, *Meetings, Manners, and Civilization*, p. 56.

17. References are to the most recent version of Satow: Ernest Satow, *Satow's Diplomatic Practice*, sixth edn., ed. Ivor Roberts (Oxford: Oxford University Press, 2009).

18. Ibid., 4.16 (as a diplomat, he documents everything in this manual in formal paragraphing), p. 53.

19. Ibid., 4.19, p. 54.

20. Quoted ibid., 40.25, pp. 626–7.

21. Quoted ibid., 40.3, pp. 618–19.

22. Joseph Nye, *Soft Power* (New York: Perseus Books, 2004).

23. La Rochefoucauld, *Collected Maxims*, trans. E. H. and A. M. Blackmore and Francine Giguère (Oxford: Oxford University Press, 2007), maxim 256, p. 73.

24. Jacques Lecoq, *The Moving Body* (not quite an accurate translation of the original French title, *Le Corps poétique*), trans. David Bradby (London: Methuen, 2002), pp. 4–5.

25. Ibid., p. 39.

26. Ibid.

CHAPTER 9. THE COMMUNITY

1. I've described at greater length the Cabrini Green project, its neighbourhood and meetings like this in Richard Sennett, *Respect in an Age of Inequality* (New York: Norton, 2003), pt. I.

2. Robert Nisbet, *The Quest for Community*, revised edn. (London: ISI Books, 2010).

3. For Chicago, the classic guide to this spatial-economic configuration is Homer Hoyt, *One Hundred Years of Land Values in Chicago* (Chicago: Beard Books, 2000).

4. A good summary of data on local economies in the global economy today is Bruno Dallago and Chiara Guglielmetti (eds.), *Local Economies and Global Competitiveness* (Basingstoke: Palgrave, 2010).

5. Saskia Sassen, *The Global City*, second edn. (Princeton: Princeton University Press, 2001) pp. 265 ff.

6. M. R. Knapp *et al.*, 'The Economics of Volunteering', *Non-Profit Studies*, 1/1 (2006) (http://kar.kent.ac.uk/26911); Roy Kakoli and Susanne Ziemek, 'On the Economics of Volunteering', cited by Knapp *et al.*; article in full at http://hdl.handle.net/10068/127795.

7. Paulo Freire, *Pedagogy of the Oppressed*, revised edn., trans. Myra Ramos (London: Penguin, 1996).

8. David Healy, *The Anti-Depressant Era* (Cambridge, Mass.: Harvard University Press, 1997).

9. Darian Leader, *The New Black: Mourning, Melancholia and Depression* (London: Penguin, 2009), pp. 183 ff.

10. Sigmund Freud, *Totem and Taboo*, trans. James Strachey (New York: Norton, 1950), p. 65.

11. Sigmund Freud, 'Mourning and Melancholia', in Freud's papers published as *On Murder, Mourning and Melancholia*, trans. Shaun Whiteside (London: Penguin, 2005), pp. 204–5.

12. Hannah Arendt, *Essays in Understanding: Formation, Exile, and Totalitarianism*, ed. Jerome Kohn (New York: Schocken, 2005).

13. Émile Durkheim, *On Suicide*, trans. Robin Buss, introd. Richard Sennett (London: Penguin, 2006).

14. Sudhir Venkatesh, *American Project: The Rise and Fall of a Modern Ghetto* (Cambridge, Mass.: Harvard University Press, 2002), and *Gang Leader for a Day* (New York: Penguin, 2008).

15. Elijah Anderson, *Code of the Street* (New York: Norton, 1999); Mitchell Duneier, *Sidewalk* (New York: Farrar, Straus and Giroux, 1999).

16. This issue is explored in Richard Sennett, *Families Against the City* (Cambridge, Mass.: Harvard University Press, 1970).

17. An excellent study of these bonds among African-Americans in the 1960s is Carol Stack, *All Our Kin* (New York: Basic Books, 1983).

18. I'm quoting from one such pep talk Kotter gave at the Harvard Business School in 2008, but this idea of planned vocation appears in almost any self-help book.

19. See the latter's autobiography: Dorothy Day, *The Long Loneliness* (New York: Harper, 1952).

20. See Sennett, *Respect*, pp. 131–4. In contrast to the cool, secular social work of Jane Addams, 'submission of the Catholic sort advocated by Mother Cabrini made for solidarity of an explicit sort – "we are all God's subjects" – and care could therefore be freely expressed' (p. 134). On a personal note, I might add that, a half-century after these Catholic centres in Chicago were founded, they kept me afloat in the Chicago slums.

21. 'The Aims and Means of the Catholic Worker', *Catholic Worker* (May 2009), pp. 4–5.

22. Dorothy Day, *Selected Writings*, ed. Robert Ellsberg (Maryknoll, NY: Orbis Books, 2009), p. 165.

23. William James, *The Varieties of Religious Experience* (London: Penguin, 1985), Lecture IX: 'Conversion'.

24. A. D. Gordon, *Selected Essays*, trans. Frances Burnce (Boston: The Independent Press, 1938).

25. A. D. Gordon, 'Man and Nature', ibid., pp. 172–3.

26. Herbert Rose, *The Life and Thought of A. D. Gordon* (New York: Bloch Publishing, 1964), p. 128.

27. A. D. Gordon, *The Nation and Labor* (Jerusalem: Jerusalem Zionist Library, 1952), pp. 235 ff.

28. See Raymond Gregory, *Norman Thomas: The Great Dissenter* (New York: Algora, 2008), an excellent account of his public career. Among Thomas's many writings, mostly assemblages of speeches, there is an

unpublished 'Autobiography' in the collection of the New York Public Library, a manuscript which is rather lacking in personal information. About Thomas's behaviour in public, I've relied on my mother's recollections.

CODA

1. Michel de Montaigne, 'An Apology for Raymond Sebond', in Montaigne, *Essays*, trans. M. A. Screech (London: Penguin, 2003), p. 505. My quotation, like the translation made by Saul Frampton, substitutes the words 'play' and 'playing' for Screech's literal 'passing time'; the original in French reads: 'qui sçait si elle passe son temps de moy plus que je ne fay d'elle.' Cf. Saul Frampton, *When I am Playing with my Cat, How do I Know She is Not Playing with Me?* (London: Faber, 2011), p. 115.

2. Cf. Montaigne, 'The Art of Conversation', in *Essays*, p. 1044, note.

3. Ibid., pp. 1054–5.

4. Montaigne, 'On Cruelty', ibid., p. 478.

5. Montaigne, 'On Habit', and 'Same Design: Different Outcomes', ibid., pp. 122–39 and 140-49; I am connecting the argument made on p. 130 to pp. 143–4. It should be noted that Montaigne, speaking as a *grand seigneur*, also praises the traditional habits as good in themselves, as on p. 134.

6. Sarah Bakewell, *How to Live: A Life of Montaigne* (London: Chatto and Windus, 2010).

7. Montaigne, 'On Experience'. Here I prefer the translation of Frampton to that of Screech: Frampton, *When I am Playing*, p. 270.

8. Montaigne, 'On Vanity', in *Essays*, p. 1132.

9. Bruno Latour, *We Have Never Been Modern*, trans. Catherine Porter (Cambridge, Mass.: Harvard University Press, 1993).

10. The phrase Burckhardt first used, absurdly, in describing the foundations of Islam, in *Gesamtausgabe* (Historical Fragments), vol. 7, ed. Albert Oeri and Emil Dürr (Basle, 1929), pp. 266 ff. The Burckhardt scholar Karl Weintraub argued, in his lectures, that the phrase modulated in Burckhardt's mind to become a label for Western modernity; this view informs Weintraub's book, *Visions of Culture* (Chicago: University of Chicago Press, 1966). It is not quite the view, I should note, of Burckhardt's recent biographer, Kurt Meyer, *Jacob Burckhardt* (Munich: Fink, 2009).

Index